Visit us at

www.syngress.com

Syngress is committed to publishing high-quality books for IT Professionals and delivering those books in media and formats that fit the demands of our customers. We are also committed to extending the utility of the book you purchase via additional materials available from our Web site.

SOLUTIONS WEB SITE

To register your book, visit www.syngress.com/solutions. Once registered, you can access our solutions@syngress.com Web pages. There you may find an assortment of valueadded features such as free e-books related to the topic of this book, URLs of related Web sites, FAQs from the book, corrections, and any updates from the author(s).

ULTIMATE CDs

Our Ultimate CD product line offers our readers budget-conscious compilations of some of our best-selling backlist titles in Adobe PDF form. These CDs are the perfect way to extend your reference library on key topics pertaining to your area of expertise, including Cisco Engineering, Microsoft Windows System Administration, CyberCrime Investigation, Open Source Security, and Firewall Configuration, to name a few.

DOWNLOADABLE E-BOOKS

For readers who can't wait for hard copy, we offer most of our titles in downloadable Adobe PDF form. These e-books are often available weeks before hard copies, and are priced affordably.

SYNGRESS OUTLET

Our outlet store at syngress.com features overstocked, out-of-print, or slightly hurt books at significant savings.

SITE LICENSING

Syngress has a well-established program for site licensing our e-books onto servers in corporations, educational institutions, and large organizations. Contact us at sales@syngress.com for more information.

CUSTOM PUBLISHING

Many organizations welcome the ability to combine parts of multiple Syngress books, as well as their own content, into a single volume for their own internal use. Contact us at sales@syngress.com for more information.

SYNGRESS®

Securing Windows Server 2008

Prevent Attacks from Outside and Inside Your Organization

Elsevier, Inc., the author(s), and any person or firm involved in the writing, editing, or production (collectively "Makers") of this book ("the Work") do not guarantee or warrant the results to be obtained from the Work.

There is no guarantee of any kind, expressed or implied, regarding the Work or its contents. The Work is sold AS IS and WITHOUT WARRANTY. You may have other legal rights, which vary from state to state.

In no event will Makers be liable to you for damages, including any loss of profits, lost savings, or other incidental or consequential damages arising out from the Work or its contents. Because some states do not allow the exclusion or limitation of liability for consequential or incidental damages, the above limitation may not apply to you.

You should always use reasonable care, including backup and other appropriate precautions, when working with computers, networks, data, and files.

Syngress Media®, Syngress®, "Career Advancement Through Skill Enhancement®," "Ask the Author UPDATE®," and "Hack Proofing®," are registered trademarks of Elsevier, Inc. "Syngress: The Definition of a Serious Security Library™," "Mission Critical™," and "The Only Way to Stop a Hacker is to Think Like One™" are trademarks of Elsevier, Inc. Brands and product names mentioned in this book are trademarks or service marks of their respective companies.

KEY	SERIAL NUMBER
001	HJIRTCV764
002	PO9873D5FG
003	829KM8NJH2
004	BAL923457U
005	CVPLQ6WQ23
006	VBP965T5T5
007	HJJJ863WD3E
008	2987GVTWMK
009	629MP5SDJT
010	IMWQ295T6T

PUBLISHED BY
Syngress Publishing, Inc.
Elsevier, Inc.
30 Corporate Drive
Burlington, MA 01803

Securing Windows Server 2008

Copyright © 2008 by Elsevier, Inc. All rights reserved. Printed in the United States of America. Except as permitted under the Copyright Act of 1976, no part of this publication may be reproduced or distributed in any form or by any means, or stored in a database or retrieval system, without the prior written permission of the publisher, with the exception that the program listings may be entered, stored, and executed in a computer system, but they may not be reproduced for publication.

Printed and bound by CPI Group (UK) Ltd, Croydon, CR0 4YY

Transferred to Digital Print 2011

ISBN 13: 978-1-59749-280-5

Publisher: Andrew Williams	Page Layout and Art: SPI
Copy Editor: Mike McGee	Indexer: Odessa & Cie
Project Manager: Gary Byrne	Cover Designer: Michael Kavish

For information on rights, translations, and bulk sales, contact Matt Pedersen, Commercial Sales Director and Rights, at Syngress Publishing; email m.pedersen@elsevier.com.

Contributing Authors

Dale Liu (CISSP, IAM, IEM, MCSE—Security, MCT) is a senior systems analyst, consultant, and trainer for Computer Revolution Enterprises. He has performed system administration, design, security analysis, and consulting for companies around the world. He currently resides in Houston, TX.

Remco Wisselink (MCT, MCSE NT4, 2000 and 2003, MCSE+messaging 2000 and 2003, MCSE+security 2000 and 2003, CCA, CCEA, SCP, and Multiple Certifications on MCTS and MCTIP) is a consultant working for the company IT-to-IT in the Netherlands. Remco has more then 10 years of experience in IT business and has multiple specialties, including ISA, Citrix, Softgrid, Exchange, and Microsoft Operating Systems in general like Windows Server 2008. Remco has been involved in several major infrastructure and mail migrations. Besides acting as a Microsoft Certified Trainer, he's also well known as a speaker on technical events.

Contents

Chapter 1

Microsoft Windows Server 2008: An Overview

Solutions in this chapter:

- Server Manager
- Server Core
- Active Directory Certificate Services
- Active Directory Domain Services

☑ Summary

☑ Solutions Fast Track

☑ Frequently Asked Questions

Introduction

With the introduction of new revisions to Microsoft products—for example, Windows, Exchange, and Communications Server—we have seen a trend toward "roles" within each product, as opposed to the various products being an all-in-one type of solution (as with Exchange 2007), or being additional features that work as a snap-in, such as DNS in Windows 2003.

With earlier versions of Windows Server 2000 or 2003, an Active Directory server was just that—an Active Directory server. What we are trying to say here is that it was more-or-less an "all-or-nothing" deal when creating a domain controller in Windows 2003. Very little flexibility existed in the way a domain controller could be installed, with the exception of whether a domain controller would also be a global catalog server or flexible single master operation (FSMO) server.

The new roles in Windows Server 2008 provide a new way for you to determine how they are implemented, configured, and managed within an Active Directory domain or forest. The new roles (and the official Microsoft definitions) are as follows:

- **Read-only domain controller (RODC)** This new type of domain controller, as its name implies, hosts read-only partitions of the Active Directory database. An RODC makes it possible for organizations to easily deploy a domain controller in scenarios where physical security cannot be guaranteed, such as branch office locations, or in scenarios where local storage of all domain passwords is considered a primary threat, such as in an extranet or in an application-facing role.

- **Active Directory Lightweight Directory Service (ADLDS)** Formerly known as Windows Server 2003 Active Directory Application Mode (ADAM), ADLDS is a Lightweight Directory Access Protocol (LDAP) directory service that provides flexible support for directory-enabled applications, without the dependencies required for Active Directory Domain Services (ADDS). ADLDS provides much of the same functionality as ADDS, but does not require the deployment of domains or domain controllers.

- **Active Directory Rights Management Service (ADRMS)** Active Directory Rights Management Services (ADRMS), a format and application-agnostic technology, provides services to enable the creation of information-protection solutions. ADRMS includes several new features that were available in Active Directory Rights Management Services (ADRMS). Essentially, ADRMS adds the ability to secure objects. For example, an e-mail can be restricted to read-only, meaning it cannot be printed, copied (using **Ctrl + C**, and so on), or forwarded.

- **Active Directory Federation Services (ADFS)** You can use Active Directory Federation Services (ADFS) to create a highly extensible, Internet-scalable, and secure identity access solution that can operate across multiple platforms, including both Windows and non-Windows environments. Essentially, this allows cross-forest authentication to external resources—such as another company's Active Directory. ADFS was originally introduced in Windows Server 2003 R2, but lacked much of its now-available functionality.

These roles can be managed with Server Manager and Server Core. Discussing Server Core is going to take considerably longer, so let's start with Server Manager.

Server Manager

Server Manager is likely to be a familiar tool to engineers who have worked with earlier versions of Windows. It is a single-screen solution that helps manage a Windows server, but is much more advanced than the previous version.

Using Server Manager to Implement Roles

Although we will be discussing Server Manager (Figure 1.1) as an Active Directory Management tool, it's actually much more than just that.

Figure 1.1 Server Manager

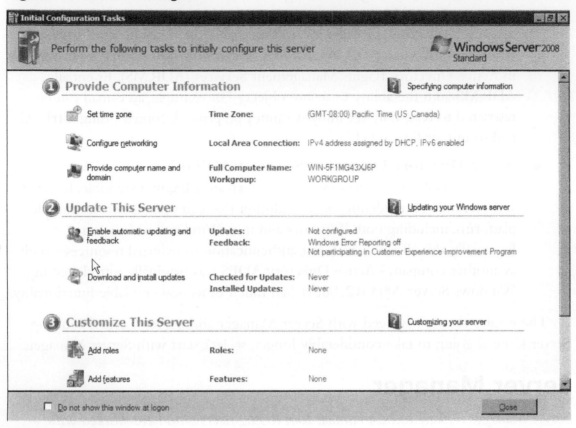

In fact, Server Manager is a single solution (technically, a Microsoft Management Console [MMC]) snap-in that is used as a single source for managing system identity (as well as other key system information), identifying problems with servers, displaying server status, enabled roles and features, and general options such as server updates and feedback.

Table 1.1 outlines some of the additional roles and features Server Manager can be used to control:

Table 1.1 Partial List of Additional Server Manager Features

Role/Feature	Description
Active Directory Certificate Services	Management of Public Key Infrastructure (PKI)
Dynamic Host Configuration Server	Dynamic assignment of IP addresses to clients
Domain Name Service	Provides name/IP address resolution
File Services	Storage management, replication, searching
Print Services	Management of printers and print servers
Terminal Services	Remote access to a Windows desktop or application
Internet Information Server	Web server services
Hyper-V	Server virtualization
BitLocker Drive Encryption	Whole-disk encryption security feature
Group Policy Management	Management of Group Policy Objects
SMTP Server	E-mail services
Failover Clustering	Teaming multiple servers to provide high availability
WINS Server	
Legacy NetBIOS name resolution	
Wireless LAN Service	Enumerates and manages wireless connections

Server Manager is enabled by default when a Windows 2008 server is installed (with the exception of Server Core). However, Server Manager can be shut off via the system Registry and can be re-opened at any time by selecting **Start | Administrative Tools | Server Manager**, or right-clicking **Computer** under the **Start** menu, and choosing **Manage** (Figure 1.2).

Figure 1.2 Opening Server Manager

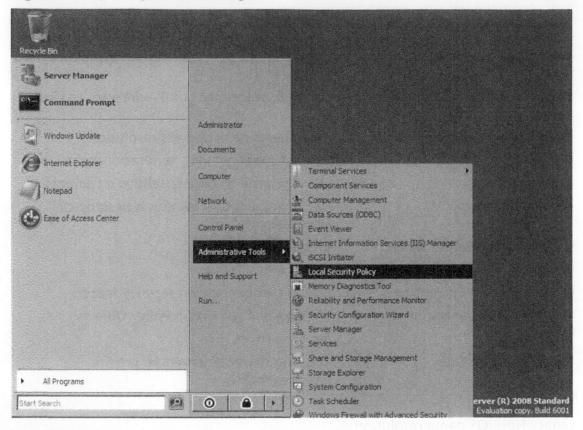

So, those are the basics of Server Manager. Now let's take a look at how we use Server Manager to implement a role. Let's take the IIS role and talk about using the Add Role Wizard to install Internet Information Services (IIS).

Tools & Traps...

Using the Add Role Wizard

Notice in Figure 1.1 that the Server Manager window is broken into three different sections:

- Provide Computer Information
- Update This Server
- Customize This Server

Under the **Customize This Server** section, click the **Add Role** icon. When the wizard opens, complete the following steps to install IIS onto the server.

1. Click the **Add Roles** icon.

2. At the **Before You Begin** window, read the information provided and then click **Next**.

3. From the list of server roles (Figure 1.3), click the check box next to **Web Server (IIS)** and then click **Next**.

4. If you are prompted to add additional required features, read and understand the features, and then click **Add Required Features**.

5. When you return to the **Select Server Roles** screen, click **Next**.

6. Read the information listed in the **Introduction to Web Server (IIS)** window and then click **Next**.

7. For purposes of this example, we will select all of the default Role Services and then click **Next**.

8. Review the Installation Summary Confirmation screen (Figure 1.4) and then click **Install**.

9. When installation is complete, click **Close**.

10. Notice that on the Server Manager screen, Web Server (IIS) is now listed as an installed role.

Figure 1.3 List of Server Roles

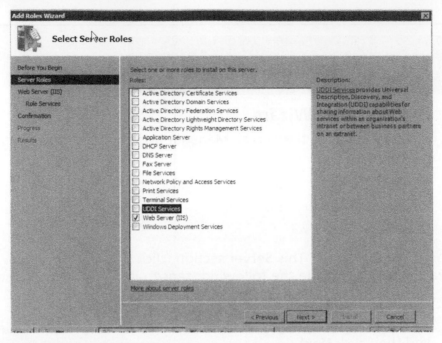

Figure 1.4 The Installation Summary Confirmation Screen

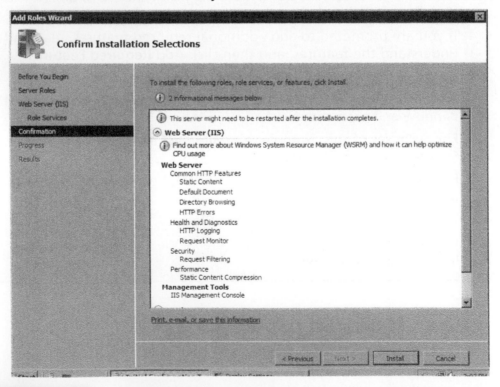

Configuring & Implementing...

Scripting vs. GUI

Sure, you can always use a wizard to implement a role, but you also have the option of using a script. Realistically speaking, it's generally not the most efficient way to deploy a role for a single server, however. Unless you are going to copy and paste the script, the chance of error is high in typing out the commands required. For example, take the following IIS script syntax:

```
start /w pkgmgr /iu:IIS-WebServerRole;IIS-WebServer;IIS-CommonHttpFeatures;
IIS-StaticContent;IIS-DefaultDocument;IIS-DirectoryBrowsing;IIS-HttpErrors;
IIS-HttpRedirect;IIS-ApplicationDevelopment;IIS-ASPNET;IIS-NetFxExtensibility;
IIS-ASP;IIS-CGI;IIS-ISAPIExtensions;IIS-ISAPIFilter;IIS-ServerSideIncludes;
IIS-HealthAndDiagnostics;IIS-HttpLogging;IIS-LoggingLibraries;IIS-Request
Monitor;IIS-HttpTracing;IIS-CustomLogging;IIS-ODBCLogging;IIS-Security;
IIS-BasicAuthentication;IIS-WindowsAuthentication;IIS-DigestAuthentication;
IIS-ClientCertificateMappingAuthentication;IIS-IISCertificateMappingAuthentica
tion;IIS-URLAuthorization;IIS-RequestFiltering;IIS-IPSecurity;IIS-
Performance;IIS-HttpCompressionStatic;IIS-HttpCompressionDynamic;IIS-WebServ
erManagementTools;IIS-ManagementConsole;IIS-ManagementScriptingTools;IIS-
ManagementService;IIS-IIS6ManagementCompatibility;IIS-Metabase;IIS-
WMICompatibility;IIS-LegacyScripts;IIS-LegacySnapIn;IIS-FTPPublishingService;
IIS-FTPServer;IIS-FTPManagement;WAS-WindowsActivationService;WAS-ProcessModel;
WAS-NetFxEnvironment;WAS-ConfigurationAPI
```

This script installs ALL of the IIS features, which may not be the preferred installation for your environment, and within the time it took to type it out, you may have already completed the GUI install!

Server Core

Server Core brings a new way not only to manage roles but also to deploy a Windows Server. With Server Core, we can say goodbye to unnecessary GUIs, applications, services, and many more commonly attacked features.

Using Server Core and Active Directory

For years, Microsoft engineers have been told that Windows would never stand up to Linux in terms of security simply because it was too darn "heavy" (too much) code, loaded too many modules (services, startup applications, and so on), and was generally too GUI heavy. With Windows Server 2008, Microsoft engineers can stand tall, thanks to the introduction of Server Core.

What Is Server Core?

What is Server Core, you ask? It's the "just the facts, ma'am" version of Windows 2008. Microsoft defines Server Core as "a minimal server installation option for Windows Server 2008 that contains a subset of executable files, and five server roles." Essentially, Server Core provides only the binaries needed to support the role and the base operating systems. By default, fewer processes are generally running.

Server Core is so drastically different from what we have come to know from Windows Server NT, Windows Server 2000, or even Windows Server 2003 over the past decade-plus, that it looks more like MS-DOS than anything else (Figure 1.5). With Server Core, you won't find Windows Explorer, Internet Explorer, a Start menu, or even a clock! Becoming familiar with Server Core will take some time. In fact, most administrators will likely need a cheat sheet for a while. To help with it all, you can find some very useful tools on Microsoft TechNet at http://technet2. microsoft.com/windowsserver2008/en/library/e7e522ac-b32f-42e1-b914-53ccc78d18161033.mspx?mfr=true. This provides command and syntax lists that can be used with Server Core. The good news is, for those of you who want the security and features of Server Core with the ease-of-use of a GUI, you have the ability to manage a Server Core installation using remote administration tools.

Figure 1.5 The Server Core Console

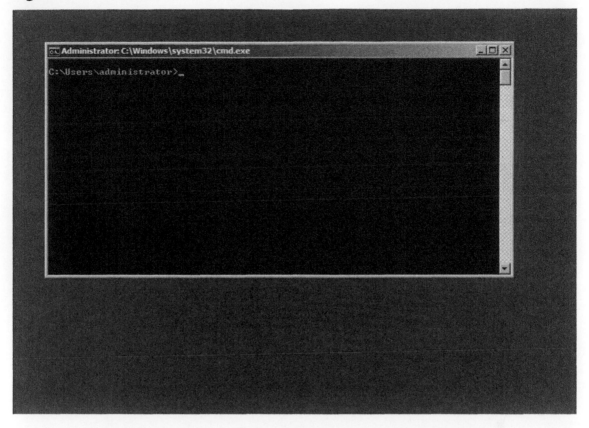

Before going any further, we should discuss exactly what will run on a Server Core installation. Server Core is capable of running the following server roles:

- Active Directory Domain Services Role
- Active Directory Lightweight Directory Services Role
- Dynamic Host Configuration Protocol (DHCP)
- Domain Name System (DNS) Services Role
- File Services Role
- Hyper-V (Virtualization) Role
- Print Services Role
- Streaming Media Services Role
- Web Services (IIS) Role

NOTE

Internet Information Server is Microsoft's brand of Web server software, utilizing Hypertext Transfer Protocol to deliver World Wide Web documents. It incorporates various functions for security, allows for CGI programs, and also provides for Gopher and FTP servers.

Although these are the roles Server Core supports, it can also support additional features, such as:

- Backup
- BitLocker
- Failover Clustering
- Multipath I/O
- Network Time Protocol (NTP)
- Removable Storage Management
- Simple Network Management Protocol (SNMP)
- Subsystem for Unix-based applications
- Telnet Client
- Windows Internet Naming Service (WINS)

NOTE

BitLocker Drive Encryption is an integral new security feature in Windows Server 2008 that protects servers at locations, such as branch offices, as well as mobile computers for all those roaming users out there. BitLocker provides offline data and operating system protection by ensuring that data stored on the computer is not revealed if the machine is tampered with when the installed operating system is offline.

The concept behind the design Server Core is to truly provide a minimal server installation. The belief is that rather than installing all the application, components, services, and features by default, it is up to the implementer to determine what will be turned on or off.

Installation of Windows 2008 Server Core is fairly simple. During the installation process, you have the option of performing a Standard Installation or a Server Core installation. Once you have selected the hard drive configuration, license key activation, and End User License Agreement (EULA), you simply let the automatic installation continue to take place. When installation is done and the system has rebooted, you will be prompted with the traditional Windows challenge/response screen, and the Server Core console will appear.

Configuring & Implementing...

Configuring the Directory Services Role in Server Core

So let's put Server Core into action and use it to install Active Directory Domain Services. To install the Active Directory Domain Services Role, perform the following steps:

1. The first thing we need to do is set the IP information for the server. To do this, we first need to identify the network adapter. In the console window, type **netsh interface ipv4 show interfaces** and record the number shown under the **Idx** column.

2. Set the IP address, Subnet Mask, and Default Gateway for the server. To do this, type **netsh interface ipv4 set address name="<ID>" source=static address=<StaticIP> mask=<SubnetMask> gateway= <DefaultGateway>**. ID represents the number from step 1, <StaticIP> represents the IP address we will assign, <SubnetMask> represents the subnet mask, and <Default Gateway> represents the IP address of the server's default gateway. See Figure 1.6 for our sample configuration.

Continued

3. Assign the IP address of the DNS server. Since this will be an Active Directory Domain Controller, we will set the DNS settings to point to itself. From the console, type **netsh interface ipv4 add dnsserver name="<ID>" address=<DNSIP> index=1. >**. ID represents the number from step 1, and <StaticIP> represents the IP address of the DNS server (in this case, the same IP address from step 2).

So, here is where things get a little tricky. When installing the Directory Services role in a full server installation, we would simply open up a Run window (or a command line) and type in DCPromo. Then, we would follow the prompts for configuration (domain name, file location, level of forest/domain security), and then restart the system. Installing the role in Server Core isn't so simple, yet it's not exactly rocket science. In order to make this installation happen, we are going to need to configure an unattended installation file. An unattended installation file (see Figure 1.7) is nothing more than a text file that answers the questions that would have been answered during the DCPromo installation. So, let's assume you have created the unattended file and placed it on a floppy disk, CD, or other medium, and then inserted it into the Server Core server. Let's go ahead and install Directory Services:

1. Sign in to the server.

2. In the console, change drives to the removable media. In our example, we will be using drive E:, our DVD drive.

3. Once you have changed drives, type **dcpromo answer:\answer.txt**. Answer.txt is the name of our unattended file (see Figure 1.7).

4. Follow the installation process as it configures directory services. Once the server has completed the installation process, it will reboot automatically.

5. When the server reboots, you will have a fully functional Active Directory implementation!

Figure 1.6 Setting an IP Address in Server Core

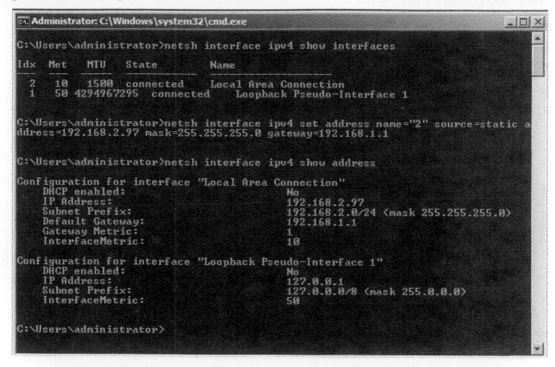

Figure 1.7 Installing Directory Services in Server Core

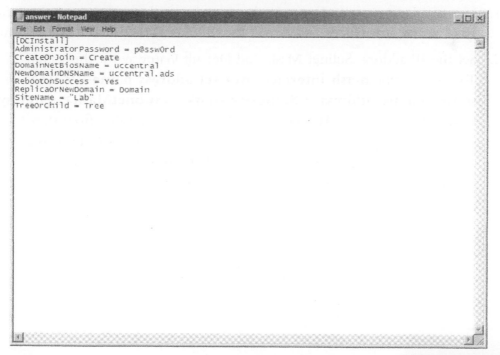

Uses for Server Core

A Windows Server 2008 Core Server Installation can be used for multiple purposes. One of the ways that Server Core can be used is to provide a minimal installation for DNS. You can manipulate, manage, and configure DNS servers through the various Windows Server 2008 DNS Graphical User Interfaces (GUIs)–DNS Manager and the Server Manager tool.

However, there are no GUIs provided with Windows Server 2008 Core Server. There are a number of advantages to running DNS within Server Core, including:

- **Smaller Footprint**. Reduces the amount of CPU, memory, and hard disk needed.

- **More Secure**. Fewer components and services running unnecessarily.

- **No GUI**. No GUI means that users cannot make modifications to the DNS databases (or any other system functions) using common/user-friendly tools.

If you are planning to run DNS within a Server Core install, there a number of steps you must perform prior to installation. The first step we must take is to set the IP information of the server. To configure the IP addressing information of the server follow these steps:

1. Identify the network adapter. In the console window, type **netsh interface ipv4 show interfaces** and record the number shown under **Idx** column.

2. Set the IP address, Subnet Mask, and Default Gateway for the server. To do this, type **netsh interface ipv4 set address name="<ID>" source=static address=<StaticIP> mask=<SubnetMask> gateway= <DefaultGateway>**. **ID** represents the interface number from step 1, **<StaticIP>** represents the IP address we will assign, **<SubnetMask>** represents the subnet mask, and **<Default Gateway>** represents the IP address of the server's default gateway. See Figure 1.8 for our sample configuration.

Figure 1.8 Setting an IP Address in Server Core

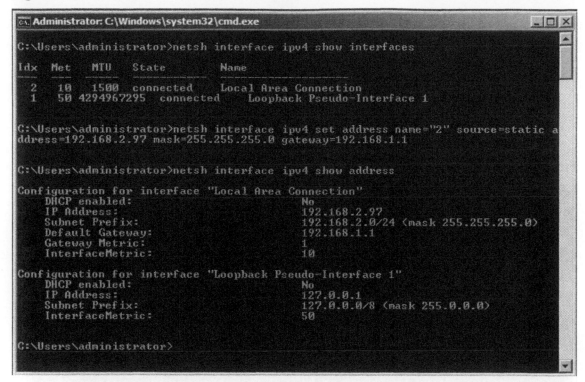

3. Assign the IP address of the DNS server. If this server were part of an Active Directory domain and replicating Active-Directory integrated zones (we will discuss those next), we would likely point this server to another AD-integrated DNS server. If it is not, we would point it to another external DNS server—commonly the Internet provider of your company. From the console, type **netsh interface ipv4 add dnsserver name="<ID>" address=<DNSIP> index=1. >. ID** represents the number from step 1, **<StaticIP>** represents the IP address of the DNS server.

   Once the IP address settings are completed—you can verify this by typing **ipconfig /all**—we can install the DNS role onto the Core Server installation.

4. To do this, from the command line type **start /w ocsetup DNS-Server-Core-Role**.

5. To verify that the DNS Server service is installed and started, type **NET START**. This will return a list of running services.

6. Next, we can use the **dnscmd** command line utility to manipulate the DNS settings. For example, you can type **dnscmd /enumzones** to list the zones hosted on this DNS server.

7. We can also change all the configuration options that we modified in the GUI section earlier by using the **dnscmd /config** option. For example, we can enable BIND secondaries by typing **dnscmd <servername> /config /bindsecondaries 1**. You can see the results in Figure 1.9.

Figure 1.9 Using the *dnscmd* Utility

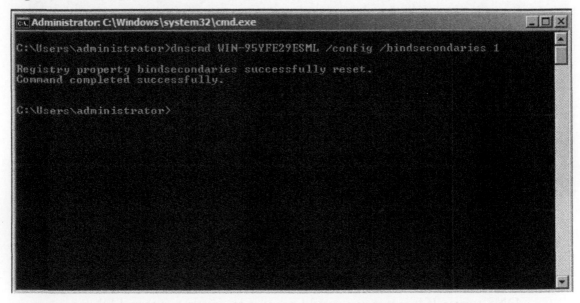

There are many, many more things you can do with the dnscmd utility. For more information on the dnscmd syntax, visit http://technet2.microsoft.com/ WindowsServer/en/library/d652a163-279f-4047-b3e0-0c468a4d69f31033.mspx.

Active Directory Certificate Services

In PKI, a digital certificate is a tool used for binding a public key with a particular owner. A great comparison is a driver's license. Consider the information listed on a driver's license:

■   Name

■   Address

- Date of birth

- Photograph

- Signature

- Social security number (or another unique number such as a state issued license number)

- Expiration date

- Signature/certification by an authority (typically from within the issuing state's government body)

The information on a state license photo is significant because it provides crucial information about the owner of that particular item. The signature from the state official serves as a trusted authority for the state, certifying that the owner has been verified and is legitimate to be behind the wheel of a car. Anyone, like an officer, who wishes to verify a driver's identity and right to commute from one place to another by way of automobile need only ask for and review the driver's license. In some cases, the officer might even call or reference that license number just to ensure it is still valid and has not been revoked.

A digital certificate in PKI serves the same function as a driver's license. Various systems and checkpoints may require verification of the owner's identity and status and will reference the trusted third party for validation. It is the certificate that enables this quick hand-off of key information between the parties involved.

The information contained in the certificate is actually part or the X.509 certificate standard. X.509 is actually an evolution of the X.500 directory standard. Initially intended to provide a means of developing easy-to-use electronic directories of people that would be available to all Internet users, it became a directory and mail standard for a very commonly known mail application: Microsoft Exchange 5.5. The X.500 directory standard specifies a common root of a hierarchical tree although the "tree" is inverted: the root of the tree is depicted at the "top" level while the other branches—called "containers"—are below it. Several of these types of containers exist with a specific naming convention. In this naming convention, each portion of a name is specified by the abbreviation of the object type or a container it represents. For example, a *CN=* before a username represents it is a "*common name*", a *C=* precedes a "*country*", and an *O=* precedes "*organization*". These elements are worth remembering as they will appear not only in discussions about X.500 and X.509, but they are ultimately the basis for the scheme of Microsoft's premier directory service, Active Directory.

X.509 is the standard used to define what makes up a digital certificate. Within this standard, a description is given for a certificate as allowing an association between a user's *distinguished name* (*DN*) and the user's public key. The DN is specified by a *naming authority* (*NA*) and used as a unique name by the *certificate authority* (*CA*) who will create the certificate. A common X.509 certificate includes the following information (see Table 1.2 and Figures 1.10 and 1.11):

Table 1.2 X.509 Certificate Data

Item	Definition
Serial Number	A unique identifier
Subject	The name of the person or company that is being identified, sometimes listed as "Issued To".
Signature Algorithm	The algorithm used to create the signature.
Issuer	The trusted authority that verified the information and generated the certificate, sometimes listed as "Issued By".
Valid From	The date the certificate was activated.
Valid To	The last day the certificate can be used.
Public Key	The public key that corresponds to the private key.
Thumbprint Algorithm	The algorithm used to create the unique value of a certificate.
Thumbprint	The unique value of every certificate, which positively identifies the certificate. If there is ever a question about the authenticity of a certificate, check this value with the issuer.

Figure 1.10 A Windows Server 2008 Certificate Field and Values

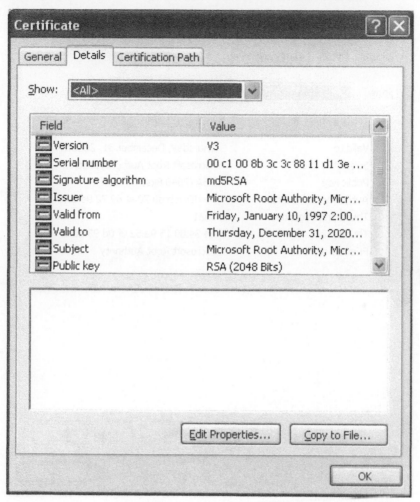

Figure 1.11 A Windows Server 2008 Certificate Field and Values

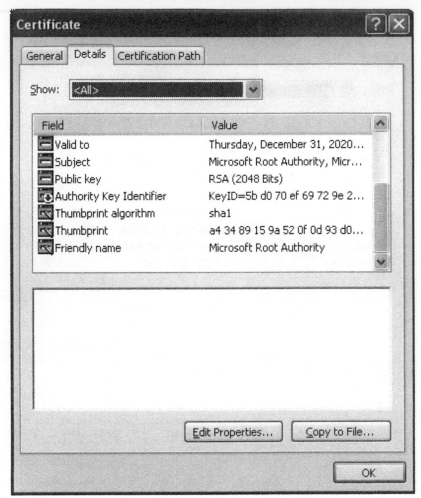

In Active Directory and Windows Server 2008, Certificate Services allow administrators to establish and manage the PKI environment. More generally, they allow for a trust model to be established within a given organization. The trust model is the framework that will hold all the pieces and components of the PKI in place. Typically, there are two options for a trust model within PKI: a *single CA model* and a *hierarchical model*. The certificate services within Windows Server 2008 provide the interfaces and underlying technology to set up and manage both of these types of deployments.

Configuring a Certificate Authority

By definition, a certificate authority is an entity (computer or system) that issues digital certificates of authenticity for use by other parties. With the ever increasing demand for effective and efficient methods to verify and secure communications, our technology market has seen the rise of many trusted third parties into the market. If you have been in the technology field for any length of time, you are likely familiar with many such vendors by name: VeriSign, Entrust, Thawte, GeoTrust, DigiCert, and GoDaddy are just a few.

While these companies provide an excellent and useful resource for both the IT administrator and the consumer, companies and organizations desired a way to establish their own certificate authorities. In a third-party, or external PKI, it is up to the third-party CA to positively verify the identity of anyone requesting a certificate from it. Beginning with Windows 2000, Microsoft has allowed the creation of a trusted *internal* CA—possibly eliminating the need for an external third party. With a Windows Server 2008 CA, the CA verifies the identity of the user requesting a certificate by checking that user's authentication credentials (using Kerberos or NTLM). If the credentials of the requesting user check out, a certificate is issued to the user. When the user needs to transmit his or her public key to another user or application, the certificate is then used to prove to the receiver that the public key inside can be used safely.

Certificate Authorities

Certificates are a way to transfer keys securely across an insecure network. If any arbitrary user were allowed to issue certificates, it would be no different than that user simply signing the data. In order for a certificate to be of any use, it must be issued by a trusted entity—an entity that both the sender and receiver trust. Such a trusted entity is known as a *Certification Authority* (CA). Third-party CAs such as VeriSign or Entrust can be trusted because they are highly visible, and their public keys are well known to the IT community. When you are confident that you hold a true public key for a CA, and that public key properly decrypts a certificate, you are then certain that the certificate was digitally signed by the CA and no one else. Only then can you be positive that the public key contained inside the certificate is valid and safe.

In the analogy we used earlier, the state driver's licensing agency is trusted because it is known that the agency requires proof of identity before issuing a driver's license. In the same way, users can trust the certification authority because they know it verifies the authentication credentials before issuing a certificate. Within an organization leveraging Windows Server 2008, several options exist for building this trust relationship. Each of these begins with the decisions made around selecting and implementing certificate authorities. With regard to the Microsoft implementation of PKI, there are at least four major roles or types of certificate authorities to be aware of:

- Enterprise CA
- Standard CA
- Root CA
- Subordinate CA

Believe it or not, beyond this list at least two variations exist: intermediate CAs and leaf CAs, each of which is a type of subordinate CA implementation.

Standard vs. Enterprise

An enterprise CA is tied into Active Directory and is required to use it. In fact, a copy of its own CA certificate is stored in Active Directory. Perhaps the biggest difference between an enterprise CA and a stand-alone CA is that enterprise CAs use Kerberos or NTLM authentication to validate users and computers before certificates are issued. This provides additional security to the PKI because the validation process relies on the strength of the Kerberos protocol, and not a human administrator. Enterprise CAs also use templates, which are described later in this chapter, and they can issue every type of certificate.

There are also several downsides to an enterprise CA. In comparison to a stand-alone CA, enterprise CAs are more difficult to maintain and require a much more in-depth knowledge about Active Directory and authentication. Also, because an enterprise CA requires Active Directory, it is nearly impossible to remove it from the network. If you were to do so, the Directory itself would quickly become outdated— making it difficult to resynchronize with the rest of the network when brought back online. Such a situation would force an enterprise CA to remain attached to the network, leaving it vulnerable to attackers.

Root vs. Subordinate Certificate Authorities

As discussed earlier, there are two ways to view PKI trust models: single CA and hierarchical. In a single CA model PKIs are very simplistic; only one CA is used within the infrastructure. Anyone who needs to trust parties vouched for by the CA is given the public key for the CA. That single CA is responsible for the interactions that ensue when parties request and seek to verify the information for a given certificate.

In a hierarchical model, a root CA functions as a top-level authority over one or more levels of CAs beneath it. The CAs below the root CA are called subordinate CAs. Root CAs serve as a *trust anchor* to all the CA's beneath it and to the users who trust the root CA. A trust anchor is an entity known to be trusted without requiring that it be trusted by going to another party, and therefore can be used as a base for trusting other parties. Since there is nothing above the root CA, no one can vouch for its identity; it must create a *self-signed* certificate to vouch for itself. With a self-signed certificate, both the certificate issuer and the certificate subject are exactly the same. Being the trust anchor, the root CA must make its own certificate available to all of the users (including subordinate CAs) that will ultimately be using that particular root CA.

Hierarchical models work well in larger hierarchical environments, such as large government organizations or corporate environments. Often, a large organization also deploys a Registration Authority (RA, covered later in this chapter), Directory Services and optionally Timestamping Services in an organization leveraging a hierarchical approach to PKI. In situations where different organization are trying to develop a hierarchical model together (such as post acquisition or merger companies or those that are partnered for collaboration), a hierarchical model can be very difficult to establish as both parties must ultimately agree upon a single trust anchor.

When you first set up an internal PKI, no CA exists. The first CA created is known as the root CA, and it can be used to issue certificates to users or to other CAs. As mentioned above, in a large organization there usually is a hierarchy where the root CA is not the only certification authority. In this case, the sole purpose of the root CA is to issue certificates to other CAs in order to establish their authority.

Any certification authority that is established after the root CA is a subordinate CA. Subordinate CAs gain their authority by requesting a certificate from either the root CA or a higher level subordinate CA. Once the subordinate CA receives the certificate, it can control CA policies and/or issue certificates itself, depending on your PKI structure and policies.

Sometimes, subordinate CAs also issue certificates to other CAs below them on the tree. These CAs are called *intermediate CAs*. Is most hierarchies, there is more than one intermediate CA. Subordinate CAs that issue certificates to end users, server, and other entities but do not issue certificates to other CAs are called *leaf CAs*.

Certificate Requests

In order to receive a certificate from a valid issuing CA, a client—computer or user—must request a certificate from a CA.

There are three ways that this request can be made:

- Autoenrollment

- Use of the Certificates snap-in

- Via a web browser

It is very likely that the most common method for requesting a certificate is autoenrollment, and we'll discuss its deployment shortly. A client can also request a certificate by use of the **Certificates** snap-in. The snap-in, shown in Figure 1.12, can be launched by clicking **Start | Run**, and then typing in **certmgr.msc** and pressing **Enter**. Note that the **Certificates** snap-in does *not* appear in the **Administrative Tools** folder as the **Certification Authority** snap-in does after installing certificate services. Once you open the Certificate Snap-in, expand the **Personal** container, and then right-clicking the **Certificates** container beneath it. You can start the **Certificate Request Wizard** by choosing **All Tasks | Request New Certificate…**, as shown in Figure 1.12.

Figure 1.12 Certificates Snap-in

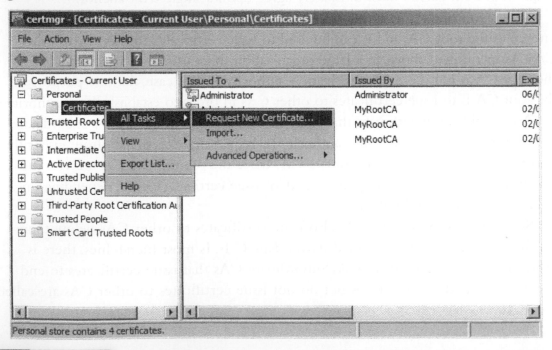

Next, you will receive the **Before You Begin** welcome screen, as shown in Figure 1.13. Click **Next**.

Figure 1.13 Before You Begin

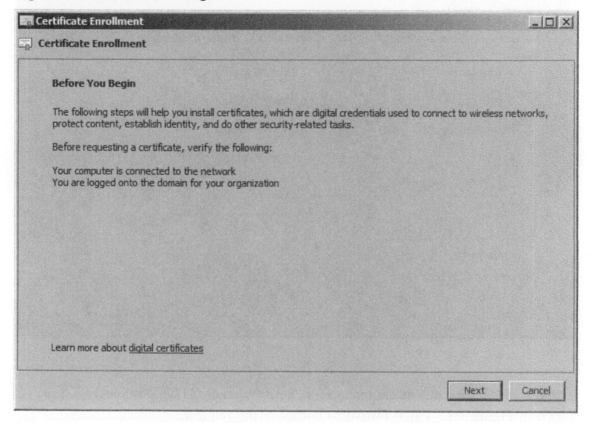

Next to Welcome screen, the wizard prompts you to choose the certificate enrollment type. Figure 1.14 shows you the available options. You can choose only a type for which the receiving CA has a template. Once you choose an appropriate template, click **Enroll**.

Figure 1.14 Request Certificates

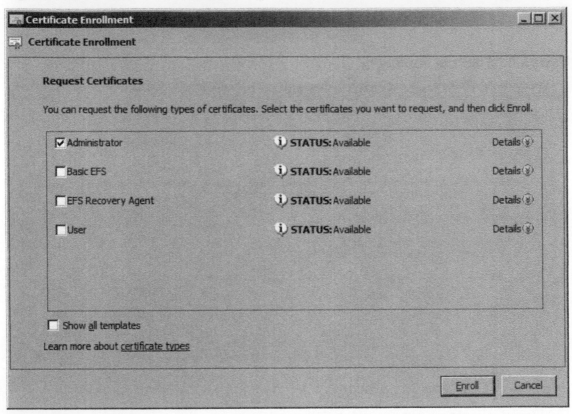

Next to Certificate Enrollment screen, verify it reads, STATUS: Succeeded, as shown in Figure 1.15. Click **Finish** to complete the request.

Figure 1.15 Certificate Installation Results

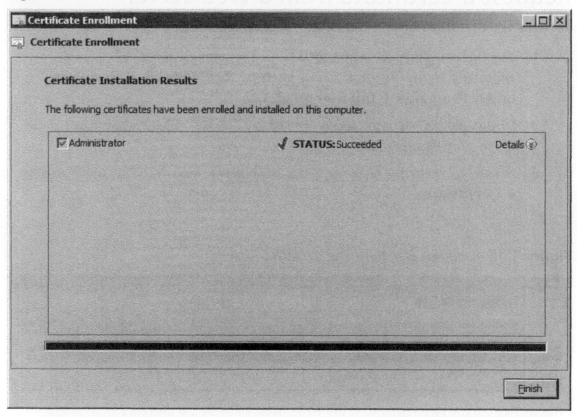

The last method for requesting a certificate is to use a Web browser on the client machine. Note that if you use this option, IIS must be installed on the CA. In the next section, we show you the steps for requesting a certificate using a client machine in this manner.

TIP

The order of component installation can be important when dealing with CAs. If you install certificate services *before* you install IIS, a client will *not* be able to connect as in the exercise below until you run the following from the command line: **certutil –vroot**. This establishes the virtual root directories necessary for Web enrollment. Note also that you must have selected the Web enrollment support option during the certificate services installation procedure.

Request a Certificate from a Web Server

To request a certificate from a Web server, follow these steps:

1. On any computer for which you want to request a certificate, launch Internet Explorer (version 5.0 or later) by clicking **Start | Programs** or **All Programs | Internet Explorer**.

2. In the address bar, type http://servername/certsrv, where servername is the name of the issuing CA.

3. When the welcome screen appears, as shown in Figure 1.16, click **Request a Certificate**.

Figure 1.16 Welcome Screen of the CA's Web Site

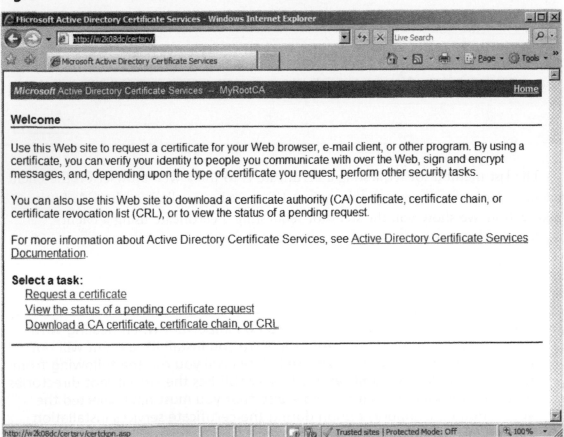

4. Click **User Certificate**, then **Submit** when the next screen appears.

5. When the **Certificate Issued** page appears, click **Install This Certificate**. Close the browser.

Certificate Practice Statement

As the use of X.509-based certificates continues to grow it becomes increasingly important that the management an organization of certificates be as diligent as possible. We know what a digital certificate is and what its critical components are, but a CA can issue a certificate for a number of different reasons. The certificate, then, must indicate exactly what the certificate will be used for. The set of rules that indicates exactly how a certificate may be used (what purpose it can e trusted for, or perhaps the community for which it can be trusted) is called a certificate policy. The X.509 standard defines certificate policies as "a named set of rules that indicates the applicability of a certificate to a particular community and/or class of application with common security requirements."

Different entities have different security requirements. For example, users want a digital certificate for securing e-mail (either encrypting the incoming messages signing outgoing mail), Syngress (as other Web vendors do) wants a digital certificate for their online store, etc. Every user will want to secure their information, and a certificate owner will use the policy information to determine if they want to accept a certificate.

It is important to have a policy in place to state what the appropriate protocol is for use of certificates—how they are requested, how and when they may be used, etc.—but it is equally as important to explain exactly how to implement those policies. This is where the Certificate Practice Statement (CPS) comes in. A CPS describes how the CA plans to manage the certificates it issues.

Key Recovery

Key recovery is compatible with the CryptoAPI architecture of Windows 2008, but it is not a necessary requirement. For key recovery, an entity's private key must be stored permanently. The storage of private keys guarantees that critical information will always be accessible, even if the information should get corrupted or deleted. On the other hand, there is a security issue in the backup of the private keys. The archived private key should be used to impersonate the private key owner only if corruption occurs on your system.

Active Directory Domain Services

Active Directory Domain Services (AD DS) stores information about users, computers, and other devices on the network. AD DS is required to install directory-enabled applications. The following are improvements made in AD DS functionality:

- Auditing (log value changes that are made to AD DS objects and their attributes)

- Fine-grained password policies (functionality to assign a special password and account lockout policies for different sets of users)

- Read-only DCs (hosts a read-only partition of the AD DS database)

- Restartable AD DS (can be stopped so that updates can be applied to a DC)

- Database mounting tool (compare different backups, eliminating multiple restores)

- User interface improvements (updated AD DS Installation Wizard)

What Is New in the AD DS Installation?

AD DS has several new installation options in Windows Server 2008, including the following:

- RODC

- DNS

- Global Catalog (GC) servers

New OS installation options include Full Install and Core Server Install.

The first thing you must do when adding a Windows Server 2008 DC to a Windows 2003 forest is to prepare the forest for the Windows 2008 server by extending the schema to accommodate the new server:

- To prepare the forest for Windows Server 2008 run the following command: *adprep /forestprep*.

- To prepare the domain for Windows Server 2008 run the following command: *adprep /domainprep*.

It is recommended that you host the primary domain controller (PDC) emulator operations master role in the forest root domain on a DC that runs Windows Server 2008 and to make this server a GC server. The first Windows Server 2008 DC in the forest cannot be an RODC. Before installing the first RODC in the forest, run the following command: *adprep /rodcprep*.

Making sure the installation was successful, you can verify the AD DS installation by checking the following:

- Check the Directory Service log in Event Viewer for errors.
- Make sure the SYSVOL folder is accessible to clients.
- Verify DNS functionality.
- Verify replication.

To run *adprep /forestprep* you have to be a member of the Enterprise Admins and Schema Admins groups of Active Directory. You must run this command from the DC in the forest that has the Schema Master FSMO role. Only one Schema Master is needed per forest.

To run *adprep /domainprep* you have to be a member of the Domain Admins or Enterprise Admins group of Active Directory. You must run this command from each Infrastructure Master FSMO role in each domain after you have run *adprep /forestprep* in the forest. Only one Infrastructure Master is needed per domain.

To run *adprep /rodcprep* you have to be a member of the Enterprise Admins group of Active Directory. You can run this command on any DC in the forest. However, it is recommended that you run this command on the Schema Master.

Summary

The new features of Windows Server 2008 are very important because understanding where changes are implemented and understanding where features have been improved will help you understand why this technology acts the way it does. Knowing how to tell what hardware components are appropriate, and which operating systems are designed for which roles and functionalities, is critical when you are choosing a new server, or deciding whether an existing server is up to the new task.

Knowledge of key features such as Server Manager, Server Core, AD Certificate Services, and AD Domain Services can help improve the user experience, improve the system administrator experience, and improve organizational security.

Solutions Fast Track

Server Manager

- ☑ Server Manager is likely to be a familiar tool to engineers who have worked with earlier versions of Windows.

- ☑ Server Manager is a single solution that is used as a single source for managing identity and system information.

- ☑ Server Manager is enabled by default when a Windows 2008 server is installed.

Server Core

- ☑ Server Core brings a new way not only to manage roles but also to deploy a Windows Server.

- ☑ Server Core is a minimal server installation option for Windows Server 2008 that contains a subset of executable files, as well as five server roles.

- ☑ Microsoft defines Server Core as "a minimal server installation option for Windows Server 2008 that contains a subset of executable files, and five server roles."

Active Directory Certificate Services

- ☑ In PKI, a digital certificate is a tool used for binding a public key with a particular owner. A great comparison is a driver's license.

- ☑ X.509 is the standard used to define what makes up a digital certificate.

- ☑ The X.500 directory standard specifies a common root of a hierarchical tree although the "tree" is inverted: the root of the tree is depicted at the "top" level while the other branches—called "containers"—are below it.

Active Directory Domain Services

- ☑ With the release of Windows Server 2008, an Active Directory domain controller can be deployed in several new ways.

- ☑ Active Directory Domain Services (AD DS) stores information about users, computers, and other devices on the network.

- ☑ AD DS has several new installation options in Windows Server 2008, including RODC and DNS.

Frequently Asked Questions

Q: Can I add Windows Server 2008 to an existing Windows 2003 Active Directory environment?

A: Yes. Adding a Windows Server 2008 DC to a current Windows 2003 Active Directory domain will make no difference to the 2003 Active Directory domain. However, you must install a full installation. The first 2008 DC cannot be a 2008 RODC, as it will need a full installation of the 2008 DC from which to replicate data.

Q: I have closed the command prompt on the Server Core terminal, and now I only see a blue background and cannot get the command prompt window back up. How do I get the command prompt window back without restarting the server?

A: Press **Ctrl + Alt + Delete** on the keyboard, open the Task Manager, and from the File menu choose **Run**, then type **cmd.exe** and click **OK**. This will bring back the command prompt window.

Q: Is an upgrade from Windows 2000 Server to Windows Server 2008 supported?

A: No. Only an upgrade from Windows Server 2003 is possible.

Q: What is Network Access Protection?

A: Network Access Protection (NAP) deals with the problem of unhealthy computers accessing the organization's network. NAP ensures that any computer that makes a connection to the network meets the requirements set out by the organization's policies. This limits access to the network and provides remediation services.

Q: My evaluation copy of Windows Server 2008 is going to expire soon. Can I extend it?

A: You can extend the 30-day grace period up to three times, for a total of 120 days. Use the SLMgr.vbs script with the *rearm* parameter to reset the counter for another 30 days. You will need to perform this step every 30 days, up to the 120 days.

Q: I am trying to install a domain controller in a domain that is in a Windows 2003 functional level. Do I have to choose Windows 2008 functional level when I install Windows Server 2008?

A: No, the functional level can always be upgraded to Windows Server 2008 at a later date.

Q: I want to be able to assign different account lockout policies to different sets of objects within Active Directory. Is this possible?

A: Yes, AD DS has a new Fine-Grained Password Policy that can be applied.

Chapter 2

Microsoft Windows Server 2008: PKI-Related Additions

Exam objectives in this chapter:

- What Is PKI?
- Digital Certificates
- Working with Certificate Services
- Working with Templates
- Creating a Custom Template

☑ Summary

☑ Solutions Fast Track

☑ Frequently Asked Questions

Introduction

Computer networks have evolved in recent years to allow an unprecedented sharing of information between individuals, corporations, and even national governments. The need to protect this information has also evolved, and network security has consequently become an essential concern of most system administrators. Even in smaller organizations, the basic goal of preventing unauthorized access while still allowing legitimate information to flow smoothly requires the use of more and more advanced technology.

That being stated, all organizations today rely on networks to access information. These sources of information can range from internal networks to the Internet. Access to information is needed, and this access must be configured to provide information to other organizations that may request it. When we need to make a purchase, for example, we can quickly check out vendors' prices through their Web pages. In order not to allow the competition to get ahead of our organization, we must establish our own Web page for the advertising and ordering of our products. Within any organization, many sites may exist across the country or around the globe. If corporate data is available immediately to employees, much time is saved. In the corporate world, any time saved is also money saved.

In the mid 1990s, Microsoft began developing what was to become a comprehensive security system of authentication protocols and technology based on already developed cryptography standards known as public key infrastructure (PKI). In Windows 2000, Microsoft used various standards to create the first Windows-proprietary PKI—one that could be implemented completely without using third-party companies. Windows Server 2008 expands and improves on that original design in several significant ways, which we'll discuss later in this chapter.

PKI is the method of choice for handling authentication issues in large enterprise-level organizations today. Windows Server 2008 includes the tools you need to create a PKI for your company and issue digital certificates to users, computers, and applications. This chapter addresses the complex issues involved in planning a certificate-based PKI. We'll provide an overview of the basic terminology and concepts relating to the public key infrastructure, and you'll learn about public key cryptography and how it is used to authenticate the identity of users, computers, and applications/services. We'll discuss different components of PKI, including private key, public key, and a trusted third party (TTP) along with PKI enhancements in Windows Server 2008. We'll discuss the role of digital certificates and the different types of certificates (user, machine, and application certificates).

You'll learn about certification authorities (CAs), the servers that issue certificates, including both public CAs and private CAs, such as the ones you can implement on your own network using Server 2008's certificate services. Next, we'll discuss the CA hierarchy and how root CAs and subordinate CAs act together to provide for your organization's certificate needs. You'll find out how the Microsoft certificate services work, and we'll walk you through the steps involved in implementing one or more certification authorities based on the needs of the organization. You'll learn to determine the appropriate CA type—enterprise or stand-alone CA—for a given situation and how to plan the CA hierarchy and provide for security of your CAs. We'll show you how to plan for enrollment and distribution of certificates, including the use of certificate requests, role-based administration, and autoenrollment deployment.

Next, we'll discuss how to implement certificate templates, different types of templates that you can use in your environment. Finally, we'll discuss the role of key recovery agent and how it works in a Windows Server 2008 environment.

What Is PKI?

The rapid growth of Internet use has given rise to new security concerns. Any company that does not configure a strong security infrastructure is literally putting the company at risk. An unscrupulous person could, if security were lax, steal information or modify business information in a way that could result in major financial disaster. To protect the organization's information, the middleman must be eliminated. Cryptographic technologies such as public key infrastructure (PKI) provide a way to identify both users and servers during network use.

PKI is the underlying cryptography system that enables users or computers that have never been in trusted communication before to validate themselves by referencing an association to a trusted third party (TTP). Once this verification is complete, the users and computers can now securely send messages, receive messages, and engage in transactions that include the interchange of data.

PKI is used in both private networks (intranets) and on the World Wide Web (the Internet). It is actually the latter, the Internet, that has driven the need for better methods for verifying credentials and authenticating users. Consider the vast number of transactions that take place every day over the internet—from banking to shopping to accessing databases and sending messages or files. Each of these transactions involves at least two parties. The problem lies in the verification of who those parties are and the choice of whether to trust them with your credentials and information.

The PKI verification process is based on the use of *keys*, unique bits of data that serve one purpose: identifying the owner of the key. Every user of PKI actually generates or receives two types of keys: a *public key* and a *private key*. The two are actually connected and are referred to as a *key pair*. As the name suggests, the public key is made openly available to the public while the private key is limited to the actual owner of the key pair. Through the use of these keys, messages can be *encrypted* and *decrypted*, allowing data to be exchanged securely (this process will be covered in a few sections later in this chapter).

The use of PKI on the World Wide Web is so pervasive that it is likely that every Internet user has used it without even being aware of it. However, PKI is not simply limited to the Web; applications such as Pretty Good Privacy (PGP) also leverage the basis of PKI technology for e-mail protection; FTP over SSL/TLS uses PKI, and many other protocols have the ability to manage the verification of identities through the use of key-based technology. Companies such as VeriSign and Entrust exist as trusted third-party vendors, enabling a world of online users who are strangers to find a common point of reference for establishing confidentiality, message integrity, and user authentication. Literally millions of secured online transactions take place every day leveraging their services within a public key infrastructure.

Technology uses aside, PKI fundamentally addresses relational matters within communications. Specifically, PKI seeks to provide solutions for the following:

- Proper authentication
- Trust
- Confidentiality
- Integrity
- Nonrepudiation

By using the core PKI elements of public key cryptography, digital signatures, and certificates, all these equally important goals can be met successfully. The good news is that the majority of the work involved in implementing these elements under Windows Server 2008 is taken care of automatically by the operating system and is done behind the scenes.

The first goal, proper *authentication*, means that you can be highly certain that an entity such as a user or a computer is indeed the entity he, she, or it is claiming to be. Think of a bank. If you wanted to cash a large check, the teller will more than likely ask for some identification. If you present the teller with a driver's license and the picture on it matches your face, the teller can then be highly certain that you are that person—that is, if the teller trusts the validity of the license itself. Because the driver's license is issued by a government agency—a trusted third party—the teller is more likely to accept it as valid proof of your identity than if you presented an employee ID card issued by a small company that the teller has never heard of. As you can see, trust and authentication work hand in hand.

When transferring data across a network, *confidentiality* ensures that the data cannot be viewed and understood by any third party. The data might be anything from an e-mail message to a database of social security numbers. In the last 20 years, more effort has been spent trying to achieve this goal (data confidentiality) than perhaps all the others combined. In fact, the entire scientific field of cryptology is devoted to ensuring confidentiality (as well as all the other PKI goals).

NOTE

Cryptography refers to the process of encrypting data; *cryptanalysis* is the process of decrypting, or "cracking" cryptographic code. Together, the two make up the science of *cryptology*.

As important as confidentiality is, however, the importance of network data *integrity* should not be underestimated. Consider the extreme implications of a patient's medical records being intercepted during transmission and then maliciously or accidentally altered before being sent on to their destination. Integrity gives confidence to a recipient that data has arrived in its original form and hasn't been changed or edited.

Finally we come to *nonrepudiation*. A bit more obscure than the other goals, nonrepudiation allows you to prove that a particular entity sent a particular piece of data. It is impossible for the entity to deny having sent it. It then becomes extremely difficult for an attacker to masquerade as a legitimate user and then send malevolent data across the network. Nonrepudiation is related to, but separate from authentication.

The Function of the PKI

The primary function of the PKI is to address the need for privacy throughout a network. For the administrator, there are many areas that need to be secured. Internal and external authentication, encryption of stored and transmitted files, and e-mail privacy are just a few examples. The infrastructure that Windows Server 2008 provides links many different public key technologies in order to give the IT administrator the power necessary to maintain a secure network.

Most of the functionality of a Windows Server 2008-based PKI comes from a few crucial components, which are described in this chapter. Although there are several third-party vendors such as VeriSign (www.verisign.com) that offer similar technologies and components, using Windows Server 2008 can be a less costly and easier to implement option—especially for small and medium-sized companies.

Components of PKI

In today's network environments, key pairs are used in a variety of different functions. This series will likely cover topics such as virtual private networks (VPNs), digital signatures, access control (SSH), secure e-mail (PGP—mentioned already—and S/MIME), and secure Web access (Secure Sockets Layer, or SSL). Although these technologies are varied in purpose and use, each includes an implementation of PKI for managing trusted communications between a host and a client.

While PKI exists at some level within the innards of several types of communications technologies, its form can change from implementation to implementation. As such, the components necessary for a successful implementation can vary depending on the requirements, but in public key cryptography there is always:

- A private key
- A public key
- A trusted third party (TTP)

Since a public key must be associated with the name of its owner, a data structure known as a public key certificate is used. The certificate typically contains the owner's name, their public key and e-mail address, validity dates for the certificate, the location of revocation information, the location of the issuer's policies, and possibly other affiliate information that identifies the certificate issuer with an organization such as an employer or other institution.

In most cases, the private and public keys are simply referred to as the private and public key certificates, and the trusted third party is commonly known as the certificate authority (CA). The certificate authority is the resource that must be available to both the holder of the private key and the holder of the public key. Entire hierarchies can exist within a public key infrastructure to support the use of multiple certificate authorities.

In addition to certificate authorities and the public and private key certificates they publish, there are a collection of components and functions associated with the management of the infrastructure. As such, a list of typical components required for a functional public key infrastructure would include but not be limited to the following:

- Digital certificates
- Certification authorities
- Certificate enrollment
- Certificate revocation
- Encryption/cryptography services

Although we have already covered digital certificates and certificate authorities at a high level, it will be well worth our time to revisit these topics. In the sections to follow, we will explore each of the aforementioned topics in greater detail.

Notes from the Underground...

PKI Enhancements in Windows Server 2008

Windows Server 2008 introduces many new enhancements that allow for a more easily implemented PKI solution and, believe it or not, the development of such solutions. Some of these improvements extend to the clients, such as the Windows Vista operating system. Overall, these improvements have increased the manageability throughout Windows PKI. For example, the revocations services have been redesigned, and the attack surface for enrollment has decreased. The following list items include the major highlights:

- **Enterprise PKI (PKIView)** PKIView is a Microsoft Management Console (MMC) snap-in for Windows Server 2008. It can be used to monitor and analyze the health of the certificate authorities and to view details for each certificate authority certificate published in Active Directory Certificate Servers.

- **Web Enrollment** Introduced in Windows Server 2000, the new Web enrollment control is more secure and makes the use of scripts much easier. It is also easier to update than previous versions.

Continued

- **Network Device Enrollment Service (NDES)** In Windows Server 2008, this service represents Microsoft's implementation of the Simple Certificate Enrollment Protocol (SCEP), a communication protocol that makes it possible for software running on network devices, such as routers and switches that cannot otherwise be authenticated on the network, to enroll for x.509 certificates from a certificate authority.

- **Online Certificate Status Protocol (OCSP)** In cases where conventional CRLs (Certificate Revocation Lists) are not an optimal solution, Online Responders can be configured on a single computer or in an Online Responder Array to manage and distribute revocation status information.

- **Group Policy and PKI** New certificate settings in Group Policy now enable administrators to manage certificate settings from a central location for all the computers in the domain.

- **Cryptography Next Generation** Leveraging the U.S. government's Suite B cryptographic algorithms, which include algorithms for encryption, digital signatures, key exchange, and hashing, Cryptography Next Generation (CNG) offers a flexible development platform that allows IT professionals to create, update, and use custom cryptography algorithms in cryptography-related applications such as Active Directory Certificate Services (AD CS), Secure Sockets Layer (SSL), and Internet Protocol Security (IPSec).

How PKI Works

Before we discuss how PKI works today, it is perhaps helpful to understand the term encryption and how PKI has evolved. The history of general cryptography almost certainly dates back to almost 2000 B.C. when Roman and Greek statesmen used simple alphabet-shifting algorithms to keep government communication private. Through time and civilizations, ciphering text played an important role in wars and politics. As modern times provided new communication methods, scrambling information became increasingly more important. World War II brought about the first use of the computer in the cracking of Germany's Enigma code. In 1952, President Truman created the National Security Agency at Fort Meade, Maryland. This agency, which is the center of U.S. cryptographic activity, fulfills two important national functions: It protects all military and executive communication from being intercepted, and it intercepts and unscrambles messages sent by other countries.

Although complexity increased, not much changed until the 1970s, when the National Security Agency (NSA) worked with Dr. Horst Feistel to establish the Data Encryption Standard (DES) and Whitfield Diffie and Martin Hellman introduced the first public key cryptography standard. Windows Server 2008 still uses Diffie-Hellman (DH) algorithms for SSL, Transport Layer Security (TLS), and IPSec. Another major force in modern cryptography came about in the late 1970s. RSA Labs, founded by Ronald Rivest, Adi Shamir, and Leonard Adleman, furthered the concept of key cryptography by developing a technology of key pairs, where plaintext that is encrypted by one key can be decrypted only by the other matching key.

There are three types of cryptographic functions. The hash function does not involve the use of a key at all, but it uses a mathematical algorithm on the data in order to scramble it. The secret key method of encryption, which involves the use of a single key, is used to encrypt and decrypt the information and is sometimes referred to as symmetric key cryptography. An excellent example of secret key encryption is the decoder ring you may have had as a child. Any person who obtained your decoder ring could read your "secret" information.

There are basically two types of symmetric algorithms. Block symmetric algorithms work by taking a given length of bits known as blocks. Stream symmetric algorithms operate on a single bit at a time. One well-known block algorithm is DES. Windows 2000 uses a modified DES and performs that operation on 64-bit blocks using every eighth bit for parity. The resulting ciphertext is the same length as the original cleartext. For export purposes the DES is also available with a 40-bit key.

One advantage of secret key encryption is the efficiency with which it takes a large amount of data and encrypts it quite rapidly. Symmetric algorithms can also be easily implemented at the hardware level. The major disadvantage of secret key encryption is that a single key is used for both encryption and decryption. There must be a secure way for the two parties to exchange the one secret key.

In the 1970s this disadvantage of secret key encryption was eliminated through the mathematical implementation of public key encryption. Public key encryption, also referred to as asymmetric cryptography, replaced the one shared key with each user's own pair of keys. One key is a public key, which is made available to everyone and is used for the encryption process only. The other key in the pair, the private key, is available only to the owner. The private key cannot be created as a result of the public key's being available. Any data that is encrypted by a public key can be decrypted only by using the private key of the pair. It is also possible for the owner to use a private key to encrypt sensitive information. If the data is encrypted by using the private key, then the public key in the pair of keys is needed to decrypt the data.

DH algorithms are known collectively as *shared secret key* cryptographies, also known as symmetric key encryption. Let's say we have two users, Greg and Matt, who want to communicate privately. With DH, Greg and Matt each generate a random number. Each of these numbers is known only to the person who generated it. Part one of the DH function changes each secret number into a nonsecret, or public, number. Greg and Matt now exchange the public numbers and then enter them into part two of the DH function. This results in a private key—one that is identical to both users. Using advanced mathematics, this shared secret key can be decrypted only by someone with access to one of the original random numbers. As long as Greg and Matt keep the original numbers hidden, the shared secret key cannot be reversed.

It should be apparent from the many and varied contributing sources to PKI technology that the need for management of this invaluable set of tools would become paramount. If PKI, like any other technology set, continued to develop without standards of any kind, then differing forms and evolutions of the technology would be implemented ad hoc throughout the world. Eventually, the theory holds that some iteration would render communication or operability between different forms impossible. At that point, the cost of standardization would be significant, and the amount of time lost in productivity and reconstruction of PKI systems would be immeasurable.

Thus, a set of standards was developed for PKI. The Public-Key Cryptography Standards (PKCS) are a set of standard protocols sued for securing the exchange of information through PKI. The list of these standards was actually established by RSA laboratories—the same organization that developed the original RSA encryption standard—along with a group of participating technology leaders that included Microsoft, Sun, and Apple.

PKCS Standards

Here is a list of active PKCS standards. You will notice that there are gaps in the numbered sequence of these standards, and that is due to the retiring of standards over time since they were first introduced.

- **PKCS #1: RSA Cryptography Standard** Outlines the encryption of data using the RSA algorithm. The purpose of the RSA Cryptography Standard is in the development of digital signatures and digital envelopes.

PKCS #1 also describes a syntax for RSA public keys and private keys. The public-key syntax is used for certificates, while the private-key syntax is used for encrypting private keys.

- **PKCS #3: Diffie–Hellman Key Agreement Standard** Outlines the use of the Diffie-Hellman Key Agreement, a method of sharing a secret key between two parties. The secret key used to encrypt ongoing data transfer between the two parties. Whitefield Diffie and martin Hellman developed the Diffie-Hellman algorithm in the 1970s as the first public asymmetric cryptographic system (asymmetric cryptography was invented in the United Kingdom earlier in the same decade, but was classified as a military secret). Diffie-Hellman overcomes the issue of symmetric key system, because management of the keys is less difficult.

- **PKCS #5: Password–based Cryptography Standard** A method for encrypting a string with a secret key that is derived from a password. The result of the method is an octet string (a sequence of 8-bit values). PKCS #8 is primarily used for encrypting private keys when they are being transmitted between computers.

- **PKCS #6: Extended-certificate Syntax Standard** Deals with extended certificates. Extended certificates are made up of the X.509 certificate plus additional attributes. The additional attributes and the X.509 certificate can be verified using a single public-key operation. The issuer that signs the extended certificate is the same as the one that signs the X.509 certificate.

- **PKCS #7: Cryptographic Message Syntax Standard** The foundation for Secure/Multipurpose Internet Mail Extensions (S/MIME) standard. It is also compatible with Privacy-Enhanced Mail (PEM) and can be used in several different architectures of key management.

- **PKCS #8: Private-key Information Syntax Standard** Describes a method of communication for private-key information that includes the use of public-key algorithm and additional attributes (similar to PKCS #6). In this case, the attributes can be a DN or a root CA's public key.

- **PKCS #9: Selected Attribute Types** Defines the types of attributes for use in extended certificates (PKCS #6), digitally signed messages (PKCS #7), and private-key information (PKCS #8).

- **PKCS #10: Certification Request Syntax Standard** Describes a syntax for certification request. A certification request consists of a DN, a public key, and additional attributes. Certification requests are sent to a CA, which then issues the certificate.

- **PKCS #11: Cryptographic Token Interface Standard** Specifies an application program interface (API) for token devices that hold encrypted information and perform cryptographic functions, such as smart cards and Universal Serial Bus (USB) pigtails.

- **PKCS #12: Personal Information Exchange Syntax Standard** Specifies a portable format for storing or transporting a user's private keys and certificates. Ties into both PKCS #8 (communication of private-key information) and PKCS #11 (Cryptographic Token Interface Standard). Portable formats include diskettes, smart cards, and Personal Computer Memory Card International Association (PCMCIA) cards. On Microsoft Windows platforms, PKCS #12 format files are generally given the extension *.pfx*. PKCS #12 is the best standard format to use when exchanging private keys and certificates between systems.

RSA-derived technology in its various forms is used extensively by Windows Server 2008 for such things as Kerberos authentication and S/MIME. In practice, the use of the PKI technology goes something like this: Two users, Dave and Dixine, wish to communicate privately. Dave and Dixine each own a key pair consisting of a public key and a private key. If Dave wants Dixine to send him an encrypted message, he first transmits his public key to Dixine. She then uses Dave's public key to encrypt the message. Fundamentally, since Dave's public key was used to encrypt, only Dave's private key can be used to decrypt. When he receives the message, only he is able to read it. Security is maintained because only public keys are transmitted—the private keys are kept secret and are known only to their owners. Figure 2.1 illustrates the process.

Figure 2.1 Public/Private Key Data Exchange

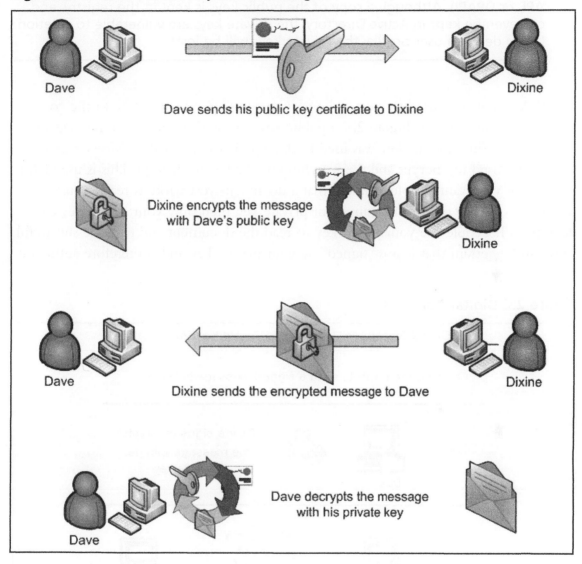

WARNING

In a Windows Server 2008 PKI, a user's public and private keys are stored under the user's profile. For the administrator, the public keys would be under *Documents and Settings\Administrator\System Certificates\My\Certificates* and the private keys would be under *Documents and Settings\Administrator*

Crypto\RSA (where they are double encrypted by Microsoft's Data Protection API, or DPAPI). Although a copy of the public keys is kept in the registry, and can even be kept in Active Directory, the private keys are vulnerable to deletion. If you delete a user profile, the private keys will be lost!

RSA can also be used to create "digital signatures" (see Figure 2.2). In the communication illustrated in Figure 2.1, a public key was used to encrypt a message and the corresponding private key was used to decrypt. If we invert the process, a private key can be used to encrypt and the matching public key to decrypt. This is useful, for example, if you want people to know that a document you wrote is really yours. If you encrypt the document using your private key, then only your public key can decrypt it. If people use your public key to read the document and they are successful, they can be certain that it was "signed" by your private key and is therefore authentic.

Figure 2.2 Digital Signatures

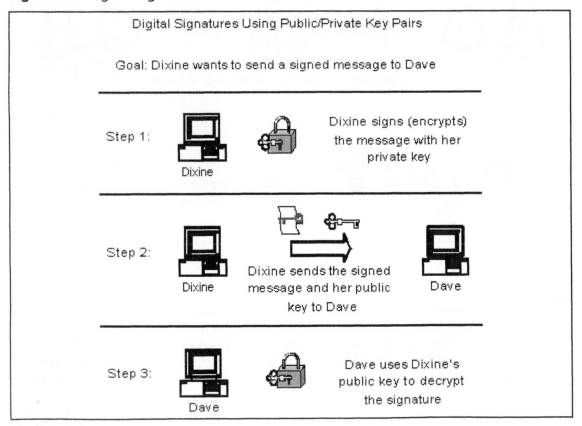

Notes from the Underground...

Modern Cryptography 101

Thanks to two mathematical concepts, prime number theory and modulo algebra, most of today's cryptography encryption standards are considered intractable—that is, they are unbreakable with current technology in a reasonable amount of time. For example, it might take 300 linked computers over 1,000 years to decrypt a message. Of course, quantum computing is expected to some day change all that, making calculations exponentially faster and rendering all current cryptographic algorithms useless—but we won't worry about that for now.

First, an explanation of the *modulo* operator. Let's go back to elementary school where you first learned to do division. You learned that 19/5 equals 3 with a remainder of 4. You also probably concentrated on the 3 as the important number. Now, however, we get to look at the remainder. When we take the modulus of two numbers, the result is the remainder—therefore, 19 mod 5 equals 4. Similarly, 24 mod 5 also equals 4 (can you see why?). Finally, we can conclude that 19 and 24 are congruent in modulo 4. So how does this relate to cryptography and prime numbers?

The idea is to take a message and represent it by using a sequence of numbers. We'll call the sequence x_i. What we need to do is find three numbers that make the following modulo equation possible: $(x^e)^d \bmod y = x$.

The first two numbers, e and d, are a pair and are completely interchangeable. The third number, y, is a product of two very large prime numbers (the larger the primes, the more secure the encryption). Prime number theory is too complex for an in-depth discussion here, but in a nutshell, remember that a prime number is only divisible by the number 1 and itself. This gives each prime number a "uniqueness."

Once we have found these numbers (although we won't go into how because this is the really deep mathematical part), the encryption key becomes the pair (e, y) and the decryption key becomes the pair (d, y). Now it doesn't matter which key we decide to make public and which key we make private because they're interchangeable. It's a good thing that Windows Server 2008 does all of the difficult work for us!

Public Key Functionality

Public key cryptography brings major security technologies to the desktop in the Windows 2000 environment. The network now is provided with the ability to allow users to safely:

- Transmit over insecure channels

- Store sensitive information on any commonly used media

- Verify a person's identity for authentication

- Prove that a message was generated by a particular person

- Prove that the received message was not tampered with in transit

Algorithms based on public keys can be used for all these purposes. The most popular public key algorithm is the standard RSA, which is named after its three inventors: Rivest, Shamir, and Adleman. The RSA algorithm is based on two prime numbers with more than 200 digits each. A hacker would have to take the ciphertext and the public key and factor the product of the two primes. As computer processing time increases, the RSA remains secure by increasing the key length, unlike the DES algorithm, which has a fixed key length.

Public key algorithms provide privacy, authentication, and easy key management, but they encrypt and decrypt data slowly because of the intensive computation required. RSA has been evaluated to be from 10 to 10,000 times slower than DES in some environments, which is a good reason not to use public key algorithms for bulk encryption.

Digital Signatures

Document letterhead can be easily created on a computer, so forgery is a security issue. When information is sent electronically, no human contact is involved. The receiver wants to know that the person listed as the sender is really the sender and that the information received has not been modified in any way during transit. A hash algorithm is implemented to guarantee the Windows 2000 user that the data is authentic. A hash value encrypted with a private key is called a digital signature. Anyone with access to the corresponding public key can verify the authenticity of a digital signature. Only a person having a private key can generate digital signatures. Any modification makes a digital signature invalid.

The purpose of a digital signature is to prevent changes within a document from going unnoticed and also to claim the person to be the original author. The document itself is not encrypted. The digital signature is just data sent along with the data guaranteed to be untampered with. A change of any size invalidates the digital signature.

When King Henry II had to send a message to his troops in a remote location, the letter would be sealed with wax, and while the wax was still soft the king would use his ring to make an impression in it. No modification occurred to the original message if the seal was never broken during transit. There was no doubt that King Henry II had initiated the message, because he was the only person possessing a ring that matched the waxed imprint. Digital signatures work in a similar fashion in that only the sender's public key can authenticate both the original sender and the content of the document.

The digital signature is generated by a message digest, which is a number generated by taking the message and using a hash algorithm. A message digest is regarded as a fingerprint and can range from a 128-bit number to a 256-bit number. A hash function takes variable-length input and produces a fixed-length output. The message is first processed with a hash function to produce a message digest. This value is then signed by the sender's private key, which produces the actual digital signature. The digital signature is then added to the end of the document and sent to the receiver along with the document.

Since the mere presence of a digital signature proves nothing, verification must be mathematically proven. In the verification process, the first step is to use the corresponding public key to decrypt the digital signature. The result will produce a 128-bit number. The original message will be processed with the same hash function used earlier and will result in a message digest. The two resulting 128-bit numbers will then be compared, and if they are equal, you will receive notification of a good signature. If a single character has been altered, the two 128-bit numbers will be different, indicating that a change has been made to the document, which was never scrambled.

Authentication

Public key cryptography can provide authentication instead of privacy. In Windows 2000, a challenge is sent by the receiver of the information. The challenge can be implemented one of two ways. The information is authenticated because only the corresponding private key could have encrypted the information that the public key is successfully decrypting.

In the first authentication method, a challenge to authenticate involves sending an encrypted challenge to the sender. The challenge is encrypted by the receiver, using the sender's public key. Only the corresponding private key can successfully decode the challenge. When the challenge is decoded, the sender sends the plaintext back to the receiver. This is the proof for the receiver that the sender is truly the sender.

For example, when Alice receives a document from Bob, she wants to authenticate that the sender is really Bob. She sends an encrypted challenge to Bob, using his public key. When he receives the challenge, Bob uses his private key to decrypt the information. The decrypted challenge is then sent back to Alice. When Alice receives the decrypted challenge, she is convinced that the document she received is truly from Bob.

The second authentication method uses a challenge that is sent in plaintext. The receiver, after receiving the document, sends a challenge in plaintext to the sender. The sender receives the plaintext challenge and adds some information before adding a digital signature.

The challenge and digital signature now head back to the sender. The digital signature is generated by using a hash function and then encrypting the result with a private key, so the receiver must use the sender's public key to verify the digital signature. If the signature is good, the original document and sender have at this point been verified mathematically.

Secret Key Agreement via Public Key

The PKI of Windows 2000 permits two parties to agreed on a secret key while they use nonsecure communication channels. Each party generates half the shared secret key by generating a random number, which is sent to the other party after being encrypted with the other party's public key. Each receiving side then decrypts the ciphertext using a private key, which will result in the missing half of the secret key.

By adding both random numbers together, each party will have an agreed-upon shared secret key, which can then be used for secure communication even though the secret key was first obtained through a nonsecure communication channel.

Bulk Data Encryption without Prior Shared Secrets

The final major feature of public key technology is that it can encrypt bulk data without generating a shared secret key first. The biggest disadvantage of using asymmetric algorithms for encryption is the slowness of the overall process, which results from the necessary intense computations; the largest disadvantage of using symmetric algorithms for encryption of bulk data is the need for a secure communication channel for exchanging the secret key. The Windows 2000 operating system combines symmetric and asymmetric algorithms to get the best of both worlds at just the right moment.

For a large document that must be kept secret, because secret key encryption is the quickest method to use for bulk data, a session key is used to scramble the document. To protect the session key, which is the secret key needed to decrypt the protected data; the sender encrypts this small item quickly by using the receiver's public key. This encryption of the session key is handled by asymmetric algorithms, which use intense computation but do not require much time, due to the small size of the session key. The document, along with the encrypted session key, is then sent to the receiver. Only the intended receiver will possess the correct private key to decode the session key, which is needed to decode the actual document. When the session key is in plaintext, it can be applied to the ciphertext of the bulk data and then transform the bulk data back to plaintext.

Digital Certificates

Let's take a moment to go on the Internet and look at a digital certificate.

1. Open up your Web browser, and go to www.syngress.com.

2. Select a book and add it to your cart.

3. Proceed to the checkout.

4. Once you are at the checkout screen, you will see a padlock in your browser. In Internet Explorer 7, this will be to the right of the address box; older browsers place the padlock in the bottom right of the window frame. Open the certificate properties. In Internet Explorer 7, you do this by clicking on the padlock and selecting "View Certificates" from the prompt; older browsers generally let you double-click the padlock.

5. Move around the tabs of the Properties screen to look at the different information contained within that certificate.

The Windows Server 2008 PKI does many things behind the scenes. Thanks in part to autoenrollment (discussed later in this chapter) and certificate stores (places where certificates are kept after their creation), some PKI-enabled features such as EFS work with no user intervention at all. Others, such as IPSec, require significantly less work than would be required without an advanced operating system.

Even though a majority of the PKI is handled by Server, it is still instructive to have an overview of how certificate services work.

1. First, a system or user generates a public/private key pair and then a certificate request.

2. The certificate request, which contains the public key and other identifying information such as user name, is forwarded on to a CA.

3. The CA verifies the validity of the public key. If it is verified, the CA issues the certificate.

4. Once issued, the certificate is ready for use and is kept in the certificate store, which can reside in Active Directory. Applications that require a certificate use this central repository when necessary.

In practice, it isn't terribly difficult to implement certificate services. Configuring the CA requires a bit more effort, as does planning the structure and hierarchy of the PKI—especially if you are designing an enterprisewide solution.

In our previous discussion of public and private key pairs, two users wanted to exchange confidential information and did so by having one user encrypt the data with the other user's public key. We then discussed digital signatures, where the sending user "signs" the data by using his or her private key. Did you notice the security vulnerability in these methods?

In this type of scenario, there is nothing to prevent an attacker from intercepting the data mid-stream, and replacing the original signature with his or her own, using of course his or her own private key. The attacker would then forward the replacement public key to the unsuspecting party. In other words, even though the data is signed, how can you be sure of who signed it? The answer in the Windows PKI is the certificate.

Think of a certificate as a small and portable combination safe. The primary purpose of the safe is to hold a public key (although quite a bit of other information is also held there). The combination to the safe must be held by someone you trust—that trust is the basis for the entire PKI system. If I am a user and want to send you my public key so that you can encrypt some data to send back to me, I can just sign the data myself, but I am then vulnerable to the attack mentioned above. However if I allow a trusted third party entity to take my public key (which I don't mind because they're trustworthy), lock it away in the safe and then send the safe to you, you can ask the trusted party for the combination. When you open the safe, you can be certain that the public key and all other information inside really belongs to me, because the safe came from a trustworthy source. The "safe" is really nothing more than a digital signature, except that the signature comes from a universally trusted third party and not from me. The main purpose of certificates, then, is to facilitate the secure transfer of keys across an insecure network. Figure 2.3 shows the properties of a Windows certificate—notice that the highlighted public key is only part of the certificate.

Figure 2.3 A Windows Server 2008 Certificate

User Certificates

Of the three general types of certificates found in a Windows PKI, the *user certificate* is perhaps the most common. User certificates are certificates that enable the user to do something that would not be otherwise allowed. The Enrollment Agent certificate is one example. Without it, even an administrator is not able to enroll smart cards and configure them properly at an enrollment station. Under Windows Server 2008, required user certificates can be requested automatically by the client and subsequently issued by a certification authority (discussed below) with no user intervention necessary.

Machine Certificates

Also known as computer certificates, *machine certificates* (as the name implies) give the system—instead of the user—the ability to do something out of the ordinary. The main purpose for machine certificates is authentication, both client-side and server-side. As stated earlier, certificates are the main vehicle by which public keys are exchanged in a PKI. Machine certificates are mainly involved with these behind-the-scenes exchanges, and are normally overseen by the operating system. Machine certificates have been able to take advantage of Windows' autoenrollment feature since 2000 Server was introduced. We will discuss auto-enrollment later in this chapter.

Application Certificates

The term *application certificate* refers to any certificate that is used with a specific PKI-enabled application. Examples include IPSec and S/MIME encryption for e-mail. Applications that need certificates are generally configured to automatically request them, and are then placed in a waiting status until the required certificate arrives. Depending upon the application, the network administrator or even the user might have the ability to change or even delete certificate requests issued by the application.

TIP

Certificates are at the very core of the Windows PKI. Make certain that you understand what certificates are, and why they are needed when using public keys. Also, be familiar with the types of certificates listed in this section and the differences between them.

Working with Certificate Services

We've just concluded a tour of most of the properties associated with a CA, but knowing what you *can* do does not mean that we know what you *should* do. To find out more about what you should do, you need to analyze the certificate needs of your organization, and then move on to create an appropriate CA structure.

According to Microsoft's TechNet, the analysis of certificate needs springs primarily from "the analysis of business requirements and the analysis of applications that benefit from PKI-based security." In other words, when designing a PKI/CA structure, you will need to understand the different uses for certificates and whether your organization needs to use certificates for each of these purposes. Examples include SSL for a secure Web server, EFS for encryption of files, and S/MIME for encryption of e-mail messages. The use of S/MIME might dictate that your CA hierarchy have a trust relationship with external CAs, and the use of SSL might lead you to implement a stand-alone CA instead of an enterprise CA. Thus, analyzing these needs *before* you implement your PKI can save you a lot of time and trouble.

Backing Up Certificate Services

1. On any computer for which you want to take a backup, Log on with administrative privileges.

2. Click **Start**, click **All Programs,** click **Administrative Tools**, and then click **Certification Authority**.

3. Right-click the name of your CA, and choose **All Tasks | Back up CA…** from the pop-up menu, as shown in Figure 2.4.

Figure 2.4 Certificate Authority Page

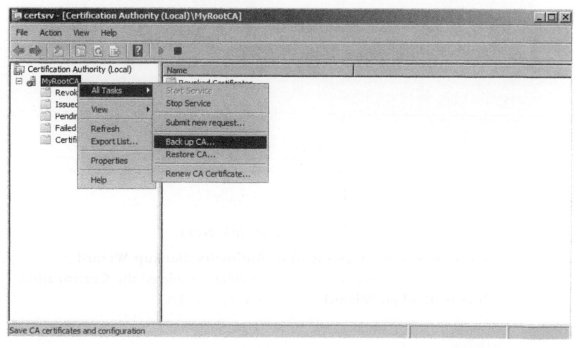

4. On the **Welcome to the Certification Authority Backup Wizard** page, click **Next** to continue.

5. **On Items to Back Up page**, click **Private key and CA certificate** and **Certificate database and certificate database log**. Type in the path of back up location, and then click Next (see Figure 2.5).

Figure 2.5 Items to Back Up

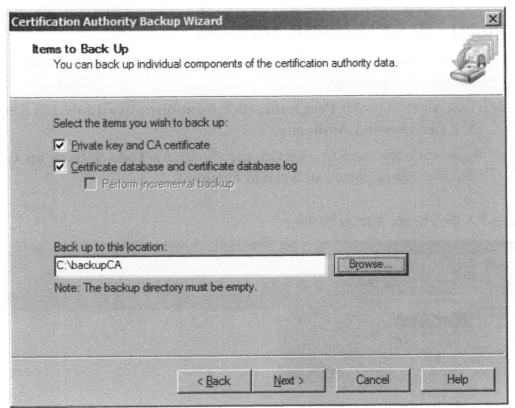

6. Type in the backup password twice and click **Next**.

7. On **Completing the Certification Authority Backup Wizard** page, verify it reads as follows: You have successfully completed the **Certification Authority Backup Wizard**, as shown in Figure 2.6.

Figure 2.6 Completing the CA Backup Wizard

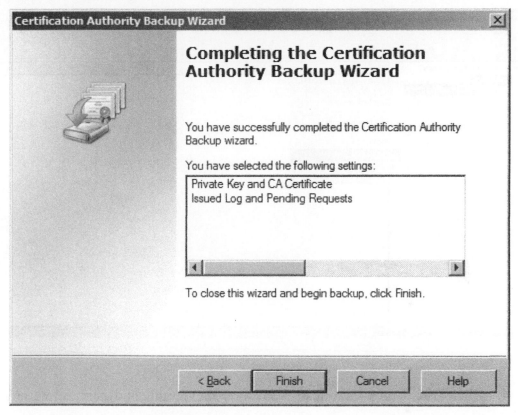

8. Click **Finish** to close the wizard.

In the next section we show you how to restore Certificate Services.

Restoring Certificate Services

1. On any computer for which you want to take a restore, Log on with administrative privileges.

2. Click **Start**, click **All Programs,** click **Administrative Tools**, and then click **Certification Authority**.

3. Right-click the name of your CA, and choose **All Tasks | Restore CA...** from the pop-up menu, as shown in Figure 2.7.

Figure 2.7 Certificate Authority page

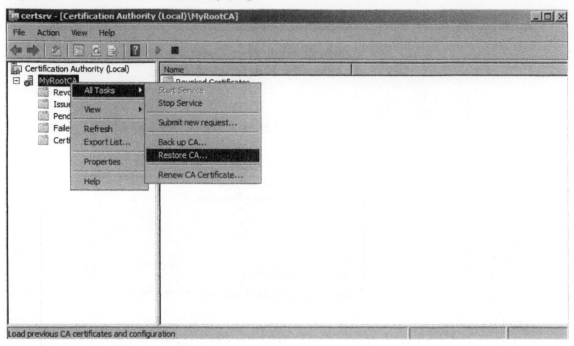

4. Click **OK** to stop Certificate Services from running and start the wizard.

5. On the **Welcome to the Certification Authority Restore Wizard** page, click **Next** to continue.

6. On **Items to Restore** page, click **Private key and CA certificate** and **Certificate database and certificate database log** to restore the backup of **Private key, CA certificate, Certificate database** and **database log file** (see Figure 2.8). Alternatively, you can choose only few components as per your requirements. Type in the path of back up location, and then click **Next**.

Figure 2.8 Items to Restore

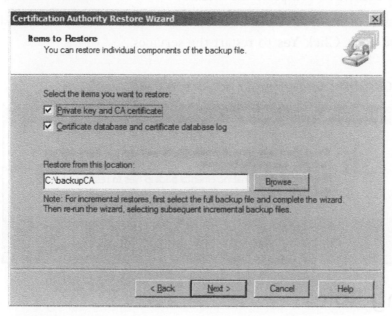

7. On the **Provide Password** page, type in the restore password, and then click **Next**.

8. On **Completing the Certification Authority Restore Wizard** page, verify it reads as You have successfully completed the **Certification Authority Restore Wizard**, as shown in Figure 2.9.

Figure 2.9 Completing the CA Restore Wizard

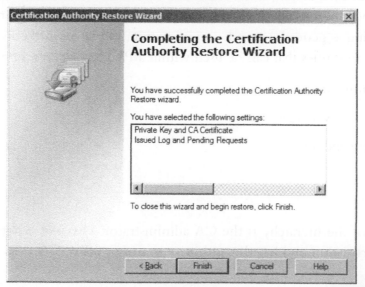

9. Click **Finish** to complete the wizard.

10. You will now be prompted to restart the certificate services, as shown in Figure 2.10. Click **Yes** to restart the services.

Figure 2.10 Certification Authority Restore Wizard

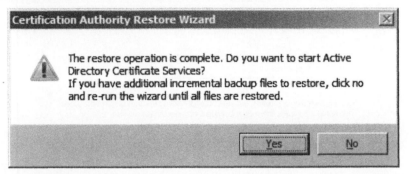

Assigning Roles

In a small network of one or two servers and just a handful of clients, administration is generally not a difficult task. When the size of the network increases, however, the complexity of administration seems to increase exponentially. Microsoft's recommendations for a large network include dividing administrative tasks among the different administrative personnel. One administrator may be in charge of backups and restores, whereas another administrator may have complete control over a certain domain and so on. The role of each administrator is defined by the tasks that he or she is assigned to, and individual permissions are granted based on those tasks. PKI administration, which can be as daunting as general network administration, can be similarly divided. Microsoft defines five different roles that can be used within a PKI to facilitate administration:

- CA Administrator
- Certificate Manager
- Backup Operator
- Auditor
- Enrollee

At the top of the hierarchy is the CA administrator. The role is defined by the *Manage CA* permission and has the authority to assign other CA roles and to renew the CA's certificate. Underneath the CA administrator is the certificate manager. The certificate manager role is defined by the *Issue and Manage Certificates* permission and has the authority to approve enrollment and revocation requests.

The Backup Operator and the Auditor roles are actually operating system roles, and not CA specific. The Backup Operator has the authority to backup the CA and the Auditor has the authority to configure and view audit logs of the CA. The final role is that of the Enrollees. All authenticated users are placed in this role, and are able to request certificates from the CA.

Enrollments

In order for a PKI client to use a certificate, two basic things must happen. First, a CA has to make the certificate available and second, the client has to request the certificate. Only after these first steps can the CA issue the certificate or deny the request. Making the certificate available is done through the use of certificate templates and is a topic that we discuss in detail below.

Like Windows Server 2003, Windows Server 2008 PKI also supports autoenrollment for user certificates as well as for computer certificates. The request and issuance of these certificates may proceed without user intervention. Group policies are used in Active Directory to configure autoenrollment. In **Computer Configuration | Windows Settings | Security Settings | Public Key Policies**, there is a group policy entitled **Automatic Certificate Request Settings**. The Property sheet for this policy allows you to choose to either **Enroll certificates automatically** or not. Also, you will need to ensure that **Enroll subject without requiring any user input** option is selected on the **Request Handling** tab of the certificate template Property sheet. Finally, be aware that doing either of the following will cause autoenrollment to fail:

- Setting the **This number of authorized signatures** option on the **Issuance Requirements** tab to higher than one.
- Selecting the **Supply in the request** option on the **Subject Name** tab.

TIP

Remember that autoenrollment is only available for user certificates if the client is Windows XP, Windows Server 2003, or Windows Server 2008.

Revocation

A CA's primary duty is to issue certificates, either to subordinate CAs, or to PKI clients. However, each CA also has the ability to revoke those certificates when necessary. Certificates are revoked when the information contained in the certificate is no longer considered valid or trusted. This can happen when a company changes ISPs (Internet Service Providers), moves to a new physical address or when the contact listed on the certificate has changed. Essentially, a certificate should be revoked whenever there is a change that makes the certificate's information "stale" and no longer reliable from that point forward.

> **NOTE**
>
> Information that has already been encrypted using the public key in a certificate that is later revoked is not necessarily invalid. Maintaining the example of a driver's license, checks that are written and authenticated by a cashier using your driver's license one week are not automatically voided if you lose your license or move states the next.

In addition to the changes in circumstance that can cause a certification revocation, certain owners may have their certificate revoked upon terminating employment. The most important reason to revoke a certificate is if the private key as been compromised in any way. If a key has been compromised, it should be revoked immediately.

> **WARNING**
>
> Certificate expiration is different from certificate revocation. A certificate is considered revoked if it is terminated prior to the end date of the certificate.

Along with notifying the CA of the need to revoke a certificate, it is equally important to notify all certificate users of the date that the certificate will no longer be valid. After notifying users and the CA, the CA is responsible for changing the status of the certificate and notifying users that it has been revoked.

When a certificate revocation request is sent to a CA, the CA must be able to authenticate the request with the certificate owner. Once the CA has authenticated the request, the certificate is revoked and notification is sent out. CAs are not the only ones who can revoke a certificate. A PKI administrator can revoke a certificate, but without authenticating the request with the certificate owner. This allows for the revocation of certificates in cases where the owner is no longer accessible or available as in the case of termination.

The X.509 standard requires that CA's publish certificate revocation lists (CRLs). In their simplest form, a CRL is a published form listing the revocation status of certification that the CA manages. There are several forms that revocation lists may take, but the two most noteworthy are *simple CRLs* and *delta CRLs*.

A simple CRL is a container that holds a list of revoked certificates with the name of the CA, the time the CRL was published, and when the next CRL will be published. It is a single file that continues to grow over time. The fact that only information about the certificates is included and not the certificate itself helps to manage the size of a simple CRL.

Delta CRLs can handle the issues that simple CRLs cannot- size and distribution. While simple CRLs contain only certain information about a revoked certificate, it can still become a large file. How, then, do you continually distribute a large file to all parties that need to see the CRL? The solution is in Delta CRLs. In an environment leveraging delta CRLs, a base CRL is sent to all end parties to initialize their copies of the CRL. Afterwards, updates know as deltas are sent out on a periodic basis to inform the end parties of any changes.

In practice within Windows Server 2008, the tool that the CA uses for revocation is the *certificate revocation list*, or CRL. The act of revoking a certificate is simple: from the **Certification Authority** console, simply highlight the **Issued Certificates** container, right-click the certificate and choose **All | Revoke Certificate.** The certificate will then be located in the **Revoked Certificates** container.

When a PKI entity verifies a certificate's validity, that entity checks the CRL before giving approval. The question is: how does a client know where to check for the list? The answer is the CDPs, or CRL Distribution Points. CDPs are locations on the network to which a CA publishes the CRL; in the case of an enterprise CA under Windows Server 2008, Active Directory holds the CRL, and for a stand-alone, the CRL is located in the *certsrv\certenroll* directory. Each certificate has a location listed for the CDP, and when the client views the certificate, it then understands where to go for the latest CRL. Figure 2.11 shows the Extensions tab of the CA property sheet, where you can modify the location of the CDP.

Figure 2.11 Extensions Tab of the CA Property Sheet

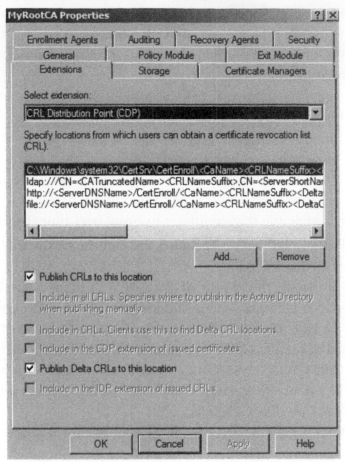

In order for a CA to publish a CRL, use the **Certificate Authority** console to right-click the **Revoked Certificates** container and choose **All Tasks | Publish**. From there, you can choose to publish either a complete CRL, or a Delta CRL.

TIP

On the day of the test, be clear as to which types of CRLs are consistently made available to users in Windows Server 2008. Since Server 203, Delta CRLs have been used to publish only the changes made to an original CRL for the purposes of conserving network traffic.

Whether you select a New CRL or a Delta CRL, you are next prompted to enter a publication interval (the most frequent intervals chosen are one week for full CRLs and one day for Delta CRLs). Clients cache the CRL for this period of time, and then check the CDP again when the period expires. If an updated CDP does not exist or cannot be located, the client automatically assumes that all certificates are invalid.

Working with Templates

A *certificate template* defines the policies and rules that a CA uses when a request for a certificate is received. Often when someone refers to building and managing a PKI for their enterprise, they are usually only thinking of the Certificate Authority and the associated infrastructure needed to support the authentication and authorization required to support the function of the CA. While this is certainly important for the proper function of the PKI, it is only half of the picture—the certificates themselves must be carefully planned to support the business goals that are driving the need to install and configure the PKI.

When you consider that certificates are flexible and can be used in scores of different scenarios, the true power of the certificate becomes apparent. While these different uses can all coexist within a single PKI, the types and functions of the certificates can be very different. Certificates that are used to support two-factor authentication on smart cards can be very different than those used to establish SSL connections to web servers, sign IPSec traffic between servers, support 802.1x wireless access through NAP, or even certificates used to sign e-mail communication.

In all of these cases, the CA and the PKI it supports are the same, but it is the certificate itself that is changing. For each of these different uses, it is important for the certificate to contain appropriate data to facilitate in the function that the designer of the PKI has intended and no more. While additional data could be provided in the certificate, the fact that these are intended to mediate security exchanges makes it inappropriate to include any more information than is necessary to complete the certificate's objective. It is the Certificate Template that specifies the data that must be included in a certificate for it to function as well as to ensure that all of the needed data are provided to ensure the certificate's validity.

Warning

Many different types of certificates can be used together within a single Public Key Infrastructure. It is the Certificate Templates that allow the certificates to differentiate themselves for different purposes ensuring that the appropriate information is stored in the cert.

For an individual certificate, there are a number of properties and settings that go into the certificate template specification. Each of these combine to build the final template that will determine the settings for the resulting Certificate.

There are many built-in templates that can be viewed using the **Certificate Templates** snap-in (see Figure 2.12). The snap-in can be run by right-clicking the **Certificate Templates** container located in the **Certification Authority** console and clicking **Manage**. You can use one of the built-in templates or create your own.

Figure 2.12 Certificate Templates Snap-in

Template Display Name ▲	Minimum Supported CAs	Ver...	Intended Purposes
Administrator	Windows 2000	4.1	
Authenticated Session	Windows 2000	3.1	
Basic EFS	Windows 2000	3.1	
CA Exchange	Windows Server 2003, Enter...	106.0	Private Key Archival
CEP Encryption	Windows 2000	4.1	
Code Signing	Windows 2000	3.1	
Computer	Windows 2000	5.1	
Cross Certification Authority	Windows Server 2003, Enter...	105.0	
Directory Email Replication	Windows Server 2003, Enter...	115.0	Directory Service Email Replication
Domain Controller	Windows 2000	4.1	
Domain Controller Authentication	Windows Server 2003, Enter...	110.0	Client Authentication, Server Authentication, Sma
EFS Recovery Agent	Windows 2000	6.1	
Enrollment Agent	Windows 2000	4.1	
Enrollment Agent (Computer)	Windows 2000	5.1	
Exchange Enrollment Agent (Offline request)	Windows 2000	4.1	
Exchange Signature Only	Windows 2000	6.1	
Exchange User	Windows 2000	7.1	
IPSec	Windows 2000	8.1	
IPSec (Offline request)	Windows 2000	7.1	
Kerberos Authentication	Windows Server 2003, Enter...	110.0	Client Authentication, Server Authentication, Sma
Key Recovery Agent	Windows Server 2003, Enter...	105.0	Key Recovery Agent
OCSP Response Signing	Windows Server 2008	101.0	OCSP Signing
RAS and IAS Server	Windows Server 2003, Enter...	101.0	Client Authentication, Server Authentication
Root Certification Authority	Windows 2000	5.1	
Router (Offline request)	Windows 2000	4.1	

Manages certificate templates that can be used by enterprise certification authorities (CAs) on the network

When creating your own template, you have multiple options that will guide the CA in how to handle incoming requests. The first step in the creation process is to duplicate an existing template. You do this by using the **Certificate Templates** snap-in, then right-clicking the template you wish to copy and selecting *Duplicate Template*. On the **General** tab that appears by default (seen in Figure 2.13), there are time-sensitive options such as validity period and renewal period. Note the default validity period of one year, and the default renewal period of six weeks. There are also general options such as the template display name and a checkbox for publishing the certificate in Active Directory.

Figure 2.13 General Tab of the New Template Property Sheet

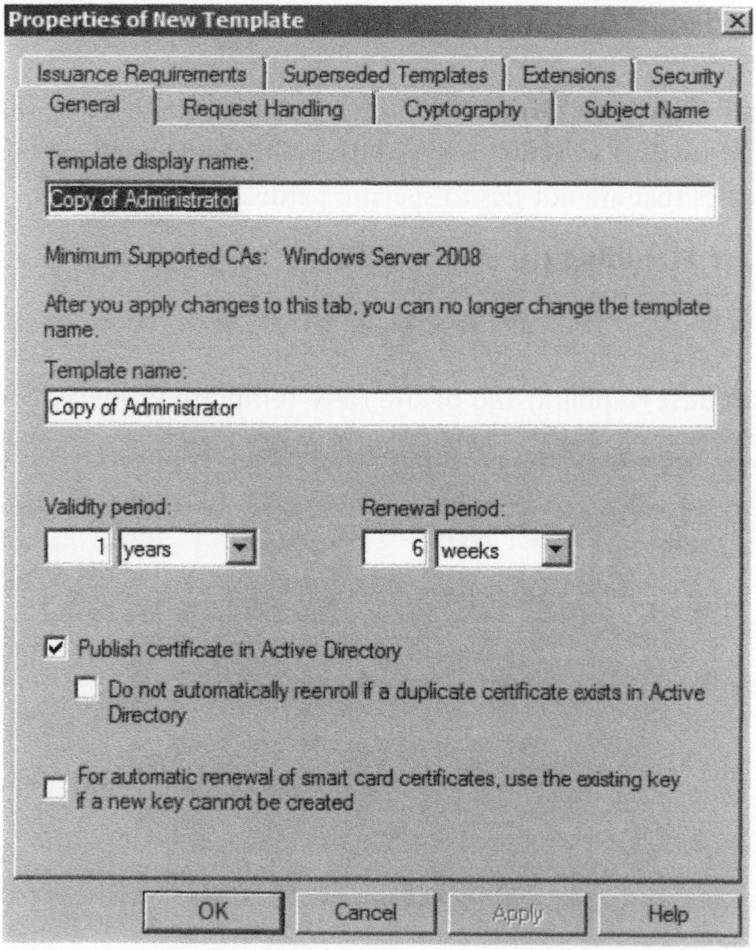

General Properties

Now we'll describe the following settings under the General tab of the new certificate template:

- **Template Display Name** It is important that the certificate that you are creating has a descriptive name accurately describes the function of the certificate. This name cannot be changed once it is assigned, but you can always recreate the certificate from another template later.

- **Validity Period** This is the period for which the derived certificates are valid. This time should be long enough so as not to create a burden on the end user, but not so long as to create a security problem.

- **Renewal Period** This is the period in which the certificate is notified of its expiration and that it will attempt to renew if this is an option for the certificate.

- **Publish in Active Directory** Some certificates can be stored in the active directory tied to security principals there. This generally applies to User certificates that are not ties to specific hardware.

The **Request Handling** tab, shown in Figure 2.14, has options to enroll without user interaction.

Figure 2.14 Request Handling Tab of the New Template Property Sheet

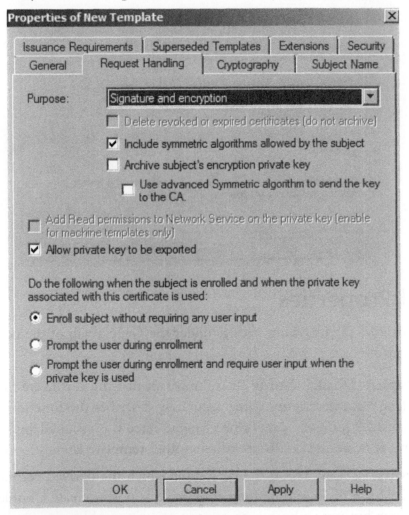

Request Handling

The Request Handling tab includes the following settings:

- **Purpose** It is important to consider the activities for which this new certificate will be responsible. Some keys can be used just to validate identity while others can also provide signing for encryption.

    - The private key can also be archived or shared with the CA so that it may be recovered in the event of loss. Otherwise, the certificate must be recreated.

- **Enrollment Actions** Different notification actions can be specified when the private key for this certificate is used. This can range from transparent usage of the key to full notification prompting the certificate owner for permission.

The **Cryptography** tab seen in Figure 2.15, gives you the choice of algorithms that can be used.

Figure 2.15 Cryptography Tab

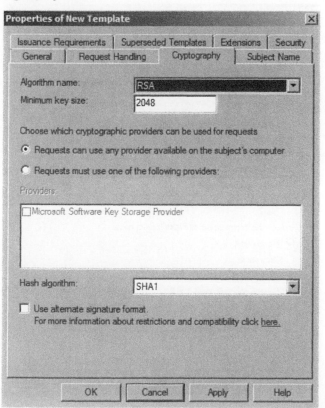

Cryptography

The Cryptography tab includes the following settings:

- **Algorithm Name** There are a number of cryptographic Algorithms that can be used to provide encryption for the keys. Valid methods under server 2008 are RSA, ECDH_P256, ECDH_P384, ECDH_P521.

  - Note: If the Purpose is changed to Signature, additional algorithms become available: ECDSA_P256, ECDSA_P384, ECDSA_P521

- **Hash Algorithm** To provide one-way hashes for key exchanges, a number of algorithms are available. These include: MD2, MD4, MD5, SHA1, SHA256, SHA384, SHA512.

The **Subject Name** tab seen in Figure 2.16, gives you the choice of obtaining subject name information from Active Directory or from the certificate request itself. In the latter case, autoenrollment (which we'll discuss later in the chapter) is not available.

Figure 2.16 Subject Name Tab of the New Template Property Sheet

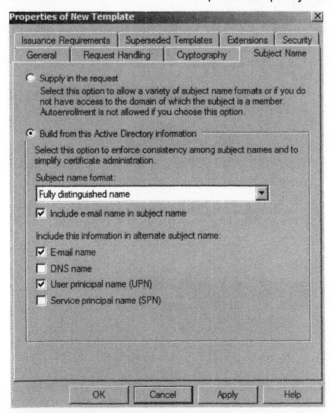

Subject Name

The Subject Name tab includes the following settings:

- **Supply in the Request** Under this option, the CA will expect to get additional subject information in the certificate request. As noted, this will not permit autoenrollment, requiring intervention to issue the certificate.

- **Build from this AD Information** Under this option, the Active Directory will be queried and the certificate will be built based on the AD files you specify.

Usually the default of the Distinguished Name is adequate for most purposes, but the common name will sometime be preferable.

The **Issuance Requirements** tab seen in Figure 2.17 allows you to suspend automatic certificate issuance by selecting the CA certificate manager approval checkbox.

Figure 2.17 Issuance Requirements Tab of the New Template Property Sheet

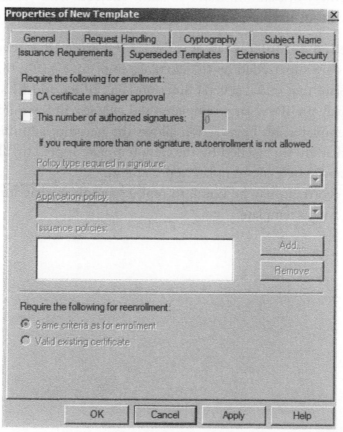

Issuance Requirements

These settings can be used to manage the approval requirements in order for a certificate to be issued. These settings allow for a workflow or approval chain to be applied to the certificate type.

- **CA Certificate Manager Approval** Using this setting will require that the CA Manager assigned in the CA approve of the certificate before it is released to the end-user of the certificate.

- **Number of Authorized Signatures** Under these settings, additional approvals steps may be required to release the certificate. In these scenarios, two or more approval authorities will have to consent before the certificate is generated.

- **Require the Following for Reenrollment** These settings specify the approval and prerequisites that are in place for renewal of the certificate. This gives the network administrator to allow subjects with valid certificates to renew without having to go through the approval chain.

The **Superseded Templates** tab, as shown in Figure 2.18, is used to define which certificates are superseded by the current template. Usually, this tab is used to configure a template that serves several functions, e.g. IPSec and EFS. In this case, a template used *only* for IPSec or a template used *only* for EFS would be placed on the superseded templates list. This section allows the network administrator to specify other templates that are superseded by the new template type. This allows control of both versioning and wholesale template replacement.

As templates evolve, it may be useful to replace templates that are already deployed in the wild with a new template.

Figure 2.18 Superseded Templates Tab of the New Template Property Sheet

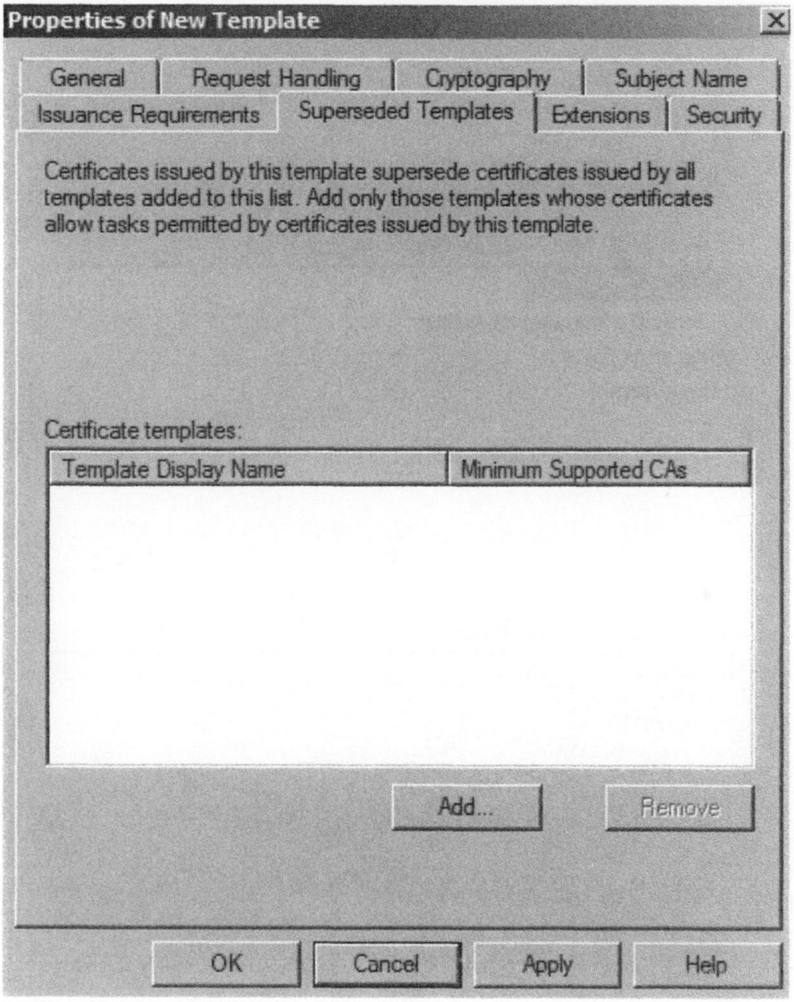

In addition to the standard usage patterns that are inherited from the parent certificate, it is sometimes important to specify new circumstances and roles that a certificate will fill. In this case, additional extensions to the certificate will be applied to provide this new functionality.

Under these settings, a new ability such as code signing can be applied to all derivative certificates to allow these new subjects the ability to complete multiple tasks.

The **Extensions** tab as seen in Figure 2.19 can be used to add such things as the Application Policies extension, which defines the purposes for which a generated certificate can be used. The Issuance Policies extension is also worth mentioning, because it defines when a certificate may be issued.

Figure 2.19 Extensions Tab of the New Template Property Sheet

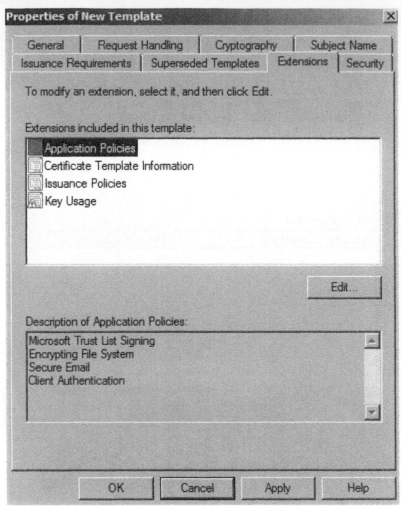

The **Security** tab is similar to the **Security** tab that we saw in Figure 2.20, except that this tab is used to control who may edit the template and who may request certificates using the template. Figure 2.20 shows the default permission level for the **Authenticated Users** group. In order for a user to request a certificate, however, the user must have at least the **Enroll** permission assigned to them for manual requests, and the **Autoenroll** permission for automatic requests.

Figure 2.20 Security Tab of the New Template Property Sheet

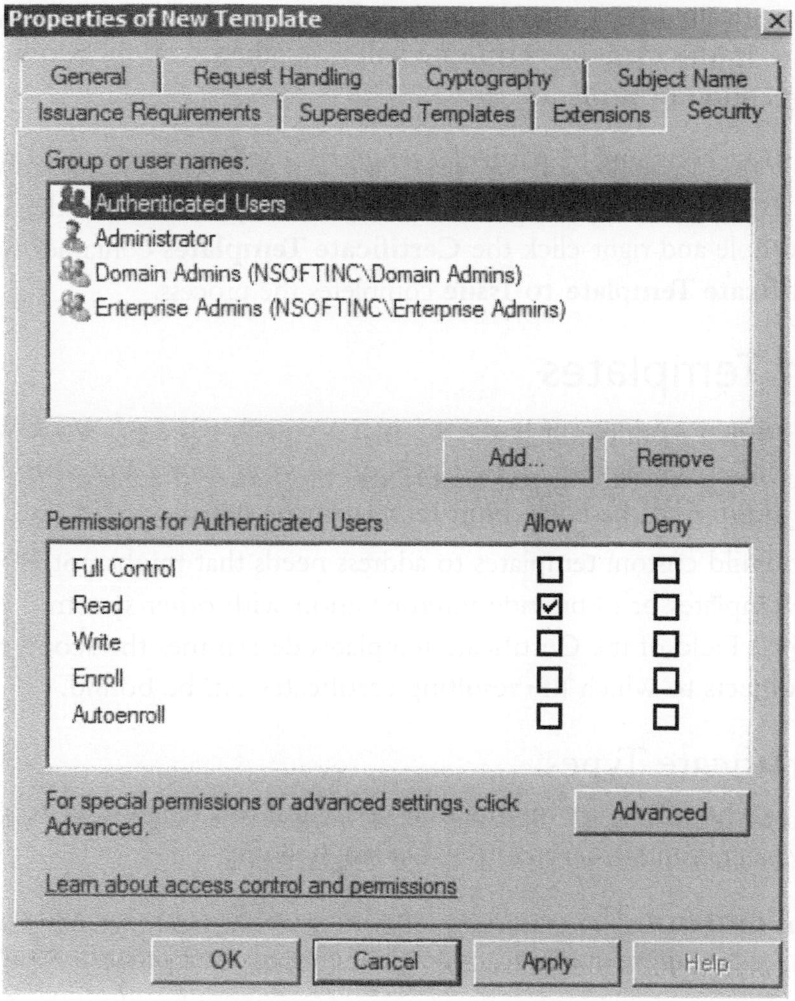

Security

The security settings control the actions that different types of users are able to perfume on a certificate template.

- **Enroll** These subjects are able to request that a certificate be created from this template and assigned to them. This enrollment process will abide by the constraints listed under the Issuance Requirements tab.

- **Autoenroll** These subjects are able to make a request to the CA and will be automatically issued the certificate if the subject meets the Issuance Requirements. In this case, the certificate will be applied without administrator intervention or assistance.

After you have configured a particular template, it still cannot be used by the CA to issue certificates until it is made *available*. To enable a template, you use the **Certification Authority** console and right-click the **Certificate Templates** container. Selecting **New | Certificate Template to Issue** completes the process.

Types of Templates

There are a number of different templates that are included with Windows Server 2008 that provide basic signing and encryption services in the Enterprise Windows PKI role. In addition to these pre-built templates, the network administrator also has the option to build custom templates to address needs that might not be covered by the standard templates or to provide interoperation with other systems.

The Subject Field of the Certificate templates determines the scope of action and the types of objects to which the resulting certificates can be bound.

User Certificate Types

User Certificate Templates are intended to be bound to a single user to provide identity and/or encryption services for that single entity.

- **Administrator** This certificate template provides signature and encryption services for administrator accounts providing account identification and trust list (CTL) management within the domain. Certificates based on the Administrator Template are stored in the Active Directory.

- **Authenticated Session** This certificate template allows users to authenticate to a web server to provide user credentials for site logon. This is often deployed for remote users as a way to validate identity without storing formation insecurely in a cookie while avoiding the need for a user to log on to the site each time.

- **Basic EFS** Certificates derived from this template are stored in Active Directory with the associated user account and are used to encrypt data using the Encrypting File System (EFS).

- **Code Signing** These certificate templates allow developers to create certificates that can be used to sign application code. This provides a check on the origin of software so that code management systems and end-users can be sure that the origin of the software is trusted.

- **EFS Recovery Agent** Certificates of this type allow files that have been encrypted with the EFS to be decrypted so that the files can be used again. EFS Recovery Agent certificates should be a part of any disaster recovery plan when designing an EFS implementation.

- **Enrollment Agent** Certificates derived from this template are used to request and issue other certificates from the enterprise CA on behalf of another entity. For example, the web enrollment application uses these certificates to manage the certificate requests with the CA.

- **Exchange Enrollment Agent** These certificates are used to manage enrollment services form within exchange to provide certificates to other entities within the exchange infrastructure.

- **Exchange Signature** Certificates derived from the Exchange Signature template are user certificates used to sign e-mail messages sent from within the Exchange system.

- **Exchange User** Certificates based on the Exchange User template are user certificates that are stored in the Active Directory used to encrypt e-mail messages sent from within the Exchange system.

- **Smartcard Logon** These certificates allow the holder of the smart card to authenticate to the active directory and provides identity and encryption abilities. This is usually deployed as a part of a two-factor security schema using smart cards as the physical token.

- **Smartcard User** Unlike the Smartcard Logon certificate template, these types of certificates are stored in the Active Directory and limit the scope of identity and encryption to e-mail systems.

- **Trust List Signing** These certificates allow the signing of a trust list to help manage certificate security and to provide affirmative identity to the signer.

- **User** This template is used to create general User Certificates—the kind that are usually thought of when talking about user certificates. These are stored in the Active Directory and are responsible for user activities in the AD such as authentication, EFS encryption, and interaction with Exchange.

- **User Signature Only** These certificates allow users to sign data and provide identification of the origin of the signed data.

Computer Certificate Types

Computer Certificate Templates are intended to be bound to a single computer entity to provide identity and/or encryption services for that computer. These are often the cornerstone of workstation authentication systems, such as NAP and 802.1x, which might require computer certificates for EAP authentication.

- **CA Exchange** These certificates are bound to Certificate Authorities to mediate key exchange between CAs allowing for PK sharing and archival.

- **CEP Encryption** Certificates of this type are bound to servers that are able to respond to key requests through the Simple Certificate Enrollment Protocol (SCEP).

- **Computer** This template is used to generate standard Computer certificates that allow a physical machine to assert its identity on the network. These certificates are extensively used in EAP authentication in identifying endpoints in secured communication tunnels.

- **Domain Controller Authentication** Certificates of this type are used to authenticate users and computers in the active directory. This allows a Domain Controller to access the directory itself and provide authentication services to other entities.

- **Enrollment Agent (Computer)** These certificates allow a computer to act as an enrollment agent against the PKI so that they can offer computer certificates to physical machines.

- **IPSec** Certificates based on this template allow a computer to participate in IPSec communications. These computers are able to assert their identity as well as encrypt traffic on the network. This is used in IPSec VPN tunnels as well as in Domain and Server Isolation strategies.

- **Kerberos Authentication** These certificates are used by local computers to authenticate with the Active Directory using the Kerberos v5 protocol.

- **OCSP Response Signing** This is a unique certificate type to Windows Server 2008 allowing a workstation to act as an Online Responder in the validation of certificate request queries.

- **RAS and IAS Server** These certificates are used to identify and provide encryption for Routing and Remote Access Server (RRAS) as well as

Internet Authorization Servers (IAS) to identify themselves in VPN and RADIUS communications with RADIUS Clients.

- **Router** This is also a new role to Windows Server 2008 providing services to provide credentials to routers making requests through SCEP to a CA.

- **Web Server** These certificates are commonly used by servers acting as web servers to provide end=point identification and traffic encryption to their customers. These kinds of certificates are used to provide Secure Socket Layer (SSL) encryption enabling clients to connect to the web server using the HTTPS protocol.

- **Workstation Authentication** Like general computer certificates, the workstation certificate allows computers that are domain members the ability to assert their identity on the network and encrypt traffic that they send across the network.

Other Certificate Types

There are a number of other certificate types that are not directly tied to either user or computer entities. These are usually infrastructure-based certificate types that are used to manage the domain or the Certificate Authorities themselves.

- **Cross-Certification Authority** These certificates are used within the Certificate Authority Infrastructure to cross -certify CAs to validate the hierarchy that makes up the PKI.

- **Directory E-mail Replication** Certificates that are derived from this type are used within the larger Exchange infrastructure to allow for the replication of e-mail across the directory service.

- **Domain Controller** This kind of certificate is only held by the Domain Controllers in the domain. These differentiate from the Domain Controller Authentication certificates as they identify the individual DC rather than facilitate authorization of inbound authentication requests.

- **Root CA** These certificates are only issued to Root Certificate Authorities to assert its identity in the Public Key Infrastructure.

- **Subordinate CA** This certificate type is used to assert the identity of Subordinate Certificate Authorities in the PKI. This type of certificate can only be issued by a computer holding the Root CA certificate or another

Subordinate CA that is the direct parent of the on to which the new certificate is being issued.

Custom Certificate Templates

In some circumstances, it might be necessary to create a custom certification type that can be used to support a specific business need. If you are using a version of Windows Server 2008 that is not either the WEB or Standard edition, you can create your own templates.

Creating a Custom Template

In this section we will create a new User Template based on the existing default user template. This new template will be valid for 10 years rather than the default 1-year expiration date.

1. Log in to your domain with an account that is a member of the Domain Admins group.

2. Navigate to **Start | Administrative Tools | Certificate Authority.**

3. Right-click the **Certificate Templates** folder on the left pane. Choose **Manage** to open the Certificate Templates Console (see Figure 2.21).

Figure 2.21 Creating a Custom Template

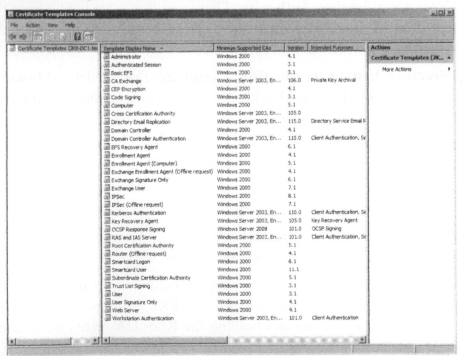

4. Right-click the **User Template**. Choose **Duplicate Template**.

5. On the Duplicate Template page, choose **Server 2008** versioning as all of our CAs are running Server 2008 (see Figure 2.22). Click **OK**.

Figure 2.22 Creating a Custom Template

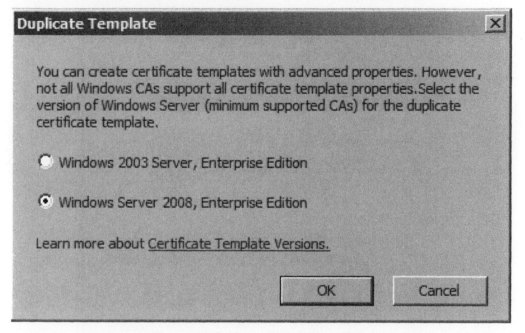

6. In the **Template display name**, enter **Long-term User.**

7. Change the **Validity Period** to 10 Years (see Figure 2.23).

Figure 2.23 Creating a Custom Template

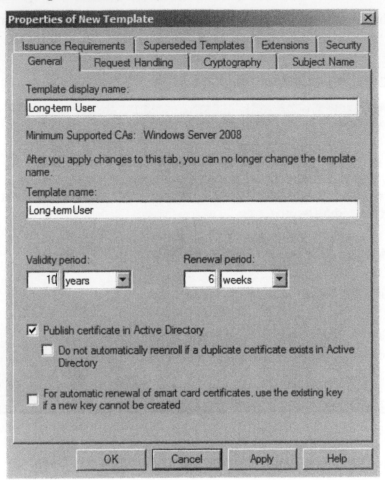

8. Click **OK**.

The new Long-term User certificate template has now been created on this CA and is ready to be used to create new derivative certificates.

Securing Permissions

With the wide set of configuration options that are available when creating a new Certificate Template, it might come as a surprise that the permissions model is relatively simple. All of the more complicated security controlling the approval process and revocation is already built into the Certificate Template itself, so there is little left to control through the more traditional Access Control Entries on the template's Access Control List.

- **Full Control** Users with this permission have access to do anything with the Certificate Template. Users with this right should be confined to the Domain Administrators and CA Managers who will be maintaining the CA and the associated Templates.

- **Read** These users will be able to read the template and view its contents. It is important for users to be able to Read the template if they are to apply it and continue to use the associated certificates issued from the template.

- **Write** Users who are able to modify and manage the template will need to have write permissions on the template. Again, this should be confined to Domain Administrators and CA Managers who will be responsible for maintaining the Templates.

- **Enroll** Users who will request certificates of this type or who already have these certs will need to have Enroll privileges.

- **AutoEnroll** Subjects that will request new certificates through the autoenrollment process will need to have autoenrollment privileges in addition to the enroll and read permissions.

NOTE

In order to keep the Certificate Authority communicating with the Active Directory, it is important that the Cert Publishers group be protected. Make sure that this group is not inadvertently destroyed or changed.

Versioning

Certificates are all tagged with version information allowing them to evolve over time. Without this feature, when a Certificate Template would get updated, all of the certificates based on the old template would have to be revoked forcing the end-users to apply for new certificates again. This is disruptive to business and introduces a large amount of risk to business continuity as the certificates are brought into compliance again.

With versioning, a new version of the Certificate Template can be issued into the production environment. Then using the autoenrollment process, these certificates can be superseded bring all of the certificate holding subjects into compliance quickly and with a minimum of both disruption to the business and administrative intervention.

WARNING

In an environment that has been upgraded from a previous version of Windows Server into the Server 2008 platform, an update to the certificate templates may be required to bring the templates into compliance. This should be done before the domain is upgraded to ensure continuity with the active directory.

Key Recovery Agent

Sometimes it is necessary to recover a key from storage. One of the problems that often arise regarding PKI is the fear that documents will become lost forever—irrecoverable because someone loses or forget their private key. Let's say that employees use Smart Cards to hold their private keys. If a user were to leave his smart card in his wallet which was left in the pants that he accidentally threw into the washing machine, then that user might be without his private key and therefore incapable of accessing any documents or e-mails that used his existing private key.

Many corporate environments implement a key recovery server solely for the purpose of backing up and recovering keys. Within an organization, there is at least one *key recovery agent*. A key recovery agent is an employee who has the authority to retrieve a user's private key. Some key recover servers require that two key recovery agents retrieve private user keys together for added security. Some key recovery servers also have the ability to function as a key escrow server, thereby adding the ability to split the keys onto two separate recovery servers, further increasing security.

Luckily, Windows Server 2008 provides a locksmith of sorts (called a Registration Authority, or RA) that earlier versions of Windows did not have. A key recovery solution, however, is not easy to implement and requires several steps. The basic method follows:

1. Create an account to be used for key recovery.
2. Create a new template to issue to that account.
3. Request a key recovery certificate from the CA.
4. Have the CA issue the certificate.
5. Configure the CA to archive certificates by using the **Recovery Agents** tab of the CA property sheet (shown in Figure 2.24).
6. Create an archive template for the CA.

Figure 2.24 Recovery Agents Tab of the CA Property Sheet

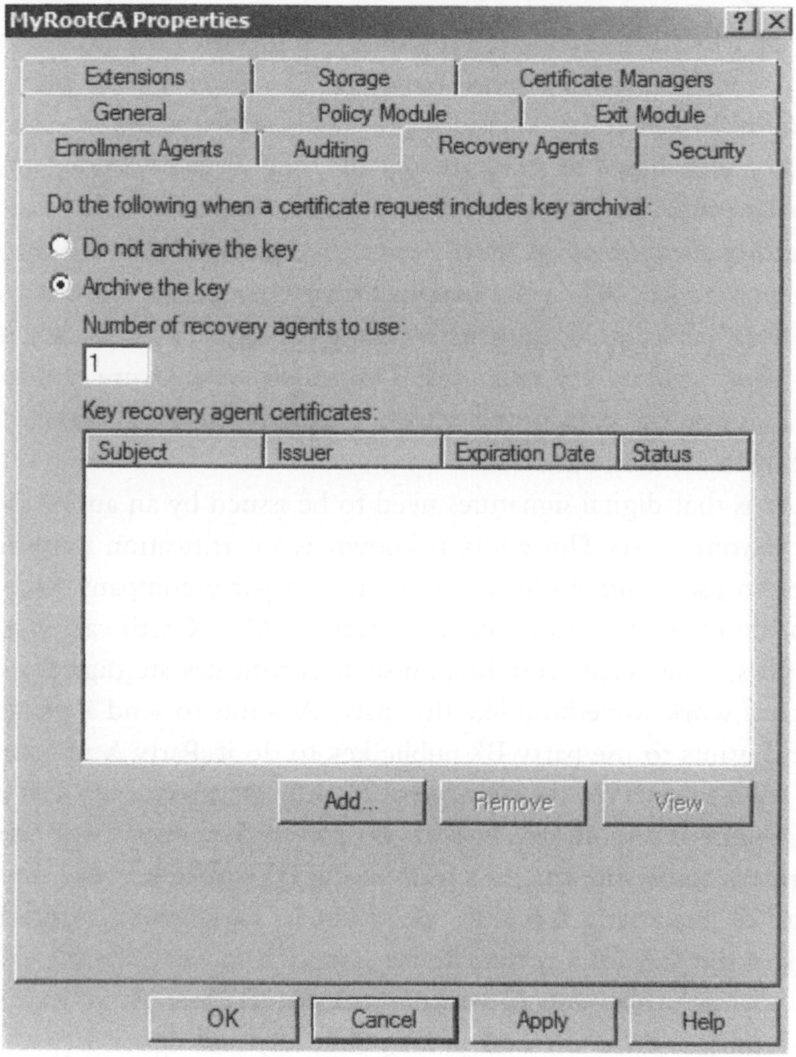

Each of these steps requires many substeps, but can be well worth the time and effort. It is worth noting again that key recovery is not possible on a stand-alone CA, because a stand-alone cannot use templates. It is also worth noting that only encryption keys can be recovered—private keys used for digital signatures cannot.

Summary

The purpose of a PKI is to facilitate the sharing of sensitive information such as authentication traffic across an insecure network. This is done with public and private key cryptography. In public key cryptography, keys are generated in pairs so that every public key is matched to a private key and vice versa. If data is encrypted with a particular public key, then only the corresponding private key can decrypt it. A digital signature means that an already encrypted piece of data is further encrypted by someone's private key. When the recipient wants to decrypt the data, he or she must first "unlock" the digital signature by using the signer's public key, remembering that only the *signer's* public key will work. This might seem secure, but because anyone at all can sign the data, how does the recipient know for certain the identity of the person who actually signed it?

The answer is that digital signatures need to be issued by an authoritative entity, one whom everyone trusts. This entity is known as a certification authority. An administrator can use Windows Server 2008, a third-party company such as VeriSign, or a combination of the two to create a structure of CAs. Certification authorities, as the name implies, issue certificates. In a nutshell, certificates are digitally signed public keys. Certificates work something like this: party A wants to send a private message to party B, and wants to use party B's public key to do it. Party A realizes that if B's public key is used to encrypt the message, then only B's private key can be used to decrypt it and since B and no one else has B's private key, everything works out well. However, A needs to be sure that he's really using B's public key and not an imposter's, so instead of just asking B for B's public key, he asks B for a certificate. B has previously asked the CA for a certificate for just such an occasion (B will present the certificate to anyone who wants to verify B's identity). The CA has independently verified B's identity, and has then taken B's public key and signed it with its own private key, creating a certificate. A trusts the CA, and is comfortable using the CA's well-known public key. When A uses the CA's public key to unlock the digital signature, he can be sure that the public key inside really belongs to B, and he can take that public key and encrypt the message.

The "I" in PKI refers to the infrastructure, which is a system of public key cryptography, certificates, and certification authorities. CAs are usually set up in a hierarchy, with one system acting as a root and all the others as subordinates at one or more levels deep. By analyzing the certificate requirements for your company, you can design your CA structure to fit your needs. Most organizations use a three-tier model, with a root

CA at the top, an intermediate level of subordinates who control CA policy, and a bottom level of subordinates who actually issue certificates to users, computers, and applications. In addition to choosing root and subordinate structure for the CA hierarchy, each CA during installation needs to be designated as either an enterprise or a stand-alone. Each of these choices has distinct advantages and disadvantages. Most CA configuration after installation is done through the Certification Authority snap-in. In addition to issuing certificates, CAs are also responsible for revoking them when necessary. Revoked certificates are published to a CRL that clients can download before accepting a certificate as valid.

Enterprise CAs use templates to know what to do when a certificate request is received and how to issue a certificate if approved. There are several built-in templates included in Server 2008, or you can configure new ones. Once a CA is ready to issue certificates, clients need to request them. Autoenrollment, Web enrollment, or manual enrollment through the Certificates snap-in are the three ways by which a client can request a certificate. Autoenrollment is available for computer certificates, and in Windows Server 2008, for user certificates as well.

Solutions Fast Track

What Is PKI?

☑ A PKI combines public key cryptography with digital certificates to create a secure environment where network traffic such as authentication packets can travel safely.

☑ Public keys and private keys always come in pairs. If the public key is used to encrypt data, only the matching private key can decrypt it.

☑ When public key-encrypted data is encrypted again by a private key, that private key encryption is called a digital signature.

Digital Certificates

☑ Digital signatures provided by ordinary users aren't very trustworthy, so a trusted authority is needed to provide them. The authority (which can be Windows-based) issues certificates, which are basically digitally signed containers for public keys and other information.

☑ Certificates are used to safely exchange public keys, and provide the basis for applications such as IPSec, EFS, and smart card authentication. A CA hierarchy is structured with a root and one or more level of subordinates— three levels are common. The bottom level of subordinates issues certificates. The intermediate level controls policies.

☑ Enterprise CAs require and use Active Directory to issue certificates, often automatically. Stand-alone CAs can be more secure, and need an administrator to manually issue or deny certificate requests.

Working with Certificate Services

☑ Certificate needs are based on which applications and communications an organization uses and how secure they need to be. Based on these needs, CAs are created by installing certificate services and are managed using the Certification Authority snap-in.

☑ CAs need to be backed up consistently and protected against attacks. Keys can be archived and later retrieved if they are lost. This is a new feature for Windows Server 2008.

☑ CAs can revoke as well as issue certificates. Once a certificate is revoked, it needs to be published to a CRL distribution point. Clients check the CRL periodically before they can trust a certificate.

Working with Templates

☑ Certificates can be requested with the Certificates snap-in or by using Internet Explorer and pointing to *http://servername/certsrv* on the CA.

☑ Machine and user certificates can be requested with no user intervention requirement by using autoenrollment. Autoenrollment for user certificates is new to Windows Server 2008.

☑ Role-based administration is recommended for larger organizations. Different users can be assigned permissions relative to their positions, such as certificate manager.

Creating a Custom Template

☑ Templates control how a CA acts when handed a request, and how to issue certificates.

☑ Templates must be enabled before a CA can use them.

☑ There are a quite a few built-in templates, or you can create your own using the Certificate Template snap-in.

Frequently Asked Questions

Q: In what format do CAs issue certificates?

A: Microsoft certificate services use the standard X.509 specifications for issued certificates and the Public Key Cryptography Standard (PKCS) #10 standard for certificate requests. The PKCS #7 certificate renewal standard is also supported. Windows Server 2003 also supports other formats, such as PKCS #12, DER encoded binary X.509, and Base64 Encoded X.509, for exporting certificates to computers running non-Windows operating systems.

Q: If certificates are so important in a PKI, why don't I see more of them?

A: Many portions of a Windows PKI are hidden to the end user. Thanks to features such as autoenrollment, some PKI transactions can be completely done by the operating system. Most of the work in implementing a PKI comes in the planning and design phase. Operations such as encrypting data via EFS use certificates, but the user does not "see" or manually handle the certificates.

Q: I've heard that I can't take my laptop overseas because it uses EFS. Is this true?

A: Maybe. The backbone of any PKI-enabled application such as EFS is encryption. Although the U.S. government now permits the exporting of "high encryption" standards, some countries still do not allow their import. The Windows Server 2008 PKI can use high encryption, and so the actual answer depends on the country in question. For information on the cryptographic import and export policies of a number of countries, see http://www.rsasecurity.com/rsalabs/faq/6-5-1.html.

Q: Can I create my own personal digital signature and use it instead of a CA?

A: Not if you need security. The purposes behind digital signatures are privacy and security, and a digital signature at first glance seems to fit the bill. The problem, however, is not the signature itself, but the lack of trust in a recipient. Impersonations become a looming security risk if you can't guarantee that the digital signatures you receive came from the people with whom they were supposed to have originated. For this reason, a certificate issued by a trusted third party provides the most secure authentication.

Q: Can I have a CA hierarchy that is five levels deep?

A: Yes, but that's probably overkill for most networks. Microsoft's three-tier model of root, intermediate, and issuing CAs will more than likely meet your requirements. Remember that your hierarchy can be wide instead of deep.

Q: Do I have to have more than one CA?

A: No. Root CAs have the ability to issue all types of certificates and can assume responsibility for your entire network. In a small organization, a single CA might be sufficient for your purposes. For a larger organization, however, this structure would not be suitable.

Q: How can I change the publishing interval of a CRL?

A: From the **Certification Authority** console, right-click the **Revoked Certificates** container and choose **Properties**. The **CRL Publishing Parameters** tab allows you to change the default interval for full and Delta CRLs.

Q: Why can't I seem to get autoenrollment for user certificates to work?

A: Remember that autoenrollment for machines is a feature that has been around since Windows 2000, but autoenrollment for user certificates is new to Windows Server 2003. In order to use this feature, you need to be running either a Windows Server 2003 or XP client and you must log on to a Windows Server 2003 domain. Finally, autoenrollment must be enabled through Active Directory's group policy. Also, you won't be able to autoenroll a user unless the user account has been assigned an e-mail address.

Q: What is the default validity period for a new certificate?

A: The default, which can be changed on the **General** tab of a new template's **Property** sheet, is one year. Other important settings, such as minimum key size and purpose of the certificate, can be found on the sheet's other tabs.

Q: If my smart card is lost or stolen, can I be reissued one?

A: Yes. The enrollment agent can enroll a new card for you at the enrollment station. Although most smart card providers allow cards to be reused (such as when they are found), a highly secure company may require old cards to be destroyed. For similar security reasons, PINs should not be reused on a newly issued card although it is possible. Remember that a card is only good to a thief if the corresponding PIN is obtained as well.

Q: When setting up smart cards for my company, can I use the MS-CHAP or MS-CHAP v2 protocols for authentication?

A: No. EAP is the only authentication method you can use with smart cards. It is considered the pinnacle of the authentication protocols under Windows Server 2003. MS-CHAP v2 is probably the most secure of the password-based protocols, but still does not provide the level of protection that smart cards using EAP do. This is because EAP is not really an authentication protocol by itself. It interfaces with other protocols such as MD5-CHAP, and is therefore extremely flexible. As a result it has been widely implemented by many different vendors. MS-CHAP and MS-CHAP v2 are Microsoft proprietary, and do not enjoy the same popularity or scrutiny applied to EAP. It is this scrutiny over the last several years that gives EAP the reputation of a highly secure protocol.

Q: How can I determine the length of time for which a certificate should be valid?

A: It is important to plan out your PKI implementation before it goes into production. In the case of certificate validity, you'll want to choose a time period that will cover the majority of your needs without being so long as to open your environment up to compromise.

If you are planning a certificate to support a traveling workforce that only connects to the corporate infrastructure once a quarter, it would be detrimental to expire certificates once a month. At the same time, specifying a certificate to be valid for 20 years might open your business up to compromise by an ex-employee long after his employment has been terminated.

Finally, you will want to ensure that your certificate lifetime is less than the lifetime for the lifetime of the CA's own cert. If the issuing CA will only be valid for a year, having a subordinate cert that is good for 5 years will lead to problems when the parent authority is revoked.

Q: My domain has been active for some time, but I have only recently implemented a Certificate Authority in my domain. I am now getting messages that my Domain Controllers do not have appropriate certificates. What should I do?

A: Make sure that you have enabled auto enrollment on your Domain Controller certificate templates. This step is often missed and can lead to a number of secondary problems, the least of which is annoying messages in the Event Logs.

Chapter 3

Microsoft Windows Server 2008: Active Directory Domain Security Changes

Solutions in this chapter:

- Configuring Audit Policies
- Fine-Grain Password and Account Lockout Policies
- Read-Only Domain Controllers (RODCs)
- Digital Rights Management Service

☑ Summary

☑ Solutions Fast Track

☑ Frequently Asked Questions

Introduction

The *domain* serves as the administrative boundary of Active Directory. It is the most basic component that can functionally host the directory. Simply put, Active Directory uses the domain as a container of computers, users, groups, and other object containers. Objects within the domain share a common directory database partition, replication boundaries and characteristics, security policies, and security relationships with other domains.

Typically, administrative rights granted in one domain are valid only within that domain. This also applies to Group Policy Objects (GPOs), but not necessarily to trust relationships. Security policies such as the password policy, account lockout policy, and Kerberos ticket policy are defined on a per-domain basis. The domain is also the primary boundary defining your DNS and NetBIOS namespaces. The DNS infrastructure is a requirement for an Active Directory domain, and should be defined before you create the domain.

There are several good reasons for a multiple-domain model, although a significant number of Active Directory implementations rely on a single-domain forest model. In the early days of Windows 2000, the most common recommendation was for a so-called empty forest root model, in which the forest root domain contains only built-in objects, and all manually created objects reside in one or more child domains. Whatever the design decision reached by your organization, it is a good practice to avoid installing additional domains unless you have a specific reason for them, as each additional domain in a forest incurs additional administrative overhead in the form of managing additional domain controllers (DCs) and replication traffic. Some of the more common reasons to create additional domains include:

- Groups of users with different security policy requirements, such as strong authentication and strict access controls.

- Groups of users requiring additional autonomy, or administrative separation for security reasons.

- A requirement for decentralized administration due to political, budgetary, time zone, or policy pressures.

- A requirement for unique namespaces.

- Controlling excessive directory replication traffic by breaking the domain into smaller, more manageable pieces. This often occurs in an extremely large domain, or due to a combination of geographical separation and unreliable WAN links.

- Maintaining a preexisting NT domain structure.

You can think of a domain tree as a DNS namespace composed of one or more domains. If you plan to create a forest with discontiguous namespaces, you must create more than one tree. The primary Active Directory partitions, also called *naming contexts*, are replicated among all DCs within a domain. These three partitions are the schema partition, the configuration partition, and the domain partition.

- The **schema partition** contains the *classSchema* and the *attributeSchema* objects that make up the directory schema. These classes and attributes define all possible types of objects and object properties within the forest. Every DC in the entire forest has a replica of the schema partition.

- The **configuration partition**, replicated identically on all DCs throughout the forest, contains Active Directory's replication topology and other configuration data.

- The **domain partition** contains the local domain objects, such as computers, users, and groups, which all share the same security policies and security relationships with other domains. If multiple DCs exist within a domain, they contain a replica of the same domain partition. If multiple domains exist within a forest, each domain contains a unique domain partition.

Because each domain contains unique principles and resources, there must be some way for other domains to locate them. Active Directory contains objects that adhere to a naming convention called the DN, or *distinguished name*. The DN contains enough detail to locate a replica of the partition that holds the object in question. Unfortunately, most users and applications do not know the DN, or what partition might contain it. To fulfill that role, Active Directory uses the *Global Catalog (GC)*, which can locate DNs based on one or more specific attributes of the needed object. (We will discuss the GC later in this chapter.)

Configuring Audit Policies

The configuration settings for auditing can be a bit trickier to understand than other group policy settings. All types of auditing use the same types of settings. You can audit the success and/or failure for a variety of tracked events. Examples of what can be tracked include logons, changes to policy, use of privileges, directory service or file access, and so forth (see Figure 3.1).

Figure 3.1 Auditing Policies

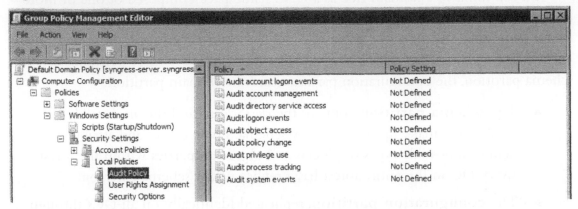

If you audit, for example, success and failure events for logons, the system will keep track of key details when users successfully log on to their accounts, and also when a logon attempt fails. Once an auditing policy item has been enabled by selecting **Define these policy settings** in its properties dialog box, four configuration options become possible (see Figure 3.2):

- Audit success is configured by selecting the **Success** setting.

- Audit failure is configured by selecting the **Failure** setting.

- Prevention of tracking auditing success is configured by unselecting the **Success** setting.

- Prevention of tracking auditing failures is configured by unselecting the **Failure** setting.

Figure 3.2 Auditing Configuration Options

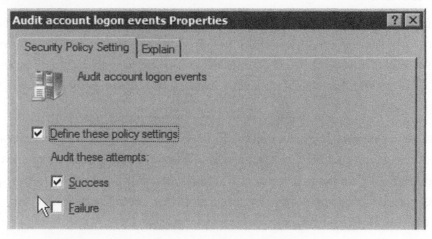

Audit account logon events. This policy needs be enabled and when processing...

...being accessed if you are logging on to your local workstation, even when...

Configuring & Implementing...

Configuring Auditing Policy

It is very important to understand how Microsoft wants you to think about auditing. It might be tempting to think that you disable auditing by deselecting the **Define these policy settings** option on individual audit settings in group policy; however, this ignores that the organization may have other group policies that are being inherited for which auditing has been enabled. To ensure that auditing is not enabled, you must explicitly configure individual policies to turn it off.

For example, let's say you have a domain policy with **Object Access** enabled for **Success** and **Failure** auditing, but you want to turn that off for one part of your organization. One way might be to block the inheritance of that GPO within Active Directory; however, for this example, we'll assume that other settings need to be applied. In this type of situation, the best option may be to create and link a GPO at just the level of Active Directory that applies to the portion of Active Directory that should have auditing disabled. In this GPO, you would configure the **Object Access** audit policy setting by selecting the option to **Define these policy settings** and making sure that **Success** and **Failure** are both unselected.

Logon Events

Logon events are among the most important to monitor. It is recommended that, at a minimum, you monitor failure events for these policy options. This allows you to spot users who are having difficulty with their logons, as well as track potentially fraudulent attempts to log on. Microsoft provides two audit policy options for monitoring logons:

- **Audit account logon events** This policy is used for credential validation, and the events audited relate to the computer which is authoritative for the credentials. For most users in a domain, this will be the DC which processes their logon, although these events can occur on any computer and may occur on both their local workstation and the DC.

- **Audit logon events** This policy tracks the creation and, when possible, the destruction of logon sessions. The actual audited event relates to the machine being accessed. If you are logging on to your local workstation (even using a domain-based user account), the event is generated on your local machine. If you accessing a resource on the network, such as files in a shared folder, this generates a logon event on the computer hosting the files.

WARNING

Microsoft often recommends auditing both **Success** and **Failure** events for logon events. Many administrators choose not to audit **Success** events because of the number of events generated. Hardcore security administrators, however, prefer to audit these events. They make the argument that auditing **Failure** does not enable you to spot potentially fraudulent successful logons that are uncharacteristic of users—for example, a successful logon from an overseas Internet Protocol (IP) address for a small company with one location in the United States.

We will now show you how to enable **Success** and **Failure** auditing for logons. You will need a Windows Server 2008 DC.

1. Open your domain's Default Domain Policy GPO using the **Group Policy Management Editor** and navigate to **Computer Configuration | Policies | Windows Settings | Security Settings | Audit Policy**, as shown earlier in Figure 3.1.

2. In the right-hand pane, right-click on **Audit account logon events** and select **Properties**.

3. In the **Audit account logon events Properties** dialog that appears, select **Define these policy settings**.

4. Under **Audit these attempts:** select **Success** and **Failure**, then click **OK**. Refer back to Figure 3.2.

5. In the right-hand pane, right-click on **Audit logon events** and select **Properties**.

6. In the **Audit logon events Properties** dialog that appears, select **Define these policy settings**.

7. Under **Audit these attempts:** select **Success** and **Failure**, and then click **OK**.

8. Close the Group Policy Management Editor.

Directory Service Access

Most Active Directory objects have their own permissions (officially called a system access control list or SACL). Any object in Active Directory that can have permissions set for it can be audited. By default, directory service auditing is not enabled in group policy; however, objects in Active Directory do come already set up with some auditing permissions assigned. For most objects this will be **Success** auditing for members of the **Everyone** group, but this does vary. For example, the domain object in Active Directory has additional auditing preconfigured for it. Setting up directory service access auditing is a two-step process: configuring a GPO to enable the directory service access auditing, and specifying what to audit on an object-by-object basis within Active Directory.

Configuring Directory Service Access Auditing in Group Policy

You configure directory service access in group policy using the following steps:

1. Open the GPO that will be used to configure auditing using the **Group Policy Management Editor** and navigate to **Computer Configuration | Policies | Windows Settings | Security Settings | Audit Policy**, as shown earlier in Figure 3.1.

2. In the right-hand pane, right-click on **Audit directory service access** and select **Properties**.

3. On the **Security Policy Setting** tab of the **Audit directory service access Properties** dialog box, configure the policy as desired by:

- Selecting **Success** to enable auditing successful object access events
- Deselecting **Success** to disable auditing successful object access events
- Selecting **Failure** to enable auditing failed object access events
- Deselecting **Failure** to disable auditing failed object access events

4. Click **OK** and close the **Group Policy Management Editor**.

Configuring Active Directory Object Auditing

To enable auditing of a specific object within Active Directory, follow these steps:

1. Open **Active Directory Users and Computers** and navigate to the object you want to audit (here, the Authors OU).

2. Right-click on the object and select **Properties** from the context menu.

3. In the **Properties** dialog box, select the **Security** tab, and click **Advanced**. See Figure 3.3.

Figure 3.3 The Properties Dialog

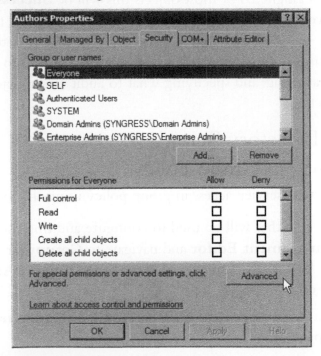

4. In the **Advanced Security Settings** dialog box, click on the **Auditing** tab (see Figure 3.4) and note that the object has inherited auditing entries. You can block these by deselecting **Include inheritable auditing entries from this object's parent**. You also can modify existing entries by clicking the **Edit** button.

Figure 3.4 The Advanced Security Settings Dialog

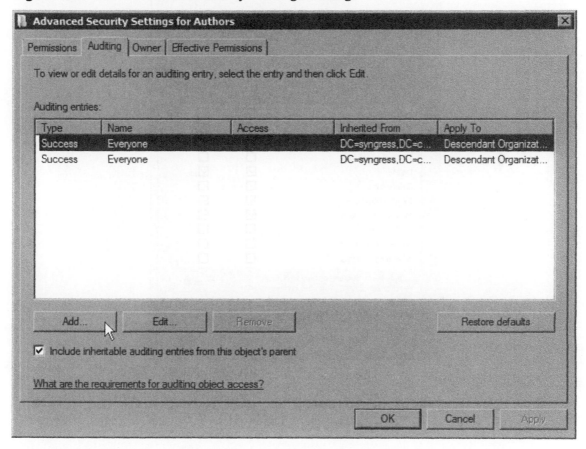

5. To add new users or groups click on the **Add** button.

6. In the **Select User, Computer, or Group** dialog box, type in or search for the users or groups you want to audit. This is a standard dialog box that works just like the permissions version. For this example, we will select **Domain Users**.

7. In the **Auditing Entry** dialog, configure the types of **Success** and/or
Failure events you want to monitor for this group and click **OK**. For this
example, we will choose **Read permissions**, **Modify permissions**, and
Delete – Success and **Failure** events. See Figure 3.5.

Figure 3.5 The Auditing Entry Dialog

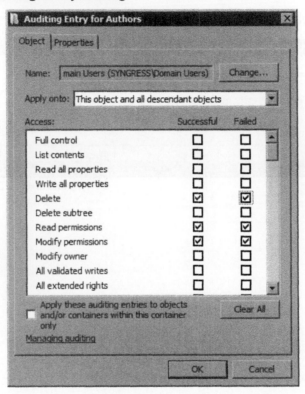

8. Click **OK** again in the **Advanced Security Settings** dialog box and **OK**
again to close the **Properties** dialog box.

Fine-Grain Password and Account Lockout Policies

When a GPO is used to apply password and account lockout policies, these policies
can be set for only the entire domain, and only one instance of each setting will be
applied to for all users in the domain. In other words, you cannot set different password
or account lockout policies for different types of users in a domain (such as administrators

and general users) using GPOs. You can do this only using a new feature, fine-grain password and account lockout policy. A key distinction between group policy-based user and account lockout enforcement and fine-grain policies is how you apply them. Unlike group policy, however, fine-grain policies are quite complex to configure.

> **W**ARNING
>
> It's important to remember that only one set of GPO account and lockout policies applies to a domain. This functionality is unchanged from Windows 2000 Server and Server 2003. Although fine-grain policies can override the settings that are configured using a GPO at the domain level, they are not GPO-based.

You can apply fine-grain policies only to users and global security groups. They are not linked to the major Active Directory container objects: sites, domains, and organizational units (OUs). It is common for organizations to organize users using these traditional Active Directory container structures, so Microsoft recommends the creation of *shadow groups* which map to an organization's domain and OU structure. In this way, you can add the global security groups to the appropriate fine-grain policy object in Active Directory one time, and use group membership to determine to whom it applies. It's possible that a user can be a member of more than one global security group and for these groups to be associated with different fine-grain policies. To accommodate this, Microsoft allows you to associate a precedence value to each fine-grain policy. A policy given a lower number will take precedence over one given a higher number if both apply to a user.

Notes from the Underground...

A Long-Awaited Password and Account Policy Solution

Fine-grain password and account lockout policy is new in Windows Server 2008. In Windows 2000 and 2003 forests, you could apply these settings only at the domain level. A single effective set of policy settings was enforced for

Continued

all users. For many midsize to large organizations, this provided an unacceptable level of security. The limitation led to all kinds of complicated technical workarounds and the use of more complex domain and forest structures, which increased management costs.

Although fine-grain policies are certainly not as easy to use as traditional GPOs, they are a step in the right direction. Most companies will no longer require their previous workarounds, and Microsoft expects that many who adopted more complex domain structures will be consolidating and simplifying their forests. Fine-grain policies also represent a major departure from Microsoft's previous instructions to administrators to adopt a site-, domain-, and OU- based management style. They cannot be applied to any of these Active Directory container objects.

Configuring a Fine-Grain Password Policy

Two new Active Directory object classes have been added to the Active Directory schema to support fine-grain policies. Policies are configured under a *Password Settings Container* (PSC). The actual policy objects themselves are called *Password Settings objects* (PSO). Creating a PSO involves using a lower-level Active Directory editing tool than you might be familiar with. There are two ways to do it. One is with the **ADSI Edit** graphics utility. The other is by using **ldifde** to script the operation at the command line. In this chapter, we'll be using **ADSI Edit**:

1. Open **ADSI Edit** by clicking **Start | Run** and type in **adsiedit.msc**.

2. Right-click on the **ADSI Edit** node in the leftmost pane and click **Connect to**. (See Figure 3.6.)

Figure 3.6 Bringing Up the Connections Settings Dialog

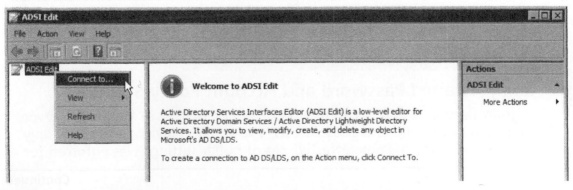

3. Accept the default naming context which appears in the **Name:** text box or type in the fully qualified domain name (FQDN) of the domain you want to use. Click **OK**. (See Figure 3.7.)

Figure 3.7 The Name: Text Box

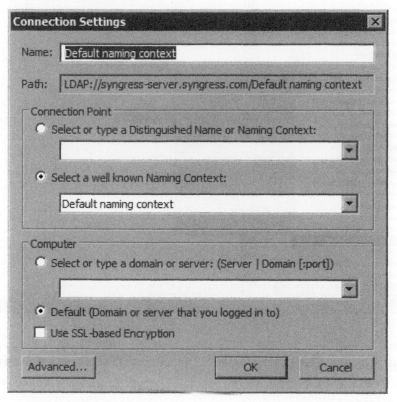

4. Expand the **Default naming context node** (if present), rxpand your **DC=DomainName** node (here, DC=syngress,DC=com), and double-click on the **CN=System** node.

5. Right-click on the **CN=Password Settings Container** node and select **New | Object**, as shown in Figure 3.8.

Figure 3.8 Creating the New Object in ADSI Edit

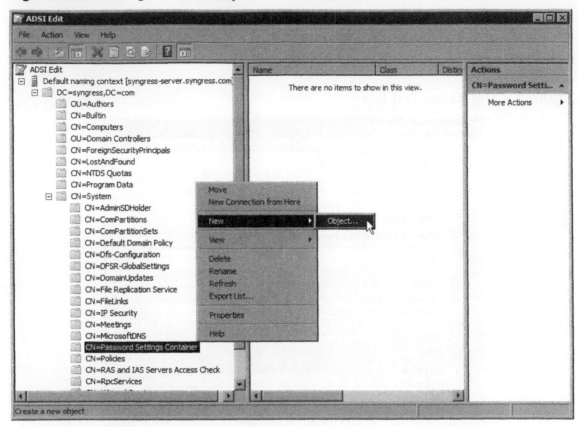

6. In the **Create Object** dialog box, select **msDS-PasswordSettings** and click **Next**. (See Figure 3.9.)

Figure 3.9 Selecting the msDS-PasswordSettings Option

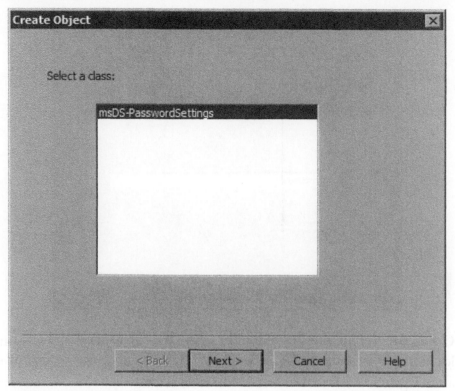

7. In the **Create Object** dialog box, enter the desired name for your PSO in
    the **Value:** text box (here, psoUsers) and click **Next**. (See Figure 3.10.)

Figure 3.10 Entering the PSO Name

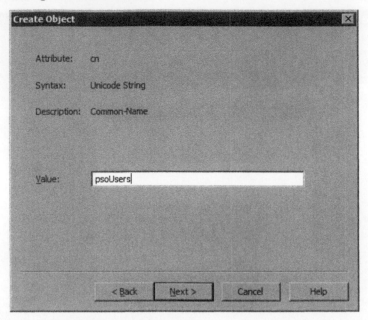

8. Configure the appropriate value for each of the password and account lockout policy settings. All are required. Refer to the information in the list after Figure 3.11 for more details on each setting.

Figure 3.11 Configuring the Fine-grain Settings

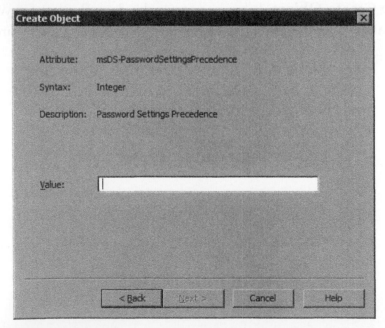

- **msDS-PasswordSettingsPrecedence** Sets the precedence value for deciding conflicts when more than one fine-grain policy applies to a user. Values greater than **0** are acceptable.

- **msDS-PasswordReversibleEncryptionEnabled** Equivalent to the **Store passwords using reversible encryption** group policy setting. Acceptable values are **TRUE** and **FALSE**.

- **msDS-PasswordHistoryLength** Equivalent to the **Enforce password history** group policy setting. Acceptable values are **0** through **1024**.

- **msDS-PasswordComplexityEnabled** Equivalent to the **Passwords must meet complexity requirements** group policy setting. Acceptable values are **TRUE** and **FALSE**.

- **msDS-MinimumPasswordLength** Equivalent to the **Minimum password length** group policy setting. Acceptable values are **0** through **255**.

- **msDS-MinimumPasswordAge** Equivalent to the **Minimum password age** group policy setting. Acceptable values are **(None)** and **days:hours: minutes:seconds** (i.e., 1:00:00:00 equals one day) through the value configured for **msDS-MaximumPasswordAge**.

- **msDS-MaximumPasswordAge** Equivalent to the **Maximum password age** group policy setting. Acceptable settings are **(Never) and msDS-MinimumPasswordAge** value through **(Never)**. This value cannot be set to **0**. It follows the **days:hours:minutes:seconds** format (i.e., 1:00:00:00 equals one day).

- **msDS-LockoutThreshold** Equivalent to the **Account lockout threshold** group policy setting. Acceptable settings are **0** through **65535**.

- **msDS-LockoutObservationWindow** Equivalent to the **Reset account lockout counter after** group policy setting. Acceptable values are **(None)** and **00:00:00:01** through **msDS-LockoutDuration** value.

- **msDS-LockoutDuration** Equivalent to the **Account lockout duration** group policy setting. Acceptable values are **(None)**, **(Never)**, and **msDS-LockoutObservationWindow** value through **(Never)**. This value follows the **days:hours:minutes:seconds** format (i.e., 1:00:00:00 equals one day).

9. After specifying the preceding values, click the **More Attributes** button, as shown in Figure 3.12.

Figure 3.12 The More Attributes Button

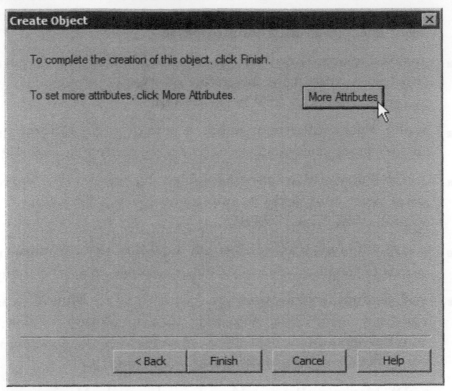

10. Although it is not required, at this point you can specify to which users or groups the fine-grain policy will apply. You can also do this in Active Directory Users and Computers (covered later). To configure this during PSO object creation:

Set **Select which properties to view:** to either **Optional** or **Both**.

Set **Select a property to view to:** to **msDS-PSOAppliesTo**.

Enter a distinguished name (DN) for a user or global security group in the **Edit Attribute:** text box and click **Add**. Multiple users and groups can be added and removed. When done, click **OK**. (See Figure 3.13.)

Figure 3.13 Associating Users and Global Security Groups

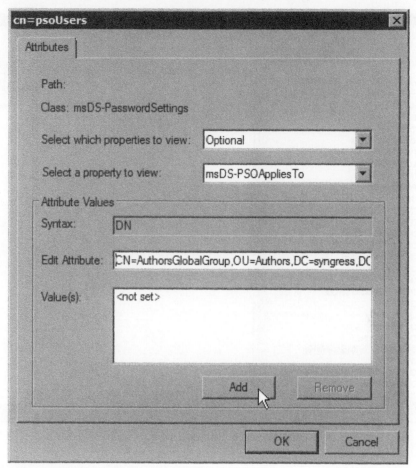

11. Click **Finish** in the Create Object dialog box. When done, **ADSI Edit**
should resemble Figure 3.14.

Figure 3.14 The ADSI Utility

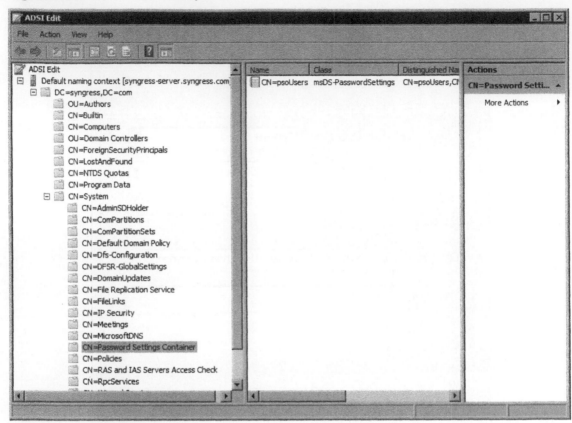

Applying Users and Groups to a PSO with Active Directory Users and Computers

In addition to using ADSI Edit to associate users and global security groups with a PSO, administrators can also use Active Directory Users and Computers:

1. Open **Active Directory Users and Computers** by clicking **Start | Administrative Tools | Active Directory Users and Computers**.

2. Ensure that **View | Advanced Features** is selected.

3. In the left pane, navigate to *Your Domain Name* **| System | Password Settings Container**.

4. In the right pane, right-click on the PSO you want to configure, and select **Properties**, as shown in Figure 3.15.

Figure 3.15 Opening the Properties for the PSO

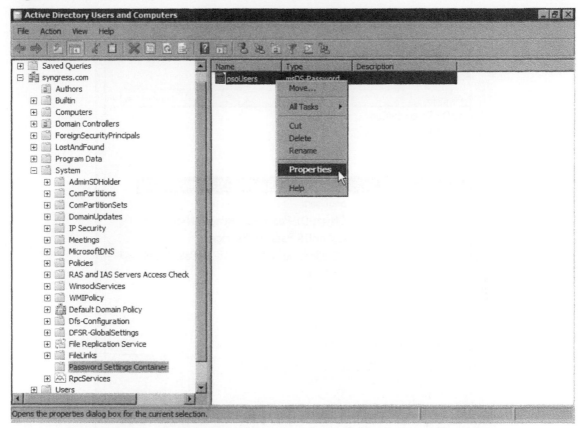

5. In the **Properties** dialog box, select the **Attribute Editor** tab. In the
   Attributes: selection window scroll down and click on **msDS–AppliesTo**
   followed by **Edit**. (See Figure 3.16.)

Figure 3.16 The Attribute Editor Tab

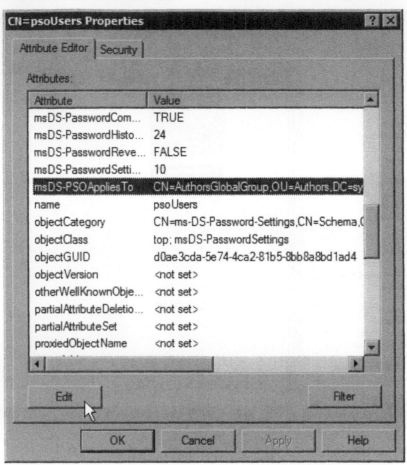

6. There are two ways to add users and global security groups using the **Multi-valued Distinguished Name with Security Principal Editor** dialog (see Figure 3.17):

    Click **Add Windows Account** to search for or type in the object name using a standard **Select Users, Computers, or Groups** dialog box.

    Click **Add DN** to type in the DN for the object you want to add.

Figure 3.17 The Multi-valued Distinguished Name with Security Principal Editor Window

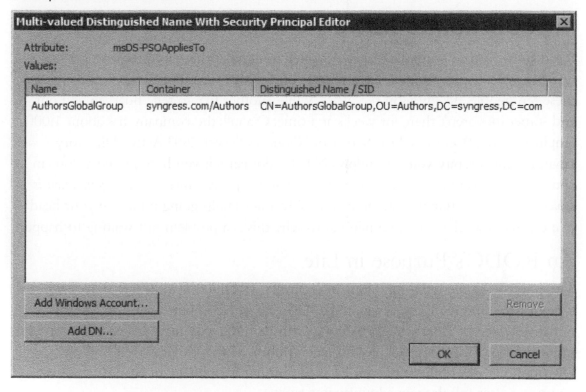

7. You can also remove accounts from the **Multi-valued Distinguished Name With Security Principal Editor** dialog by highlighting the account in the **Values:** selection box and clicking the **Remove** button. When you are done adding and deleting accounts from this PSO, click **OK**.

8. In the **Properties** window, click **OK**.

Read-Only Domain Controllers (RODCs)

One of the biggest mistakes IT organizations make is underestimating the security risk presented by remote offices. Many organizations (big and small) make major investments in their corporate IT security strategy and then place a domain controller on top of a desk in a small/remote office—right next to an exit. Several times during the course of the day, employees, delivery people, solicitors, and more walk by this door—and often the server itself. Typically, little exists to stop these people from walking out the door and selling their newly found (stolen) hardware on eBay.

And this is probably a best-case scenario. What would happen if the information on this server actually ended up in the *wrong* hands?

Introduction to RODC

Read-only domain controllers were designed to combat this very problem. Let's take a scenario where a corporation has a remote office with ten employees. On a daily basis, these ten people are always in the office, while another five to ten "float" in and out and sometimes aren't there for weeks at a time. Overall, the company has about 1,000 employees. In a Windows 2000 Server or Windows Server 2003 Active Directory environment (or, pity you, a Windows NT 4.0 domain), if you have placed a domain controller in this remote office, *all information for every user account in the organization is copied to this server.* Right now, there's probably a light bulb going off above your head (we can see it all the way from here) as to why this is a problem just waiting to happen.

An RODC's Purpose in Life

The purpose of the read-only domain controller (RODC) is to deal directly with this type of issue, and many issues like it. RODCs are one component in the Microsoft initiative to secure a branch office. Along with RODCs, you may also want to consider implementing BitLocker (whole-disk encryption), Server Core, as well as Role Distribution—the ability to assign local administrator rights to an RODC without granting a user full domain administrator rights.

RODC Features

A number of features come with an RODC, which focus on providing heightened security without limiting functionality to the remote office users. Some of the key points here are:

- **Read-only replicas of the domain database:** Clients are not allowed to write changes directly to an RODC (much like a Windows NT BDC). RODC holds all the Active Directory Domain Services (AD DS) objects and attributes that a writable domain controller holds, with the exception of account passwords. Clients, however, are not able to write changes directly to the RODC.

- **Filtered Attribute Sets:** The ability to prevent certain AD attributes from being replicated to RODCs.

- **Unidirectional Replication:** Since clients cannot write changes to an RODC, there is no need to replicate *from* an RODC *to* a full domain controller.

This prevents potentially corrupt (or hijacked) data from being disbursed, and also reduces unnecessary bandwidth usage.

- **Read-only DNS:** Allows one-way replication of application directory partitions, including ForestDNSZones and DomainDNSZones.

- **Cached accounts:** By caching accounts, if the RODC were ever compromised, only the accounts that have been compromised need to be reset. The full DCs are aware of which accounts are cached, and a report can be generated for auditing purposes.

So these are the key features of a read-only domain controller. Now let's step through the installation process.

Configuring RODC

Configuring an RODC isn't all that different from adding a traditional domain controller. The most important thing to remember about an RODC is that a writable domain controller *must* exist somewhere in the domain. Once this prerequisite is met, we can go ahead and configure our RODC. Let's assume that our writable DC is in place, using the domain information from the previous exercise.

Configuring & Implementing...

Adding an RODC to an Existing Forest

A read-only domain controller can be added to a preexisting forest, but this will require that schema changes be made to the forest for this to work properly. The process is fairly simple. Using the *adprep* tool with the */rodcprep* switch (the actual syntax would be **adprep /rodcprep**), we can add the necessary schema changes to support our RODC.

Let's begin configuring our RODC:

1. Click **Start | Administrative Tools | Server Manager**.
2. Scroll down to Role Summary, click **Add roles**.

3. When the Before You Begin page opens, click **Next**.

4. On the Select Server Roles page, choose **Active Directory Domain Services** and then click **Next**.

5. Click **Next** again on the Active Directory Domain Services page.

6. On the Confirm Installation Selections page (Figure 3.18), click **Install**.

Figure 3.18 Confirming Installation Selections

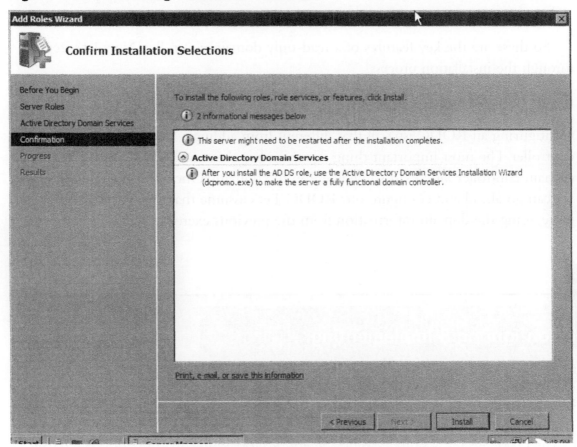

7. When installation is complete, click **Close**.

8. If the Server Manager window has closed, re-open it.

9. Expand **Roles**, and then click **Active Directory Domain Services**.

10. Under Summary (Figure 3.19), click the link to **Run The Active Directory Domain Services Installation Wizard**.

Figure 3.19 The Summary Page

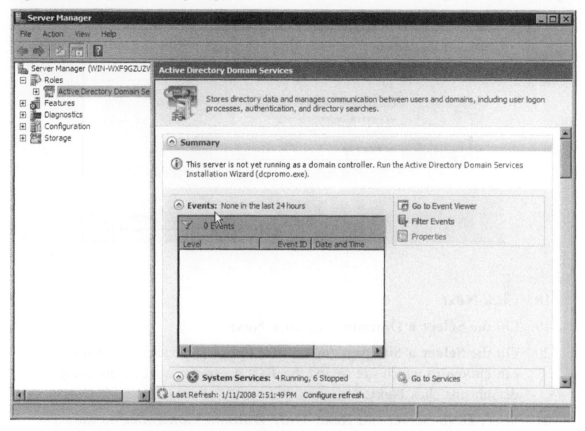

11. Click **Next** on the **Welcome To The Active Directory Domain Services Installation Wizard** page.

12. On the **Operating System Compatibility** page, click **Next**.

13. On the **Choose A Deployment Configuration** page, click **Existing Forest**.

14. Ensure **Add A Domain Controller To An Existing Domain** is selected and then click **Next**.

15. On the **Network Credentials** page, verify that your domain is listed and click **Set**.

16. In the **User Name** field, type **<domain>/administrator**.

17. In the **Password** field, type your administrator password and then click **OK** (see Figure 3.20).

Figure 3.20 Setting Account Credentials

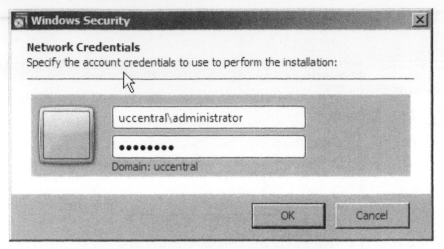

18. Click **Next**.

19. On the **Select a Domain** page, click **Next**.

20. On the **Select a Site** page (if you have Sites and Services configured), you can choose to which site to add this RODC. In this case, we are using the default site, click **Next**.

21. Select **DNS Server** and **Read-Only Domain Controller** on the Additional Domain Controller Options page and then click **Next**.

22. In the **Group Or User** field, type **<domain>\administrator**, and then click **Next**.

23. Verify the file locations, and click **Next**.

24. On the **Active Directory Domain Services Restore Mode Administrator Password** page, type and confirm a restore mode password, and then click **Next**.

25. On the **Summary** page, click **Next**.

26. The Active Directory Domain Services Installation Wizard dialog box appears. After installation, reboot the server.

TIP

It is possible to "stage" an RODC and delegate rights to complete an RODC installation to a user or group. In order to do this, you must first create an account in Active Directory for the RODC in Active Directory Users and Computers. Once inside of ADU&C, you must right-click the **Domain Controllers** OU container, and select **Pre-create Read-Only Domain Controller Account**. From here, you can set the alternate credential for a user who can then finish the installation. On the server itself, the user must type **dcpromo /UseExistingAccount:Attach** in order to complete the process.

Removing an RODC

There may come a time when you need to remove an RODC from your forest or domain. Like anything in this world, there is a right way and a wrong way to go about doing this. For the exam, you'll want to make sure you know the right way. Removing a read-only domain controller is almost as simple as adding an RODC. One important thing to remember with an RODC is that it cannot be the first—or the last—domain controller in a domain. Therefore, all RODCs must be detached before removing a final writable domain controller. Fewer steps make up the removal process. Let's take a look at how this is done.

1. Choose **Start | Run**.
2. In the **Run** window, type **dcpromo.exe**.
3. At the **Welcome To Active Directory Domain Services Installation Wizard** screen, click **Next**.
4. On the **Delete The Domain** window, make sure the check box is not checked, and then click **Next**.
5. Enter your administrator password, and then click **Next**.
6. Click **Next** in the **Summary** window, and then click **Next** again.
7. When removal is complete, reboot the server.

8. When the server reboots, sign back in.

9. Select **Start | Administrative Tools | Server Manager**.

10. Scroll down to **Role Summary**.

11. Expand **Roles**, and then click **Remove Roles**.

12. On the **Before You Begin** page, click **Next**.

13. Remove the checkmark from **Active Directory Domain Services and DNS Server** and click **Next**.

14. Review the confirmation details, and then click **Remove**.

15. Review the results page, and click **Close**.

16. Restart the server if necessary.

Digital Rights Management Service

When you need to protect how content is used you will need to use Digital Rights Management (DRM). DRM applies a policy based on who is accessing the content that dictates elements such as where and for how long you can view content. Common places where you will see DRM is in pay-per-view and subscription content scenarios. The Windows Media platform delivers DRM functionality through various components. Windows Media Server's role in the DRM scenario is as a content delivery mechanism. The license issuing and management are handled by either a service provider or a custom-developed license server based on the Windows Media Rights Manager SDK. For more information on the Rights Manager SDK visit www.microsoft.com/windows/windowsmedia/forpros/drm/sdksandversions.aspx, and for a list of partners who provide DRM services visit www.microsoft.com/windows/windowsmedia/forpros/partner.aspx.

Notes from the Underground...

Administrative Changes to AD RMS

Even if you have used AD RMS in the past, you should plan to spend some time working with this new release. There have been enough changes between releases to the administrative interface to warrant a deeper look at the product. The setup process has changed to allow smaller organizations to implement AD RMS with less effort than was required in previous releases. The extensibility opens AD RMS up to the rigorous needs of a full-scale enterprise deployment as well. As you experiment with AD RMS, you might find it useful to implement in your existing organization once you realize how little effort is required to get it up and running!

Summary

You can use group policy settings to enforce security-related settings across multiple Windows 2000 and later computers. Password and account lockout group policy items must be linked at the domain level to be effective. Windows Server 2008 creates a Default Domain Policy GPO and links it to the domain level for each domain in the forest. The domain password policy allows administrators to specify a combination of password security options, including how frequently users change their passwords, how long passwords must be, how many unique passwords must be used before a user can reuse one, and how complex passwords must be. Account lockout is used to prevent successful brute force password guessing. If it is not enabled, an attacker can continue to guess username and password combinations very rapidly using software. The proper combination of settings can effectively block these types of security vulnerabilities by either locking the account out permanently or requiring long waiting times between a low number of incorrect guesses.

Only one password and account lockout policy will be effective for all users and computers in the domain unless fine-grain policies are used. Although more difficult to create than standard GPOs, these fine-grain policy objects, called Password Settings objects, allow administrators to apply different password and account lockout settings to user accounts and global security groups. You can create them using ldifde or ADSI Edit, and you can modify them using either of these tools as well as Active Directory Users and Computers.

You can also use group policy objects to enable auditing. Auditing is used to track authorized and unauthorized resource access, usage, and change. Administrators can audit the success and/or failure for a number of tracked events. Examples of what can be tracked include logons, changes to policy, use of privileges, directory service or file access, and so forth. Some objects such as the Active Directory directory service, the file system, Registry keys, and printers require two steps to enable auditing. Administrators must enable auditing in group policy and on the specific objects they want to track. You can configure these resources to track individual and group accounts, as well as specific actions such as changing permissions on or deleting the object. Most objects have a sizable number of possible auditing options. Unlike the other items in the previous list, some Active Directory objects already have auditing configured for them. Despite this convenience, administrators should always double-check the objects they specifically want to audit and ensure that the settings are appropriate for the information they want to receive.

Solutions Fast Track

Configuring Audit Policies

☑ Auditing is used to track authorized and unauthorized resource access, usage, and change within Windows Server 2008.

☑ You can audit the success and/or failure for a variety of tracked events. Examples of what can be tracked include logons, changes to policy, use of privileges, directory service or file access, and so forth.

☑ Some objects such as directory services, the file system, Registry keys, and printers require two steps to enable auditing. You must enable auditing in group policy and on the specific objects you want to track.

Fine-Grain Password and Account Lockout Policies

☑ Windows Server 2008 creates a Default Domain Policy GPO for every domain in the forest. This domain is the primary method used to set some security-related policies such as password expiration and account lockout.

☑ You can use fine-grain password and account lockout policy to apply custom password and account lockout policy settings to individual users and global security groups within a domain.

☑ The domain password policy allows you to specify a range of password security options, including how frequently users change their passwords, how long passwords must be, how many unique passwords must be used before a user can reuse one, and how complex passwords must be.

☑ You can use account lockout to prevent successful brute force password guessing. If it's not enabled, someone can keep attempting to guess username/password combinations very rapidly using a software-based attack. The proper combination of settings can effectively block these types of security vulnerabilities.

Read-Only Domain Controllers (RODCs)

☑ RODC holds all of the Active Directory Domain Services (AD DS) objects and attributes that a writable domain controller holds, with the exception of account passwords.

☑ Unidirectional replication prevents RODCs from replicating information to a writable domain controller.

☑ The installation of read-only domain controllers can be delegated to other users.

Configuring Active Directory Rights Management Services

☑ AD RMS can only be installed on full installations of Windows Server 2008.

☑ It provides protection in a format- and application-agnostic manner.

☑ You can define your trust boundary to include specific users within your organization, users in other organizations, or the public at large through Windows Live ID.

☑ The Microsoft Office suite is the primary authoring tool made available by Microsoft. You will require the Professional edition or later to author content.

☑ Policy templates provide a uniform way for users to apply a consistent set of usage rights to a document.

☑ You should decommission a server and resave protected content in an unprotected state before removing it.

Frequently Asked Questions

Q: I created a GPO with specific password and account lockout settings and applied it to an OU in my Active Directory domain. Why weren't the settings applied?

A: A GPO with password and account lockout settings is applied only when linked at the domain level of Active Directory.

Q: My security administrator is concerned about brute force password attacks. Are there any Windows Server 2008 features which can help to manage those risks?

A: Account lockout can be used to minimize risks from brute force password attacks by setting an appropriate combination of values for the **Account lockout duration**, **Account lockout threshold**, and **Reset account lockout counter after** options.

Q: I'm concerned about users going for too long without changing their passwords, or using passwords that are really simple and easy to guess. What can I do about this in Windows Server 2008?

A: Windows Server 2008 group policy allows you to specify a range of password security options, including how frequently users change their passwords, how long passwords must be, how many unique passwords must be used before a user can reuse one, and how complex passwords must be when initially specified or changed.

Q: How can I apply a different set of password and account lockout policy to administrators?

A: In Windows Server 2008, a new feature called fine-grain password and account lockout policy can be used to apply custom password and account lockout policy settings to individual users and global security groups within a domain.

Q: What can I monitor using auditing in Windows Server 2008?

A: Auditing can be used to track successful and failed resource access, usage, and change, including logon events, directory service objects, file system objects, Registry objects, printers, exercise of user privileges and rights, system events, account management changes, and much more.

Q: It seems like auditing file system and directory service objects would produce too many log entries to sort through. Is there a way to limit this?

A: In addition to enabling auditing of these types of objects, you can also specify exactly what you want to track on an object-by-object basis. This includes both who changed an object and what was specifically changed.

Q: I see that two types of logon events can be audited. What is the difference between them?

A: The **Audit account logon events** policy is used for credential validation, and the events audited relate to the computer which is authoritative for the credentials. For most users in a domain, this will be the DC which processes their logon regardless of the location of the resources being accessed. The **Audit logon events** policy relates directly to where the resources being accessed are located.

Q: I'd like to restrict some users from being able to change their workstation's time, shut down servers, and so forth. This doesn't seem to be configurable with permissions. How can I accomplish this?

A: The User Rights Assignment node in group policy can be used to configure options such as this. Administrators can grant a wide array of user rights, including the ability to log on to a server locally or from a network connection, the ability to shut down a server, the ability for certain accounts to be able to log on as a service, and many others.

Q: Does Rights Management work with mobile devices?

A: Yes, there is a mobile module for Rights Management Services. However, only Windows Mobile devices are supported with Rights Management. Check with your wireless vendor or mobile manufacturer for support and availability on particular models.

Q: Can an RODC replicate to another RODC?

A: No. RODCs can only replicate with full domain controllers. This is a feature of the RODC, which is meant to be—as the name implies—a read-only server. Since neither RODC would have write capabilities in this example, it would be pointless to have them replicate to one another.

Q: Can an RODC exist in a mixed–mode (Windows 2003 and Windows 2008) domain?

A: Yes, but you must run *adprep* with the proper switches in order for it to succeed. If the domain is not prepped for this new Windows Server 2008 role, the RODC installation will fail almost immediately. *adprep* is required to add the appropriate schema modifications for RODC.

Chapter 4

Microsoft Windows Server 2008: Network Security Changes

Solutions in this chapter:

- Network Policy Server
- Network Policy and Access Services Role
- 802.1x Wired and Wireless Access

☑ Summary

☑ Solutions Fast Track

☑ Frequently Asked Questions

Introduction

Organizations rely on networking and communications to meet the challenging requirements necessary to compete in the global marketplace. All members of these organizations need to have constant access to files. This requires the ability to connect to the network wherever they may be and from any device that they have available to them at the time. In addition, those outside the vendor's network will require the ability to interact smoothly with the key resources they require. Partners and clients want to be able to also conduct quick and fluid transactions through the network. Security is more important than ever in networking because of the constant threat of infiltration and exposure to the Internet. Successfully navigating all of these concerns relies on the knowledge of how to configure network access efficiently and provide the most secure yet accessible connection possible to your organization and its members.

As an administrator, you must accommodate these needs using the latest and most practical tools in your arsenal. To help accomplish this there have been a number of networking and communications enhancements made to Windows Server 2008 to address connectivity. This will help you to improve the ease of use, reliability, management, and security of your organization's assets. By applying what Windows Server 2008 has to offer with its latest features you will have more flexibility when managing your network infrastructure. Windows Server 2008 allows for a total system health by deploying settings for authenticated wireless and wired connections through Group Policy or scripts, and deploying protected traffic scenarios. In order to take on this task, a number of features from former versions of Windows Server have been improved upon or replaced with new updated features, which will allow you to provide the highest level of efficiency and security to your organization.

In this chapter, we will discuss the many new and powerful changes to Microsoft Windows Server 2008 that include innovative enhancements to networking technologies and network access configuration. We will discuss Network Policy Server and show you how to use Windows Server 2008's Network Policy and Access Services Role to install Network Policy Server (NPS) and Routing and Remote Access (RRAS), as well as configure Kerberos to utilize different methods of authentication. We'll also discuss 802.1x wired and wireless access.

Network Policy Server

Windows Server 2008 offers exceptional ease of use and configuration for remote access. All features previously available are featured in Windows Server 2008. There is also the additional replacement of Internet Authentication Service (IAS) with Network Policy Server and Network Access Protection (NAP).

The change to Windows Server 2008 in regards to remote access is the addition of Secure Socket Tunneling Protocol (SSTP). SSTP is the latest form of VPN tunnel created for use with Windows Server 2008. It contains many new features that enable traffic to pass through firewalls that block Point-to-Point Tunneling Protocol (PPTP) and Layer 2 Tunneling Protocol (L2TP)/Internet Protocol Security (IPSec) traffic. In addition, SSTP uses the Secure Sockets Layer (SSL) channel of the Hypertext Transfer Protocol Secure (HTTPS) protocol by making use of a process that encapsulates PPP traffic. PPP is very versatile. It enables you to use strong authentication methods such as Extensible Authentication Protocol-Transport Layer Security (EAP-TLS), which were not possible in past versions of Windows for VPN. All traffic will be channeled through the TCP port 443, which is typically used for Web access, because of the use of HTTPS. Security features include transport level security with enhanced key negotiation, encryption, and integrity checking capabilities by using SSL.

In the RRAS there are a number of snap-in roles that can be used in configuring and setting up your network access needs for Windows Server 2008. In previous incarnations of Windows Server 2003, Internet Authentication Service (IAS) snap-in was Microsoft's implementation of a Remote Authentication Dial-in User Service (RADIUS) server and proxy. It was capable of performing localized connection AAA Protocol for many types of network access, including wireless and VPN connections.

For Windows Server 2008, Microsoft has replaced IAS with a new snap- in called Network Policy Server (NPS). NPS is the Microsoft implementation of a RADIUS server and proxy in Windows Server 2008, and it promises to be even simpler to use than IAS.

NPS is not just a replacement for IAS; it does what IAS did but also offers another role called Network Access Protection (NAP). When you install NPS you will find that you have a lot of new functionality.

NPS does many of the same things that IAS did such as:

- Routing of LAN and WAN traffic.
- Allowing access to local resources through VPN or dial-up connections.
- Creating and enforcing network access through VPN or dial-up connections.

For example, NPS can provide these functions:

- VPN services
- Dial-up services
- 802.11 protected access
- RRAS
- Authentication through Windows Active Directory
- Control of network access with policies

What NPS does that is new are all the functions related to NAP. NAP when used in unison with NPS creates a "total system health policy enforcement platform," which helps in the creation of health policies for your network, as shown in Figure 4.1.

Figure 4.1 NPS and NAP Health Policy Overview

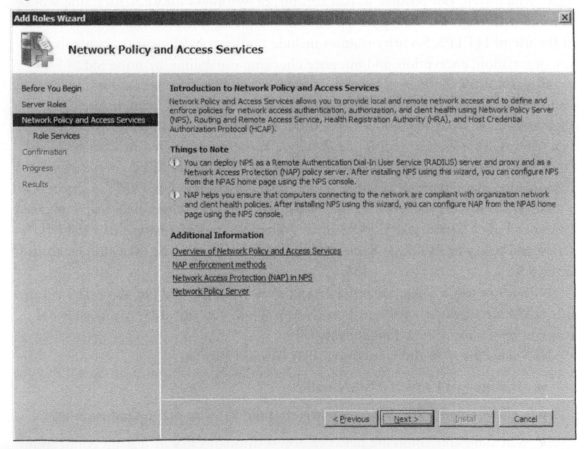

NAP is designed to enhance a corporate VPN. This is accomplished when clients establish a VPN session with a Windows Server 2008 system that is running the RRAS. Once a connection is made, a NPS will validate the remote system and determine the status of its health. The NPS collects information and compares the remote computer's configuration against a pre-determined network access policy that can be customized by the administrator. Policies can be configured to either monitor or isolate based on the administrators preference as, shown in Figure 4.2.

Figure 4.2 NPS Policy Configuration

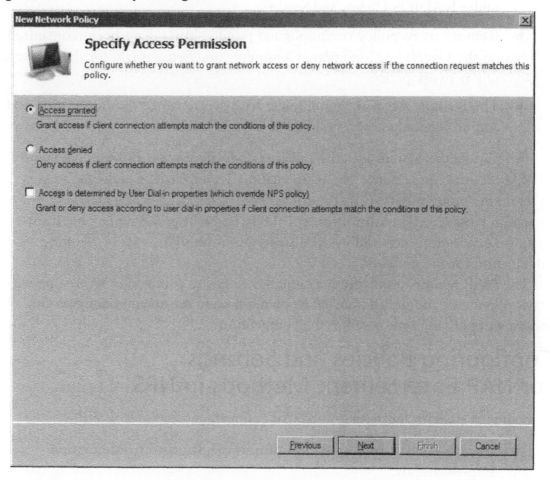

Although monitoring will not prevent any PCs from gaining access to your network, each PC logging on to the network will be recorded for compliance. Isolation will put non-compliant users onto an isolated segment of the network, where it cannot interfere with production or resources. Of course, the administrator is ultimately responsible for configuring what access non-compliant computers will be allowed.

If you are already familiar with Windows Server 2003 and the IAS snap-in, you will notice many changes to the NPS snap-in:

- Network policies have replaced remote access policies and have been moved to the policies node.

- RADIUS Clients and Servers node has replaced the RADIUS Client node.

- There is no Connection Request Processing node.

- Policies and the Remote RADIUS Server Groups node have been moved under RADIUS Clients and Servers.

- Remote access policy conditions and profile settings have been reorganized on the Overview, Conditions, Constraints, and Settings tabs for the properties of a network policy.

- The Remote Access Logging folder has been renamed the Accounting node, and no longer has the Local File or SQL Server nodes.

In addition, the System Health Validators node allows you to set up and adjust all NAP health requirements. The Remediation Server Groups node allows you to set up the group of servers that restricted NAP clients can access for the VPN and Dynamic Host Configuration Protocol (DHCP) NAP enforcement methods. Last, the Accounting node allows you to set up how NPS stores accounting information for the network.

The NAP wizard automatically configures all of the connection request policies, network policies, and health policies. Knowing how to set up and configure this feature will put you steps ahead of the competition.

Configuring Policies and Settings for NAP Enforcement Methods in NPS

To configure policies and settings for NAP enforcement methods in NPS:

1. Select **Network Access Protection** in the Standard Configuration drop-down box.

2. Click Configure NAP.

To configure policies and settings for VPN or dial-up network access:

1. Select RADIUS server for Dial-Up or VPN Connections from the drop-down box.

2. Click **Configure VPN** or **Dial-Up**.

To configure policies and settings for 802.1X-authenticated wired or wireless access:

1. Select **RADIUS server for 802.1X Wireless or Wired Connections** from the drop-down box.

2. Click **Configure 802.1X**.

The wizard will guide you through the configuration process for your chosen scenario. The NAP wizard for VPN enforcement has a number of policy creation options, including ones for compliant NAP clients, noncompliant NAP clients, and non-NAP capable clients. It also includes two health policies for compliant and noncompliant NAP clients. The new NAP wizards and other wizards contained within will help you with creating RADIUS clients, remote RADIUS server groups, connection request policies, and network policies. Overall, this will make it that much easier to configure NPS for a variety of network access scenarios, and this will make your job and exam all the more simple.

Network Policy and Access Services Role

Windows Server 2008 authentication is a two-part process involving authentication of the user (interactive login) and access control to network resources. When users log in, their identities are verified through Active Directory (AD) Domain Services, and this provides controlled access to Active Directory objects. As users attempt to access various network resources, their network authentication credentials are used to determine whether or not they have permission to access those resources. Also part of AD are user accounts and groups that impact network access. Authentication can also occur through a public key infrastructure (PKI), which uses digital certificates and certification authorities to verify and authenticate entities including users, computers, and services. Group Policy is used to manage configuration settings for servers, clients, and users. Remote Authentication Dial-In User Service (RADIUS) is a protocol that originally was created for dial-in authentication and authorization service. Now, its role has expanded to include wireless access point access, authenticating Ethernet switches, virtual private network servers, and more. In Windows Server 2008, the RADIUS function is now handled by the Network Policy and Access Services role.

As you can see from Figure 4.3, the Network Policy and Access Services role installs Network Policy Server (NPS) and Routing and Remote Access (RRAS). Under the NPS node, you'll find RADIUS Clients and Servers, Policies, Network Access Protection (NAP) and Accounting. Under the Routing and Remote Access node, you'll find Network Interfaces, Remote Access Logging & Policies, IPv4 and IPv6.

Figure 4.3 Network Policy and Access Services Server Manager Interface

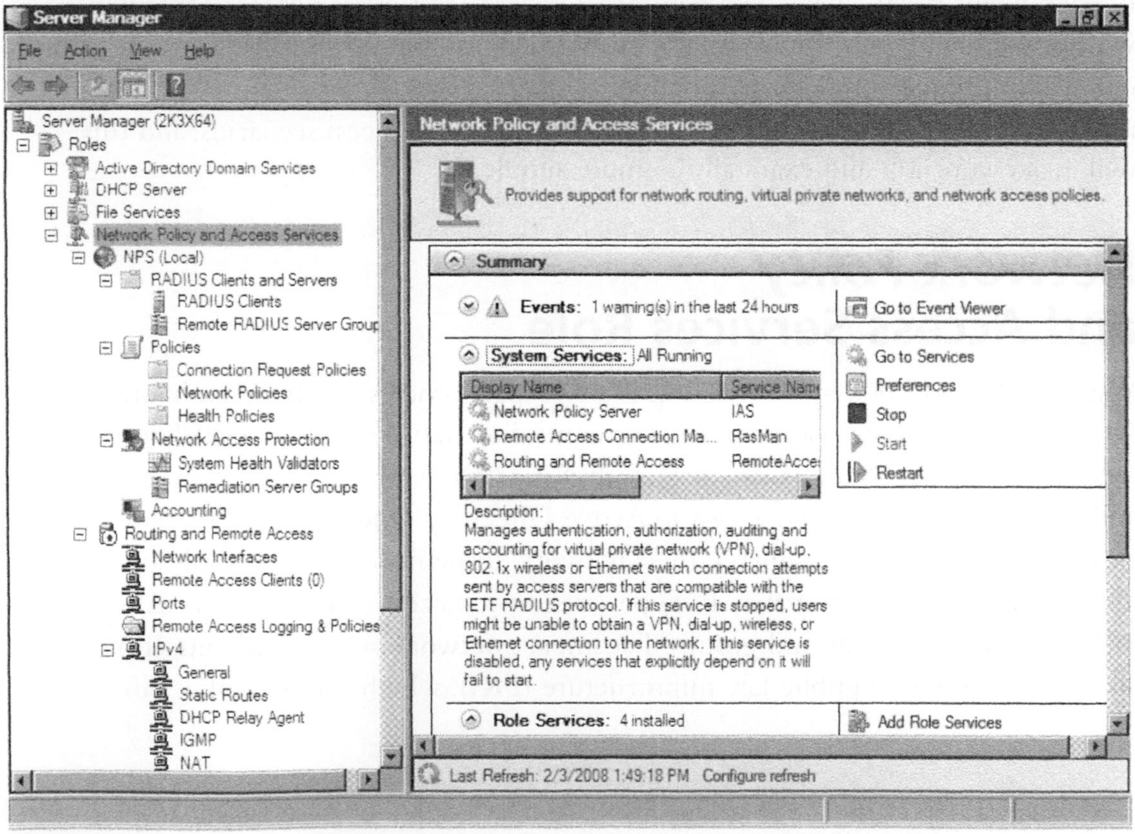

NPS is the Microsoft implementation of a RADIUS server and proxy in Windows Server 2008, and it is expected to be even simpler to use than IAS. You will need to know how to set up a RADIUS server using NPS. Begin by installing NPS and setting up your RADIUS Server.

1. Open **Server Manager** and click on the **Add Roles.**
2. Choose the **Network Policy and Access Services** shown in Figure 4.4, and review the overview screen (see Figure 4.5).

Figure 4.4 Choosing the NPS Role

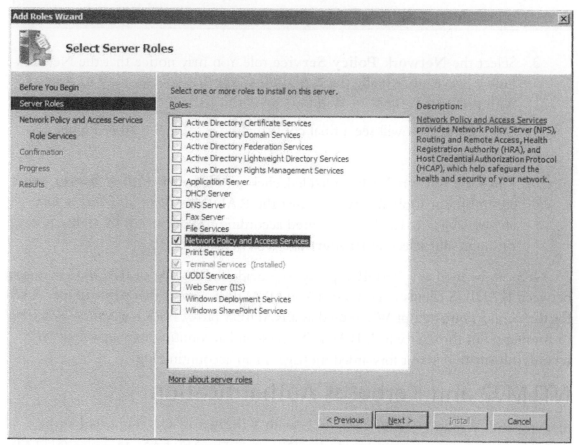

Figure 4.5 Overview Screen on NPS

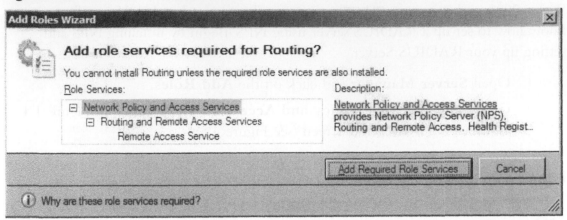

3. Select the **Network Policy Service** role. You may notice that the Network Policy Service is actually the RADIUS server that you are used to seeing with previous versions of Windows Server in IAS.

4. Click **Next**. You will see a final confirmation screen, as seen in Figure 4.5.

5. Click **Install**.

6. Once the software has been loaded, click on **Network Policy Server** under administrator tools. You will see that the RADIUS Client and Server Tabs are available and can be configured according to your needs by right-clicking on them and selecting **Properties**.

NPS can be used as a RADIUS proxy to provide the routing of RADIUS messages between RADIUS clients (access servers) and RADIUS servers that perform user AAA for the connection attempt. When used as a RADIUS proxy, NPS is a central switching or routing point through which RADIUS access and accounting messages flow. NPS records information about forwarded messages in an accounting log.

NTLMv2 and Kerberos Authentication

Starting with Windows 2000, Kerberos Version 5 (Kerberos) was supported as the default authentication protocol in Active Directory. The NT LAN Manager (NTLM) protocol is still supported for authentication with clients that required NTLM (i.e., for backward compatibility only). You can control how NTLM is used through Group Policy. The default authentication level in most cases is "Send NTLMv2 Response Only." With this level of authentication, NTLMv2 is used with clients that use this authentication protocol and session security only if the server supports it.

You can configure Kerberos to utilize different methods of authentication, and these can be set via NPS for the network as well as in the IPSec Settings tab of the Windows Firewall with Advanced Security Properties.

To begin, install this role on your Windows Server 2008 computer, if it's not already installed. To do so, open Server Manager, choose **Add Roles** from the interface option, and then select **Network Policy and Access Services**. Follow the on-screen prompts to complete configuration, which are self-explanatory. In order to install *Health Registration Authority* (HRA) and *Host Credential Authorization Protocol* (HCAP), you also need to have web services (IIS) installed. For our purposes, we will disregard these two options and focus just on network access. Once Network Policy and Access Services are installed, you can access the services through the Server Manager interface. As shown in Figure 4.3, you can start, stop, or check the status of a service as well as set Preferences. Note that you can deploy NPS in a number of ways at various points in your forest or domain. It is beyond the scope of this chapter to discuss these options in detail.

802.1x Wired and Wireless Access

IEEE 802.1x standards define an effective framework for controlling and authenticating clients to a wired or wireless protected network—in this case a NAP infrastructure. These standards define port-based authentication on supported devices. These devices could be switches or wireless access points that support the IEEE 802.1x standard. The IEEE standard is significant because it has been accepted by hardware and software vendors—their products will be designed with the standards in mind. What does this mean for you and me? All hardware that is 802.1x based should work with RADIUS and NAP.

An 802.1x deployment consists of three major components that allow for the authentication process to work correctly (see Figure 4.6).

- **Supplicant** a device that requests access to our network and is connected via a pass-through authenticator.

- **Pass-through authenticator** a switch or access point that is 802.1x compliant.

- **Authentication server** when the supplicant connects to the pass-through authenticator, the request is passed to the authentication server by the pass-through authenticator. The authentication server decides whether the client is granted access or denied.

Figure 4.6 Components of 802.1x

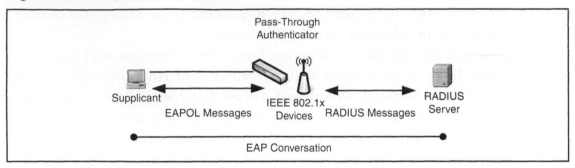

Authentication is handled using the Extensible Authentication Protocol (EAP). EAP messages used in the authentication process are transmitted between the supplicant and pass-through authenticator using EAP over LAN (EAPoL). The pass-through authenticator talks to the RADIUS using RADIUS messages and EAP.

When NAP uses IEEE 802.1x, the authenticating pass-through authenticator uses the RADIUS protocol. NPS instructs the pass-through authenticator (wireless access-point or switch) to place supplicants that are not in compliance with NPS into a restricted network. The restricted network could be a separate VLAN or a network with IP filters in place to isolate it from the secured network.

WLAN Authentication Using 802.1x and 802.3

NPS is responsible for network security and is used to provide secure wireless access through NPS. Windows Server 2008 also provides features that enable you to deploy 802.1x authenticated wired service for IEEE 802.3 Ethernet network clients. In conjunction with 802.1x capable switches and other Windows Server 2008 features, you can control network access through Wired Network Policies in Windows Server 2008 Group Policies. Recall that NPS is used to configure remote connections. The 802.3 wired network specification allows you to use the 802.1x specification to provide wired networking access. This is configured via NPS and uses Protected Extensible Authentication Protocol (PEAP) authentication. It is outside the scope of this book to discuss how to plan, configure, and deploy a WLAN authentication method, but we will discuss these concepts to the extent you need to understand the changes in the Windows Server 2008 environment.

Let's start with some definitions as a review. The 802.11 standard defined the shared key authentication method for authentication and Wired Equivalent Privacy (WEP) for encryption for wireless communications. 802.11 ultimately ended up being a relatively weak standard and newer security standards are available and recommended for use. The 802.1x standard that existed for Ethernet switches was adapted to the 802.11 wireless LANs to provide stronger authentication than the original standard. 802.1x is designed for medium to large wireless LANs that have an authentication infrastructure, such as AD and RADIUS in the Windows environment. With such an infrastructure in place, the 802.1x standard supports dynamic WEP, which are mutually determined keys negotiated by the wireless client and the RADIUS server. However, the 802.1x standard also supports the stronger Wi-Fi Protected Access (WPA) encryption method. The 802.11i standard formally replaces WEP with WPA2, an enhancement to the original WPA method.

Wireless and Wired Authentication Technologies

Windows Server 2008 supports several authentication methods for authenticating that a computer or user is attempting to connect via a protected wireless connection. These same technologies support 802.1x authenticated wired networks as well. These Extended Authentication Protocols (EAP) methods are:

- EAP–TLS
- PEAP–TLS
- PEAP–MS–CHAPv2

Extended Authentication Protocol–Transport Layer Security (EAP–TLS) and Protected Extended Authentication Protocol–Transport Layer Security (PEAP–TLS) are used in conjunction with Public Key Infrastructure (PKI) and computer certificates, user certificates, or smart cards. Using EAP–TLS, a wireless client sends its certificate (computer, user, or smart card) for authentication and the RADIUS server sends its computer certificate for authentication. By default, the wireless client authenticates the server's certificate. With PEAP–TLS, the server and client create an encrypted session before certificates are exchanged. Clearly, PEAP–TLS is a stronger authentication method because the authentication session data is encrypted.

If there are no computer, user, or smart card certificates available, you can use PEAP-Microsoft Challenge Handshake Authentication Protocol version 2 (PEAP-MS-CHAPv2). This is a password-based authentication method in which the exchange of the authentication traffic is encrypted (using TLS), making it difficult for hackers to intercept and use an offline dictionary attack to access authentication exchange data. That said, it's the weakest of these three options for authentication because it relies on the use of a password.

A Windows-based client running Windows Vista or Windows Server 2008 can be configured in the following ways:

- Group Policy
- Command line
- Wired XML profiles

Using Group Policy, you can configure the Wired Network (IEEE 802.3) Policies Group Policy extension, which is part of Computer configuration Group Policy that can specify wired network settings in the AD environment. The Group Policy extension applies only to Windows Server 2008 and Windows Vista computers. The command line can be used within the **netsh** context using the **lan** command (**netsh lan**). You can explore the available comments by typing **netsh lan /?** at the command line prompt. Wired XML profiles are XML files that contain wired network settings. These can be imported and exported to Windows Server 2008 and Windows Vista clients using the **netsh** context as well. You can use **netsh lan export profile** or **netsh lan add profile** to export or import a wired profile using the command line.

For Windows XP SP2 or Windows Server 2003-basec computers, you can manually configure wired clients by configuring 802.1x authentication settings from the Authentication tab of the properties dialog box of a LAN connection in the Network Connections folder, as shown in Figure 4.7, which shows the Network Connections Properties dialog box from a Windows XP Pro SP2 computer.

Figure 4.7 802.1x Settings on Wired Windows XP SP2 Client

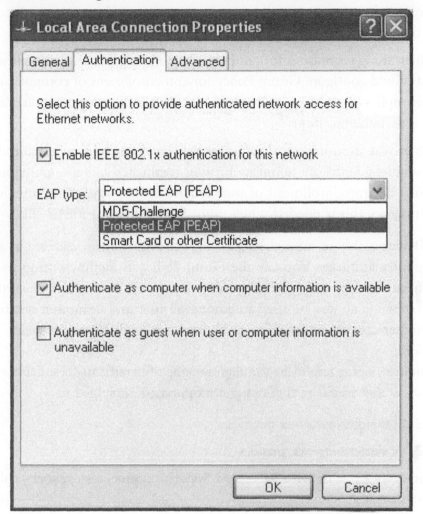

Implementing Secure Network Access Authentication

Although it's outside the scope of this chapter to go into the details of PKI, it is useful to look at some of the ways PKI can be used as part of a Windows-based authentication infrastructure for secure network access using the protocols discussed in this section.

- When using PEAP–MS-CHAPv2 for network access authentication, configure Group Policy for autoenrollment of computer certificates to install computer certificates on the NPS servers.

- When using certificates for computer-level network access authentication, you should configure Group Policy for autoenrollment of computer certificates. This applies if you're using EAP–TLS or PEAP–TLS for computer-level wireless authentication.

- When you are using certificates for user-level network access authentication, configure a certificate template for user certificates and also configure Group Policy for autoenrollment of user certificates. As with computer-level certificates, this is needed when using EAP–TLS and PEAP–TLS.

Group Policy is also an important part of securing network access and authenticating computers and users. You can use Group Policy to deploy settings to install a root certificate on a domain member computer to validate computer certificates of the NPS servers. It can also be used to autoenroll user and computer certificates on domain member computers for user- and computer-level certificate-based authentication.

In addition to being useful in the deployment of certificate-based authentication, Group Policy is also useful in deploying configuration settings for:

- 802.11 wireless network profiles

- 802.1x wired network profiles

- Windows Firewall with Advanced Security connection security rules to protect traffic

- NAP client configuration

Notes from the Underground…

Changes to Authentication Protocols

PPP-based connections no longer support the SPAP, EAP-MD5-CHAP and MS-CHAPv1 authentication protocols. Remote access PPP-based connections now support the use of Protected EAP (PEAP) with PEAP-MS-CHAP v2 and PEAP-TLS. Keep this in mind as you plan out your new Windows Server 2008 remote access options.

EAPHost architecture in Windows Server 2008 and Windows Vista includes new features not supported in Windows Server 2003 and Windows XP including:

- Support for additional EAP methods
- Network discovery (as defined in RFC 4284)
- RFC 3748 compliance and support for expanded EAP types including vendor-specific EAP types
- Coexistence of multiple EAP types (Microsoft and Cisco, for example)

Configuring 802.1x Settings in Windows Server 2008

You can configure wired policies from the **Computer Configuration | Policies | Windows Settings | Security Settings | Wired Network (IEEE 802.3) Policies** node in the **Group Policy Management Editor snap-in** via the MMC. By default, there are no wired policies in place. To create a new policy, use the following steps:

1. Right-click the **Wired Network (IEEE 802.3) Policies** in the console tree of the GP Editor snap-in.

2. Click **Create A New Windows Vista Wired Policy**.

3. The **New Windows Vista Wired Policy Properties** dialog is displayed, shown in Figure 4.8. It has two tabs: General and Security. The **General** tab is selected by default. Enter the policy name and description and ensure the checkbox for "Use Windows Wired Auto Config service for clients" is checked.

Figure 4.8 New Vista Wired Network Policy Properties Security Tab

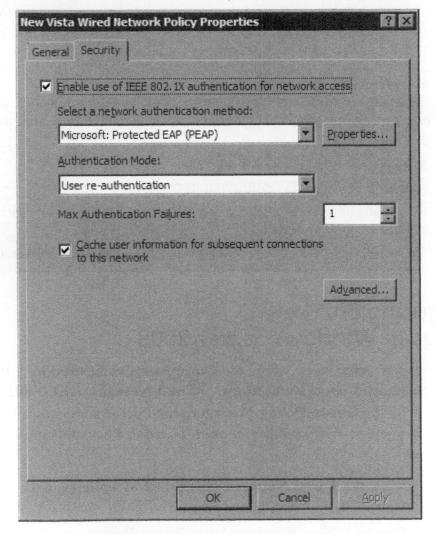

4. Click the **Security** tab to set security options. On this tab, click the checkbox next to "Enable use for IEEE 802.1X authentication for network access" then click the dropdown box to select a network authentication method

(EAP, PEAP, MS-CHAPv2). Also select the "Authentication Mode" from the second dropdown box. The options are User re-authentication, computer only, user authentication, or guest authentication. Also select the number of times the authentication can fail before it is abandoned (1 is the default). The last setting in the Security tab is a checkbox whether to "Cache user information for subsequent connections to this network." If this checkbox is cleared, the credential data is removed when the user logs off. If the checkbox is checked, the credential data will be cached after user log off.

5. To access advanced settings, click the **Advanced** button on the Security tab. There are two Advanced segments: **IEEE 802.1X** and **Single Sign On**, shown in Figure 4.9.

Figure 4.9 Advanced Settings for New Vista Wired Network Policy Properties

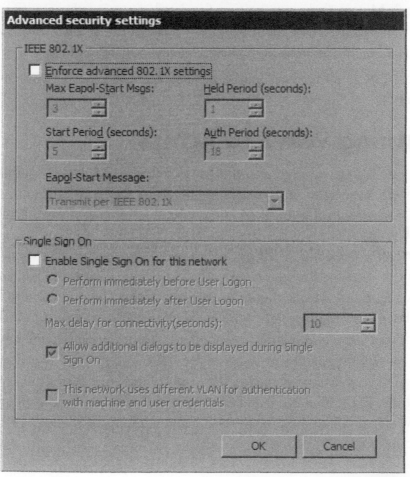

6. In the **IEEE 802.1X** section, click the checkbox to the left of "Enforce advanced 802.1X settings" to enable these options: Max Eapol-Start Msgs:, Held Period (seconds), Start Period (seconds), Auth Period (seconds), Eapol-Start Message. In most cases, the default settings are fine; it you believe you need these advanced settings, check the Microsoft documentation for details on how to set these.

7. In the **Single Sign On** section, click the checkbox next to "Enable Single Sign On for this network" to enable the following options: Perform immediately before User Logon, Perform immediately after User Logon, Set Max. delay for connectivity (seconds), Allow additional dialogs to be displayed during Single Sign On, and This network uses different VLAN for authentication with machine and user credentials. Again, as with the IEEE 802.1X Advanced settings, these can be modified if you have a specific need to do so. Check Microsoft documentation for details on using these options within your network environment. A good starting place is www.microsoft.com/ technet/technetmag/issues/2008/02/CableGuy/default.aspx.

8. Click **OK** to accept configuration; click **Cancel** to exit without saving changes.

Configuring Wireless Access

Increased use of laptop computers and other wireless access devices within an enterprise along with an increase in worker mobility, have fueled the demand for wireless networks in recent years. Up until recently, wireless technology was plagued with incompatibility issues and vendor-specific products. The technology was slow, expensive, and reserved for mobile situations or hostile environments where cabling was impractical or impossible. In recent years, the maturing of industry standards has caused a leveling point. This is thanks to industry-enforced compatibility standards and the deployment of lightweight wireless networking hardware. All of these factors have allowed wireless technology to come of age in the modern company.

Wireless networking hardware requires the use of technology that deals with radio frequencies as well as data transmission. The most widely used standard is 802.11 produced by the IEEE. This is a standard defining all aspects of radio frequency wireless networking. There have been several amendments to the 802.11 standard, the most recent being 802.11.

Many wireless networks use an AP to gain connectivity. In this type of network, the AP acts like a hub, providing connectivity for the wireless computers. It can connect the wireless LAN to a wired LAN, allowing wireless computer access to LAN resources. This includes such resources as file servers or existing internet connectivity. This type of wireless network is said to run in infrastructure mode.

An ad hoc or peer-to-peer wireless network is one in which a number of computers each equipped with a wireless networking interface card, can connect without the use of an AP. Each computer communicates with all of the other wireless-enabled computers directly. This allows for the sharing of files and printer services, but may not be able to access wired LAN resources. The exception to this is if one of the computers acts as a bridge or AP to the wired LAN using special software.

As you might be familiar with in Windows Server 2003, Wireless Auto Configuration will attempt to pair up configured preferred wireless networks with the wireless networks that are broadcasting their network name. If no such available networks exist that match a preferred wireless network, Wireless Auto Configuration will then send a number of probe requests to attempt to find a match. These are to try and determine if the preferred networks in the ordered list are non-broadcast networks. The end result of this total process should be that broadcast networks are connected to before non-broadcast networks. This even includes situations where a non-broadcast network is higher in the preferred list than a broadcast network. A big downside of this method, however, is that a Windows XP or Windows Server 2003 wireless client has to advertise its list of preferred wireless networks when sending probe requests. This leaves clients vulnerable while sending these probe requests.

Windows Server 2008 presents a better option. By configuring the wireless networks as broadcast, the wireless network names will be included in the Beacon frames sent by the wireless AP. If you set the wireless network as non-broadcast, the Beacon frame contains a wireless network name. This name is set to NULL, which results in Wireless Auto Configuration attempting connection to the wireless networks in the preferred network list order. This is regardless of whether they are broadcast or non-broadcast. By explicitly marking wireless networks as broadcast or non-broadcast, Windows Server 2008 wireless clients only send probe requests for non-broadcast wireless networks. This reduces wireless client side vulnerability and enhances security.

Previously, if a preferred wireless network could not be connected to and the wireless client was configured in a way that prevented automatic connections not in the preferred list by default, then Wireless Auto Configuration would create a random wireless network name. Then it would place the wireless network adapter in infrastructure mode. The random wireless network does not have a security configuration, making it possible for all kinds of malicious users to connect to the wireless client, thereby using the random wireless network name.

For computers running Windows Server 2008 that use updated wireless drivers designed for Windows Vista, Wireless Auto Configuration will remove this vulnerability by parking the wireless network adapter in a passive listening mode. A parked wireless device does not send probe request frames for a random wireless network name. It also does not allow for any other names, so malicious users cannot connect to the wireless client.

If you are using a wireless network adapter driver that was designed for Windows XP, computers running Windows Vista or Windows Server 2008 will use the behavior of the Wireless Client Update for Windows XP with Service Pack 2 (a random wireless network name with a security configuration).

Windows Server 2008 troubleshooting wireless connections is made much easier through the following features:

- **Network Diagnostics Framework** The Network Diagnostics Framework is an extensible architecture that provides users with a means to recover from and troubleshoot problems with network connections. In the case of a failed wireless connection, Network Diagnostics Framework will give the user the option to identify and correct the problem. Wireless support for the Network Diagnostics Framework tries to discover the source of the failed connection and will automatically fix the problem. Also based on your security considerations, it can be made to prompt the user to make the appropriate configuration change themselves.

- For a failed wireless connection attempt, the wireless components of Windows Server 2008 now records detailed information about the connection attempt in the Windows event log. Support professionals can now access and use these records to perform troubleshooting tasks, and attempt to resolve the problem quickly if the wireless diagnostics either could not resolve the problem or when it could resolve the problem, but the problem cannot be fixed by changing wireless client settings. This will cut down on the time needed to resolve wireless connection support problems. These can also be automatically collected by network administrators using Microsoft Operations Manager, to be analyzed for patterns and wireless infrastructure design changes.

- You can now gain access to in-depth information about the computer's state and wireless components in Windows, and their interaction when the problem occurred. This can be done using information from *wireless diagnostics tracing* in Windows Server 2008. To use wireless diagnostics tracing, you must start tracing, reproduce the problem, stop tracing, and then collect the tracing report. To view the tracing report, in the console tree of the Reliability and Performance Monitor snap-in open **Reports | System | Wireless Diagnostics**.

Windows Server 2003 and Windows XP do not have a command-line interface that allows you to configure the wireless settings that are available from the wireless dialog boxes in the Network Connections folder, or through the Wireless Network (IEEE 802.11) Policies Group Policy settings. Command-line configuration of wireless settings can help deployment of wireless networks in the following situations:

- **Automated script support for wireless settings without using Group Policy Wireless Network (IEEE 802.11) Policies Group Policy settings only apply in an Active Directory domain**. For an environment without Active Directory or a Group Policy infrastructure, a script that automates the configuration of wireless connections can be run either manually or automatically, such as part of the login script.

- **Bootstrapping of a wireless client onto the protected organization's wireless network**. A wireless client computer that is not a member of the domain cannot connect to the organization's protected wireless network. Furthermore, computers are not able to join the domain until a successful connection has occurred to the organization's secure wireless network. A command-line script provides a method to connect to the organization's secure wireless network to join the domain.

In Windows Server 2008, you can use **Netsh** commands in the **netsh wlan** context to do the following:

- Save all wireless client settings in a named profile including general settings (the types of wireless networks to access), 802.11 settings (SSID, type of authentication, type of data encryption), and 802.1X authentication settings (EAP types and their configuration).

- Specify the list of allowed and denied wireless network names.

- Specify the order of preferred wireless networks.

- Display a wireless client's configuration.

- Remove the wireless configuration from a wireless client.

- Migrate a wireless configuration setting between wireless clients.

Many applications are not network aware, resulting in customer confusion and developer overhead. For example, an application cannot automatically adjust its behavior based on the currently attached network and conditions. Users might have to reconfigure application settings depending on the network to which they are attached (their employer's private network, the user's home network, the Internet). To remove the configuration burden, application developers can use low-level Windows APIs, data constructs, and perhaps even probing the network themselves to determine the current network and adjust their application's behavior accordingly.

To provide an operating system infrastructure to allow application developers to more easily reconfigure application behavior based on the currently attached network, the Network Awareness APIs in Windows Server 2008 make network information available to applications and enables them to easily and effectively adapt to these changing environments. The Network Awareness APIs allow applications to obtain up-to-date network information and location change notification.

Let's take a look at how to deal with the variety of elements available with Windows Server 2008 in regards to wireless network access and how they will be applied to your exam.

Set Service Identifier (SSID)

The Service Set Identifier (SSID) is a 32-character unique identifier attached to the header of packets that are sent over a Wireless Local Area Network (WLAN). The SSID acts as a password when a mobile device tries to connect to the BSS. The SSID differentiates one WLAN from another. This way all APs and all devices attempting to connect to a specific WLAN must use the same SSID in order to succeed. No device will be permitted to join the BSS unless it can provide the unique SSID. SSID is not a security measure, because it can very easily be sniffed due to being stored in plain text.

In Windows Server 2008, an additional wireless network configuration setting has been added that can indicate whether a wireless network is broadcast or non-broadcast. This setting can be configured locally through the "Manually connect to a wireless network" dialog box, the properties of the wireless network, or through Group Policy. The "Connect even if the network is not broadcasting" check box determines whether the wireless network broadcasts or does not broadcast its SSID. Once selected, Wireless Auto Configuration sends probe requests to discover if the non-broadcast network is in range.

Configured wireless networks are now openly marked as broadcast or non-broadcast. Windows Server 2008-based wireless clients only send probe requests for wireless networks that are configured for automatic connection and as non-broadcast.

This method allows Windows Server 2008-based wireless clients to detect non-broadcast networks when they are in range. Therefore, even though they are not broadcasting the name of their wireless network, they will appear in the list of available wireless networks when they are in range. The wireless client detects whether the automatically connected, non-broadcast networks are in range based on the probe request responses. Then Wireless Auto Configuration attempts to connect to the wireless network in the preferred networks list order. This is regardless of whether they are configured as broadcast or non-broadcast. By only sending probe requests for automatically connected, non-broadcast networks, Windows Server 2008-based wireless clients reduce the number of situations in which they disclose their wireless network configuration.

You can also configure manually connected, non-broadcast wireless networks. In doing so, you can control exactly when to send probe requests. Manually connected, non-broadcast wireless networks are always displayed in the list of available networks, allowing users to initiate connections as needed.

Despite the improvements in non-broadcast network support in Windows Server 2008, Microsoft recommends against using non-broadcast wireless networks.

Wi-Fi Protected Access (WPA)

Wi-Fi Protected Access (WPA) was designed to provide a much higher level of security for wireless users than existing WEP standards provide. The WPA specification makes allowances both for network-based authentication for corporate networks, and for a special home mode for use in a SOHO or home-user environment. WPA is capable of interoperating with WEP devices, although in cases of interoperability, the default security for the entire wireless infrastructure reverts to the WEP standard. WPA's network-based authentication can make use of existing authentication technologies such as RADIUS servers, so adding the secure technology that WPA represents won't disrupt existing network infrastructures too much. Windows Server 2008 offers full support and configuration for WPA through the Wireless Group Policy settings.

TIP

Remember to know your hardware. The installed wireless network adapter must be able to support the wireless LAN or wireless security standards that you require. For example, Windows Server supports configuration options for the Wi-Fi Protected Access (WPA) and Wi-Fi Protected Access 2 (WPA2) security standards. However, if the wireless network adapter does not support WPA2, you cannot enable or configure WPA2 security options.

Wi-Fi Protected Access 2 (WPA2)

Windows Server 2008 includes built-in support to configure WPA2 authentication options with both the standard profile (locally configured preferred wireless networks), and the domain profile with Group Policy settings. WPA2 is a product certification available through the Wi-Fi Alliance that certifies wireless equipment as being compatible with the IEEE 802.11i standard. WPA2 in Windows Server 2008 supports both WPA2-Enterprise (IEEE 802.1X authentication) and WPA2-Personal (pre-shared key authentication) modes of operation.

Windows Server 2008 also includes full support for WPA2 for an ad hoc mode wireless network including the *Fast Roaming* settings. Fast roaming is an advanced capability of WPA2 wireless networks that allow wireless clients to more quickly roam from one wireless AP to another by using pre-authentication and pair wise master key (PMK) caching in infrastructure mode. With Windows Server 2008, you can configure this feature using the Wireless Group Policy settings.

Ad Hoc vs. Infrastructure Mode

To set up an ad hoc wireless network, each wireless adapter must be configured for ad hoc mode versus the alternative infrastructure mode. In addition, all wireless adapters on the ad hoc network must use the same SSID and the same channel number.

An ad hoc network tends to feature a small group of devices all in very close proximity to each other.

Performance suffers as the number of devices grows, and a large ad hoc network quickly becomes difficult to manage. Ad hoc networks cannot bridge to wired LANs or to the Internet without installing a special-purpose gateway.

Ad hoc networks make sense when needing to build a small, all-wireless LAN quickly and spend the minimum amount of money on equipment. Ad hoc networks also work well as a temporary fallback mechanism if normally available infrastructure mode gear (APs or routers) stop functioning.

Most installed wireless LANs today utilize infrastructure mode that requires the use of one or more APs. With this configuration, the AP provides an interface to a distribution system (e.g., Ethernet), which enables wireless users to utilize corporate servers and Internet applications.

As an optional feature, however, the 802.11 standard specifies ad-hoc mode, which allows the radio network interface card (NIC) to operate in what the standard refers to as an independent basic service set (IBSS) network configuration. With an IBSS, APs are not required. User devices communicate directly with each other in a peer-to-peer manner.

Ad hoc mode allows users to form a wireless LAN with no assistance or preparation. This allows clients to share documents such as presentation charts and spreadsheets by switching their NICs to ad hoc mode to form a small wireless LAN within their meeting room. Through ad hoc mode, you can easily transfer the file from one laptop to another. With any of these applications, there's no need to install an AP and run cables.

The ad hoc form of communications is especially useful in public-safety and search-and-rescue applications. Medical teams require fast, effective communications when attempting to find victims. They can't afford the time to run cabling and install networking hardware.

Before making the decision to use ad hoc mode, you should consider the following:

- **Cost Efficiency** Without the need to purchase or install an AP, you'll save a considerable amount of money when deploying ad hoc wireless LANs.

- **Rapid Setup Time** Ad hoc mode only requires the installation of radio NICs in the user devices. As a result, the time to set up the wireless LAN is much less than installing an infrastructure wireless LAN.

- **Better Performance Possible** The question of performance with ad hoc mode is very debatable. Performance can be higher with ad hoc mode because there is no need for packets to travel through an AP. This only applies to a small number of users, however. If you have many users, then you will have better performance by using multiple APs to separate users onto non-overlapping channels. This will help to reduce medium access contention and collisions. Also, because of a need for sleeping stations to wake up during each beacon interval, performance can be lower with ad hoc mode due to additional packet transmissions if you implement power management.

- **Limited Network Access** There is no distribution system with ad hoc wireless LANs. Because of this, users have limited effective access to the Internet and other wired network services. Ad hoc is not a good solution for larger enterprise wireless LANs where there's a strong need to access applications and servers on a wired network.

- **Difficult Network Management** Network management can become a nightmare with ad hoc networks, because of the fluidity of the network topology and lack of centralized devices. The lack of an AP makes it difficult for network managers to monitor performance, perform security audits, and manage their network. Effective network management with ad hoc wireless LANs requires network management at the user device level. This requires a significant amount of overhead packet transmission over the wireless LAN. This again disqualifies ad hoc mode away from larger, enterprise wireless LAN applications.

Infrastructure mode requires a wireless AP for wireless networking. To join the WLAN, the AP and all wireless clients must be configured to use the same SSID. The AP is then cabled to the wired network to allow wireless clients access to, for example, Internet connections or printers. Additional APs can be added to the WLAN to increase the reach of the infrastructure and support any number of wireless clients.

Compared to the alternative, ad hoc wireless networks, infrastructure mode networks offer the advantage of scalability, centralized security management, and improved reach.

The disadvantage of infrastructure wireless networks is simply the additional cost to purchase AP hardware.

Wireless Group Policy

New technology makes it easier for mobile workers to connect to hotspots or corporate LANS, by eliminating the need for manual configuration of the network connection. Enterprises can better manage guest access on their network and provide payment plans such as pay-per-use or monthly Internet access to customers, but in order to do so a strict wireless group, policy must be maintained to better control access.

Wireless network settings can be configured locally by users on client computers, or centrally. To enhance the deployment and administration of wireless networks, you need to take advantage of Group Policy. In doing so, you can create, modify, and assign wireless network policies for Active Directory clients and members of the wireless network. When you use Group Policy to define wireless network policies, you can configure wireless network connection settings, enable IEEE 802.1X authentication for wireless network connections, and specify the preferred wireless networks that clients can connect to. By default, there are no Wireless Network (IEEE 802.11) policies.

Creating a New Policy

To create a new policy:

1. Right-click **Wireless Network (IEEE 802.11) Policies** in the console tree of the **Group Policy** snap-in.

2. Click **Create Wireless Network Policy**.

3. The Create Wireless Network Policy Wizard is started, from which you can configure a name and description for the new wireless network policy. You can create only a single wireless network policy for each Group Policy object.

4. To modify the settings of a **Wireless Network Policy**, double-click its name in the details pane.

5. Locate the **General** tab for the **Wireless Network Policy** you wish to update.

6. Click on the **General** tab and configure the following:

    ■ **Name** Specifies a friendly name for the wireless network policy.

    ■ **Description** Provides a description for the wireless network policy.

- **Check for Policy Changes Every...** Specifies a time period in minutes, after which wireless clients that are domain members will check for changes in the wireless network policy.

- **Networks to Access** Specifies the types of wireless networks with which the wireless client is allowed to create connections to. Select either **Any available network** (AP preferred), **Access point** (infrastructure) networks only, or **Computer-to-computer** (ad hoc) networks only.

7. Select the **Windows to configure wireless network settings for clients** check box if you wish to enable the Wireless Auto Configuration.

8. Click the **Automatically connect to non-preferred networks** check box if you wish to allow automatic connections to wireless networks that are not configured as preferred networks.

9. Click the **Preferred** tab of the **Wireless Network Policy** pane to configure these options:

- **Networks** Displays the list of preferred wireless networks.

- **Add/Edit/Remove** Creates, deletes, or modifies the settings of a preferred wireless network.

- **Move Up/Move Down** Moves preferred wireless network up or down in the Networks list.

10. Click on a **Preferred Wireless Network** to open up advanced configuration options.

Summary

You should be aware of the need for remote access in the business environment. This includes what features of remote access are supported such as dial up, VPNs, NAT, and RADIUS, and how each of these aspects can be configured and installed. You should also be aware of the newest VPN protocol for Windows Server 2008, SSTP, and how it compares to other VPN protocols. You should now be able to set up an SSL VPN network from start to finish using the RRAS, NPS, and NAP. Additionally, you should be aware of all of the necessary installation methods for these snap-in features.

Lastly you should have a good grasp of wireless access methods such as infrastructure mode and ad hoc mode, and be able to distinguish which of these options is best for the situation you are presented with. This also includes the security methods that are supported for wireless access in Windows Server 2008, such as WEP, WPA, and WPA2. You should be confident in how to distinguish the advantages and disadvantages of each of these methods and also be able to Group Policy for each of them.

Solutions Fast Track

Network Policy Server

☑ Windows Server 2008 Microsoft has replaced IAS with a new feature called Network Policy Server (NPS). NPS is the Microsoft implementation of a RADIUS server and proxy in Windows Server 2008, and promises to be even simpler and more secure to use than IAS.

☑ RADIUS is protocol used for controlling access to network resources by authenticating, authorizing, and accounting for access, referred to as an AAA protocol. RADIUS is the unofficial industry standard for this type of access.

☑ NAP, when used in unison with NPS, creates a "total system health policy enforcement platform." NAP is designed to enhance a corporate VPN. This is accomplished when clients establish a VPN session with a Windows Server 2008 system that is running the RRAS. Once a connection is made, a NPS will validate the remote system and determine the status of its health.

Network Policy and Access Services Role

☑ Remote Authentication Dial-In User Service (RADIUS) is a protocol that originally was created for dial-in authentication and authorization service. Now, its role has expanded to include wireless access point access, authenticating Ethernet switches, virtual private network servers, and more. In Windows Server 2008, the RADIUS function is now handled by the Network Policy and Access Services role.

☑ The Network Policy and Access Services role installs Network Policy Server (NPS) and Routing and Remote Access (RRAS).

☑ NPS is the Microsoft implementation of a RADIUS server and proxy in Windows Server 2008, and it is expected to be even simpler to use than IAS.

802.1x Wired and Wireless Access

☑ In Windows Server 2008, an additional wireless network configuration setting has been added that can indicate whether a wireless network is broadcast or non-broadcast. This allows Windows Server 2008-based wireless clients to detect non-broadcast networks when they are in range. Even though they are not broadcasting the name of their wireless network, they will appear in the list of available wireless networks when they are in range.

☑ Windows Server 2003 and Windows XP do not have a command-line interface that allows you to configure the wireless settings that are available from the wireless dialog boxes in the Network Connections folder, or through the Wireless Network (IEEE 802.11) Policies Group Policy settings. Windows Server 2008 has a command-line configuration of wireless settings that can help deployment of wireless networks.

☑ Windows Server 2008 includes full support for WPA2 for an ad hoc mode wireless network, including the Fast Roaming settings. Fast roaming is an advanced capability of WPA2 wireless networks, that allows wireless clients to more quickly roam from one wireless AP to another by using pre-authentication and PMK caching.

Frequently Asked Questions

Q: What changes have been made to Windows Server 2008 in regards to routing?

A: These are the major changes present in Windows Server 2008 in regards to routing:

- BAP is no longer supported by Windows Server 2008.

- X.25 is also no longer supported.

- SLIP, an encapsulation of IP meant for use over serial ports and modems, has also been excluded due to infrequency of use. All SLIP-based connections will automatically be updated to PPP-based connections.

- ATM, which was used to encode data traffic into small fixed cells, has been discarded.

- IP over IEEE 1394 is no longer supported.

- NWLink IPX/SPX/NetBIOS Compatible Transport Protocol has been omitted.

- Services for Macintosh (SFM).

- OSPF routing protocol component in Routing and Remote Access is no longer present.

- Basic Firewall in Routing and Remote Access has been replaced with the new Windows Firewall feature.

- Static IP filter APIs for Routing and Remote Access are no longer viable, and have been replaced with Windows Filtering Platform APIs.

- SPAP, EAP-MD5-CHAP, and MS-CHAP authentication protocols for PPP-based connections are no longer used by Windows Server 2008.

Q: Is IAS still a feature of Windows Server 2008 and if not, what has replaced it?

A: In previous incarnations of Windows Server 2003 IAS snap-in was Microsoft's implementation of a RADIUS server and proxy. It was capable of performing localized connection AAA Protocol for many types of network access, including wireless and VPN connections. For Windows Server 2008, Microsoft has replaced IAS with a new snap in called NPS. NPS is the Microsoft implementation of a RADIUS server and proxy in Windows Server 2008, and promises to be even simpler to use than IAS.

Q: When does ad hoc mode work best for wireless access?

A: Ad hoc networks work best when building a small, all-wireless LAN quickly, with the lowest cost possible for equipment. Ad hoc networks also work well as a temporary fallback mechanism if normally available infrastructure mode gear (APs or routers) fail to function.

Chapter 5

Microsoft Windows Server 2008: Data Protection

Solutions in this chapter:

- BitLocker
- Active Directory Rights Management Services
- Authorization

☑ Summary

☑ Solutions Fast Track

☑ Frequently Asked Questions

Introduction

Computer and network security is of paramount importance for companies in the global marketplace, and a large percentage of these companies have Microsoft infrastructures in place, including domain controllers (DCs), Exchange servers, and Vista and XP workstations. A Windows server provides a number of useful functions in a company's network infrastructure. In this chapter we explain how BitLocker, Digital Rights Management Services, and authentication can help you secure your data.

BitLocker

Everyone has heard the new reports about laptops being stolen, temporarily misplaced, or lost. The data stored on the hard drive can be retrieved by means other than through the operating system. Things such as bootable CDs or USB keys can be used to bypass the operating system and get directly to the information stored on the physical media without the need to know any passwords. Once the operating system has been bypassed, all the files on the drive can be viewed, edited, or copied. The best safeguard to defend against this security issue is encryption.

BitLocker is Microsoft's answer to providing better security by encrypting the data stored on the drive's operating system volume, and is available only in the Enterprise and Ultimate versions of Vista. This new security feature goes a long way toward helping users and organizations protect their data.

You can set up BitLocker in the following configurations:

- **TPM only** In this configuration, only the hardware microchip is used to protect the data stored on the drive. The Trusted Platform Module (TPM) stores the encryption key and verifies that there have been no changes to the hard drive.

- **TPM and USB flash drive** In this configuration, the TPM will still verify the validity of the hard drive, but in addition, part of the encryption key is stored on the USB flash drive. The USB flash drive is required each time the computer starts.

- **TPM and PIN** This configuration is also a two-layer security approach. After successful verification of the drive, you will be required to enter the correct PIN for the start process to continue.

NOTE

It is important to create a recovery password in case there are any hardware failures that may prevent the system from booting. Things such as motherboard failures and USB flash drive failures, where applicable, will affect the system. If a hardware failure occurs, the only way to recover the data is through the recover mode, and a recovery password is required. There are no other ways to restore the data without the recovery password.

The default configuration for BitLocker is to be used in conjunction with a TPM. The TPM is a hardware microchip embedded into the motherboard that is used to store the encryption keys. This protects the hard drive even if it has been removed from the computer and installed into another computer. You can also use BitLocker on systems that don't have the TPM hardware manufactured on the mother board. You can do this by changing the BitLocker's default configurations with either a Group Policy or a script. When you use BitLocker without a TPM, you must store the key on a USB flash drive and insert the USB flash drive into the computer for the system to boot.

Tools & Traps...

BitLocker Vulnerabilities

BitLocker is a new security feature in Vista. As with all security technology, some people are working on creating vulnerabilities or ways around this security, so you must always be aware that new threats are coming out all the time. Therefore, BitLocker is just another technical challenge to many hackers in the world.

To use a BitLocker-enabled system, the key must be stored in RAM while the system is up and running. Universities have found that when a system is shut down, it's possible to retrieve the key from RAM for up to several minutes, giving a hacker complete control over the entire system and all files

Continued

stored on the drive. The main way to avoid this, of course, is to never leave a system unattended in an unsecured area in the first place. The next step is to completely shut down the system so that the RAM can be allowed to fully discharge.

When Vista is used in a domain environment, it is important for the domain administrators to be able to retrieve the information stored on a system in case of any emergency or other type of event. In a case where a user isn't able to work or is asked to leave the company, the information on the hard drive still needs to be accessed and recoverable. Active Directory domains in Server 2003 and 2008 provide administrators with the safeguard to set up Group Policies and have the BitLocker key backed up and stored in Active Directory on the servers.

The hardware and software requirements for BitLocker are:

- A computer that is capable of running Windows Server 2008
- A Trusted Platform Module version 1.2, enabled in BIOS
- A Trusted Computing Group (TCG)-compliant BIOS.
- Two NTFS disk partitions, one for the system volume and one for the operating system volume

Trusted Platform Modules

Developed by the Trusted Platform Group—an initiative by vendors such as AMD, Hewlett-Packard, IBM, Infineon, Intel, Microsoft, and others—a TPM is a semiconductor built into your computer motherboard. It is capable of generating cryptographic keys, limiting the use of those keys, and generating pseudo-random numbers.

Each TPM has a unique RSA key (the *endorsement key*) burnt into it that cannot be altered. The key is used for data encryption (a process known as *binding*). A TPM also provides facilities for *Secure I/O, Memory curtaining, Remote Attestation*, and *Sealed Storage*. You can secure your TPM module by assigning a TPM owner password.

With secure input and output (which is also known as *trusted path*), it is possible to establish a protected path between the computer user and the software that is running. The protected path prevents the user from capturing or intercepting data sent from the user to the software process, for example playing a media file. The trusted path is implemented in both hardware (TPM) and software and uses checksums for the verification process.

Memory curtaining provides extended memory protection. With memory curtaining, even the operating system does not have full access to the protected memory area.

Remote attestation creates a hashed summary of the hardware and software configuration of a system. This allows changes to the computer to be detected.

Sealed storage protects private information in a manner that the information can be read only on a system with the same configuration. In the preceding example, sealed storage prevents the user from opening the file on a "foreign" media player or computer system. In conjunction, it even prevents the user from making a copy (*memory curtaining*) or capturing the data stream that is sent to the sound system (*secure I/O*).

A Practical Example

You download a music file from an online store. Digital rights management protects the file. All security methods are enforced: the file plays only in media players provided by the publisher (*remote attestation*). The file can be played only on your system (*sealed storage*), and it can neither be copied (*memory curtaining*) nor digitally recorded by the user during playback (*secure I/O*).

The major features of BitLocker are full-volume encryption, checking the integrity of the startup process, recovery mechanisms, remote administration, and a process for securely decommissioning systems.

Full Volume Encryption

Windows BitLocker provides data encryption for volumes on your local hard drive. Unlike Encrypting File System (EFS), BitLocker encrypts all data on a volume— operating system, applications and their data, as well as page and hibernation files. In Windows Server 2008, you can use BitLocker to encrypt the whole *drive*, as compared to Windows Vista where you can encrypt *volumes*. BitLocker operation is transparent to the user and should have a minimal performance impact on well-designed systems. The TPM *endorsement key* is one of the major components in this scenario.

Startup Process Integrity Verification

Because Windows Startup components must be unencrypted for the computer to start, an attacker could gain access to these components, change the code, and then gain access to the computer, thereby gaining access to sensitive data such as BitLocker keys or user passwords as a consequence.

To prevent such attacks, BitLocker Integrity checking ensures that startup components (BIOS, Master Boot Record (MBR), boot sector, and boot manager code) have not been changed since the last boot.

Each startup component checks its code each time the computer starts, and calculates a hash value. This hash value is stored in the TPM and cannot be replaced until the next system restart. A combination of these values is also stored.

These values are also used to protect data. For this to work, the TPM creates a key that is bound to these values. The key is encrypted by the TPM (with the endorsement key) and can be decrypted only by the same TPM. During computer startup, the TPM compares the values that have been created by startup components with the values that existed when the key was created (see Figure 5.1). It decrypts the key only if these values match.

Figure 5.1 Startup Component Integrity Verification Flowchart

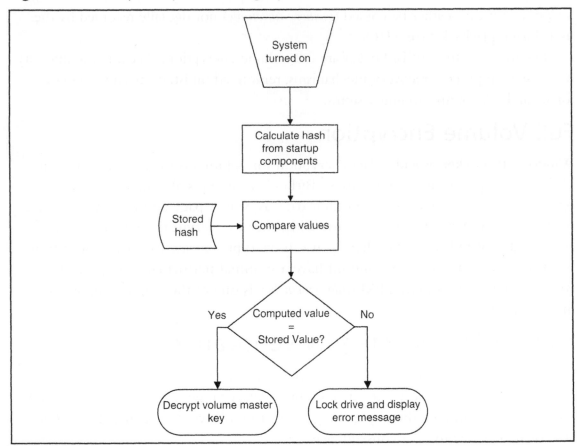

Recovery Mechanisms

BitLocker includes a comprehensive set of recovery options to make sure data not only is protected, but also available. When BitLocker is enabled, the user is asked for a recovery password. This password must be either printed out, saved to file on a local or network drive, or saved to a USB drive.

In an enterprise environment, however, you would not want to rely on each user to store and protect BitLocker keys. Therefore, you can configure BitLocker to store recovery information in Active Directory. We will cover key recovery using Active Directory later in this chapter.

Remote Administration

Especially in environments with branch offices, it is desirable to have a remote management interface for BitLocker. A WMI script provided by Microsoft allows for BitLocker remote administration and management. You will find the script in the **\Windows\System32** folder after you install BitLocker.

To manage a BitLocker protected system via script:

1. Log on as an administrator.

2. Click **Start**, click **All Programs**, click **Accessories**, and then click **Command Prompt**.

3. At the command prompt type **cd /d C:\Windows\System32**.

4. For example, to view the current status of BitLocker volumes, type **cscript manage-bde.wsf –status**.

Secure Decommissioning

If you decommission or reassign (maybe donate) equipment it might be necessary to delete all confidential data so that it cannot be reused by unauthorized people. Many processes and tools exist to remove confidential data from disk drives. Most of them are very time consuming, costly, or even destroy the hardware.

BitLocker volume encryption makes sure that data on a disk is never stored in a format that can be useful to an attacker, a thief, or even the new owner of the hardware. By destroying all copies of the encryption key it is possible to render the disk permanently inaccessible. The disk itself can then be reused.

There are two scenarios when deleting the encryption key:

■ Deleting all key copies from volume metadata, while keeping an archive of it in a secure location such as a USB flash drive or Active Directory. This approach allows you to temporarily decommission hardware. It also enables you to safely transfer or ship a system without the risk of data exposure.

■ Deleting all key copies from volume metadata without keeping any archive. Thus, no decryption key exists and the disk can no longer be decrypted.

Notes from the Underground...

New Group Policy Settings to Support BitLocker

To support centralized administration of BitLocker, Group Policy (GPO) has been extended in Windows Server 2008 Active Directory. The new set of GPO settings allows for configuration of BitLocker as well as TPM. These can be found under Computer Configuration/Administrative Templates/Windows Components/ BitLocker Drive Encryption and Computer Configuration/Administrative Templates /System/Trusted Platform Module. To configure these settings, make sure you have at least one Windows Vista or Windows Server 2008 Computer in your Active Directory to create a policy with the new settings available.

BitLocker Architecture

Once Integrity verification is successful, a filter driver encrypts and decrypts disk sectors transparently as data is written or read from the protected volume. The filter driver is a component of Windows Server 2008 or Vista and is inserted into the file system stack during BitLocker installation (see Figure 5.2), thus requiring a system restart. After the initial encryption of the volume is completed, BitLocker operation is completely transparent to the user.

Figure 5.2 Filter Driver Inserted into the File System Stack

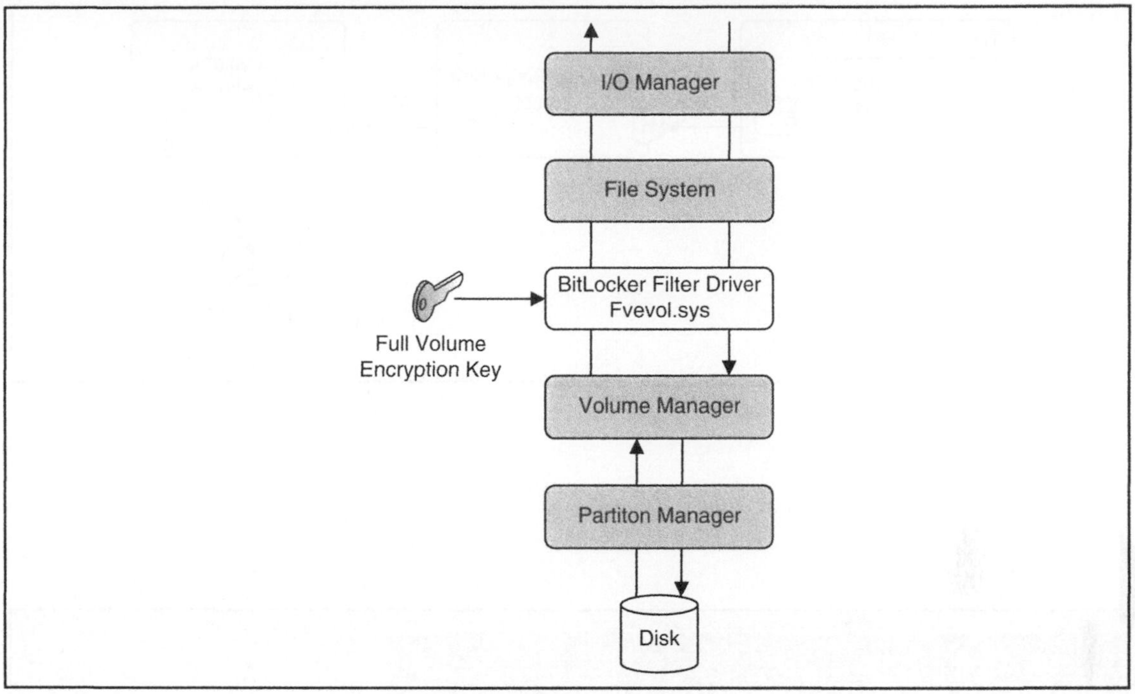

Keys Used for Volume Encryption

Volume encryption does not simply create a single key, which it will use to encrypt the volume. In fact, a *full volume encryption key* is used to encrypt the entire volume. This key is a 256-bit Advanced Encryption Standard (AES) key. BitLocker encrypts the full volume key with a *volume master key*. The volume master key is also 256-bit AES. Finally, the volume master key is encrypted with the TPM *endorsement key*. As mentioned before, the endorsement key is a RSA key (see Figure 5.3).

Figure 5.3 Keys Used for Volume Encryption

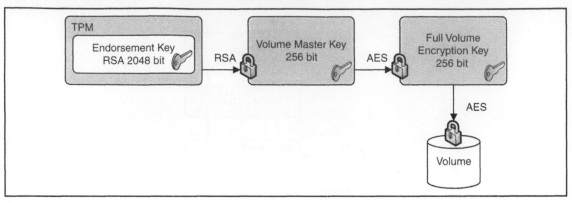

Notes from the Underground…

New Group Policy Settings to Support BitLocker

Why does BitLocker use a volume master key? Wouldn't it be easier to encrypt the full volume encryption key directly with the TPM endorsement key? At first glance, this would make sense. However, without the volume master key you would have to decrypt and reencrypt the entire volume in case an upstream key is lost or compromised.

Hardware Upgrades on BitLocker Protected Systems

Thanks to the use of *volume master key*, upgrades of hardware such as CPU, motherboard, and such are not very time consuming. To do so you have to disable BitLocker. Disabling BitLocker will *not* decrypt protected volumes. Instead, the volume master key will be encrypted with a symmetric key, which is stored unencrypted on the hard drive. Moving the disk to another BitLocker-enabled system and activating the volume is possible without any additional steps. Because the encryption key for the volume master key is stored unencrypted on the disk, administrators can boot the system and the reenable BitLocker.

By reenabling BitLocker the unencrypted key is removed from the disk, the volume master key is keyed and encrypted again, and BitLocker is turned back on.

BitLocker Authentication Modes

After Installation BitLocker can be configured to seamlessly integrate into the boot process (TPM only)—therefore being transparent to the user—or can require additional information in the form of a PIN or a startup key to initiate the boot process (TPM with PIN or startup key). The later scenarios add an additional layer of security through the use *multifactor authentication* options. TPM with PIN requires something the user *knows* (e.g., the PIN), TPM with startup key requires something the user *has* (e.g., a USB device).

TPM Only

In this scenario, you enable BitLocker with a TPM only. No additional authentication options are used. BitLocker operation is completely transparent to the user and requires no interaction during the boot process.

TPM with PIN Authentication

Using TPM with PIN authentication, the administrator sets up a PIN during BitLocker initialization. The PIN is hashed using SHA-256 and the first 160 bits of the hash are used as authorization data for the TPM. The TPM uses the PIN data to seal the volume master key. Both the TPM and the PIN now protect the volume master key. During system startup or resume from hibernation, the user has to input the PIN to unseal the volume master key and initiate the boot process (see Figure 5.4).

Figure 5.4 Accessing a BitLocker-Enabled Disk That Is Secured with TPM+PIN

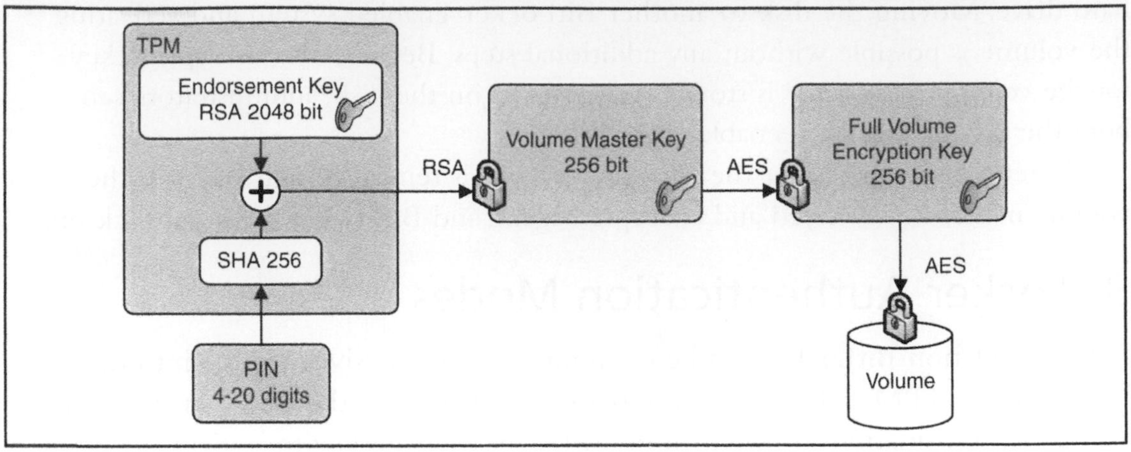

TPM with Startup Key Authentication

In this scenario the administrator creates a startup key during BitLocker initialization and stores it on any USB device that can be enumerated by the computer BIOS. During system startup or resume from hibernation, the user must insert the device. The device can be removed after the system has successfully booted.

Startup Key-Only

In this scenario, the administrator enables BitLocker on a computer without a TPM module. The startup key for the computer is generated during initialization and is stored on a USB flash drive. The computer user has to insert the USB flash drive each time the computer starts or resumes from hibernation.

A system configured to use a startup key-only configuration will not provide the same level of security as a system using one of the TPM modes. It will not check the integrity of system startup components. Using this scenario, make sure you create a Backup copy of the startup key! You do this by using the Control Panel BitLocker applet. The system saves the startup key with a .bek extension.

When to Use BitLocker on a Windows 2008 Server

In shared or unsecured environments such as branch offices, BitLocker can provide an additional level of security to a server. By securing the startup process and encrypting the operating system volume and all data volumes, BitLocker protects data from unauthorized access.

The BitLocker feature is not installed by default on Windows Server 2008. You would install it using Server Manager. Setup and maintenance are performed either by GUI tools or from the command line using a script, which also allows for remote management. On Windows Server 2008, BitLocker also integrates with Extensible Firmware Interface (EFI) computers to support IA64 hardware platforms. EFI is a newer, more flexible alternative to classical BIOS implementations. You should not install and enable BitLocker on a Windows Server 2008 Cluster machine, as it is a nonsupported scenario.

Encryption of data volumes on Windows Server 2008 is also supported. Data volumes are encrypted the same way as operating system volumes. Windows Server 2008 will automatically mount and decrypt these volumes on startup when configured to do so.

Support for Multifactor Authentication on Windows Server 2008

Multifactor authentication extends the security of BitLocker protected drives, although there are some constraints that you should think about when you plan to implement it.

PIN Authentication

Although it might not be desirable to use BitLocker with multifactor authentication on a Server, PIN authentication is a supported scenario on Windows Server 2008. If you manage a server remotely and have to reboot, who would enter the PIN?

Of course, there are third-party solutions to overcome this limitation. Most of the modern server boxes offer a built-in remote management solution that is independent of the operating system. For example, Hewlett-Packard offers a so-called Integrated Lights Out (ILO) board to remotely connect to a server and transfer the screen to your desk.

If no remote management solutions were available, another possibility would be to instruct a trustworthy person at the branch office on how and when to enter the pin.

Startup Key Authentication

Of course, startup key support also is built into Windows Server 2008 BitLocker. All the facts mentioned for PIN support apply also to the startup key scenario, plus an additional one: startup keys protect the server only if the key is not left in the server after startup completes. Hence, there must be someone to insert and remove the USB device every time you reboot the server.

Enabling BitLocker

Due to its tight integration into the operating system, enabling BitLocker is straightforward. Before you begin installing and configuring, make sure that the machine you want to secure meets all software and hardware requirements. To enable BitLocker you must be a member of the local administrators group on your computer.

Partitioning Disks for BitLocker Usage

For BitLocker to work your system must have at least two partitions configured. The first, unencrypted partition is the system partition, which contains boot information. The second partition is the boot volume, which is encrypted and contains the operating system. Both partitions must be created before you install the operating system.

If you forgot to partition your system accordingly, there's no way of reconfiguring your partitions (see Figure 5.5). Therefore, you must repartition your hard disk and reinstall the operating system from scratch.

Figure 5.5 BitLocker Refuses to Configure the System Due to an Invalid Partition Scheme

The drive configuration is unsuitable for BitLocker Drive Encryption. To use BitLocker, please re-partition your hard drive according to the BitLocker requirements.

Set up your hard disk for BitLocker Drive Encryption

Creating Partitions for a Bitlocker Installation

In this section we'll show you how to create partitions for a Bitlocker installation.

1. Start the computer from the Windows Server 2008 Product DVD.

2. In the Install Windows screen, choose your **Installation language**, **Time and currency format and Keyboard layout**, and then click **Next**.

3. In the **Install Windows** screen, click **Repair your Computer**.

4. In the **System Recovery Options** dialog box, make sure no operating system is selected. Then click **Next**.

5. In the **System Recovery Options** dialog box, click **Command Prompt**.

6. At the command prompt type **Diskpart** and then type **Enter**.

7. Type **select disk 0**.

8. Type **clean** to erase all existing partitions.

9. Type **create partition primary size=1500**. This will create a primary partition with a size of 1.5 GB.

10. Type **assign letter=B** to give this partition drive letter B.

11. Type **activate** to set the partition as the active partition.

12. Type **create partition primary** to create a partition with the remaining space. Windows Server 2008 will be installed on this partition.

13. Type **assign letter=c**.

14. Type **list volume** to see a display of all the volumes on this disk.

15. Type **exit**.

16. Type **format c: /y /f /fs:ntfs** to format the C volume.

17. Type **format b: /y /f /fs:ntfs** to format the B volume.

18. Type **exit**.

19. Close the **System Recovery Options** window by clicking the close window icon in the upper right (do not click Shut Down or Restart).

20. Click **Install now** to install Windows Server 2008. Use the larger partition for installation.

Installing BitLocker on Windows Server 2008

As we already mentioned, BitLocker is a *Feature* of Windows Server 2008 and is not installed by default. To install BitLocker you use Server Manager as you would with all other roles and features. Be aware that a restart is required after installation. You can also install BitLocker from the command line by typing **ServerManagerCmd -install BitLocker –restart**.

Here are the steps to follow to install Bitlocker on Windows Server 2008.

1. Log on as an administrator.

2. Click **Start | Administrative Tools | Server Manager**.

3. Scroll down to **Feature Summary**; click **Add Features**.

4. On the **Select Features** page, choose **BitLocker Drive Encryption** (see Figure 5.6), and then click **Next**.

Figure 5.6 Selecting the BitLocker Feature in Server Manager

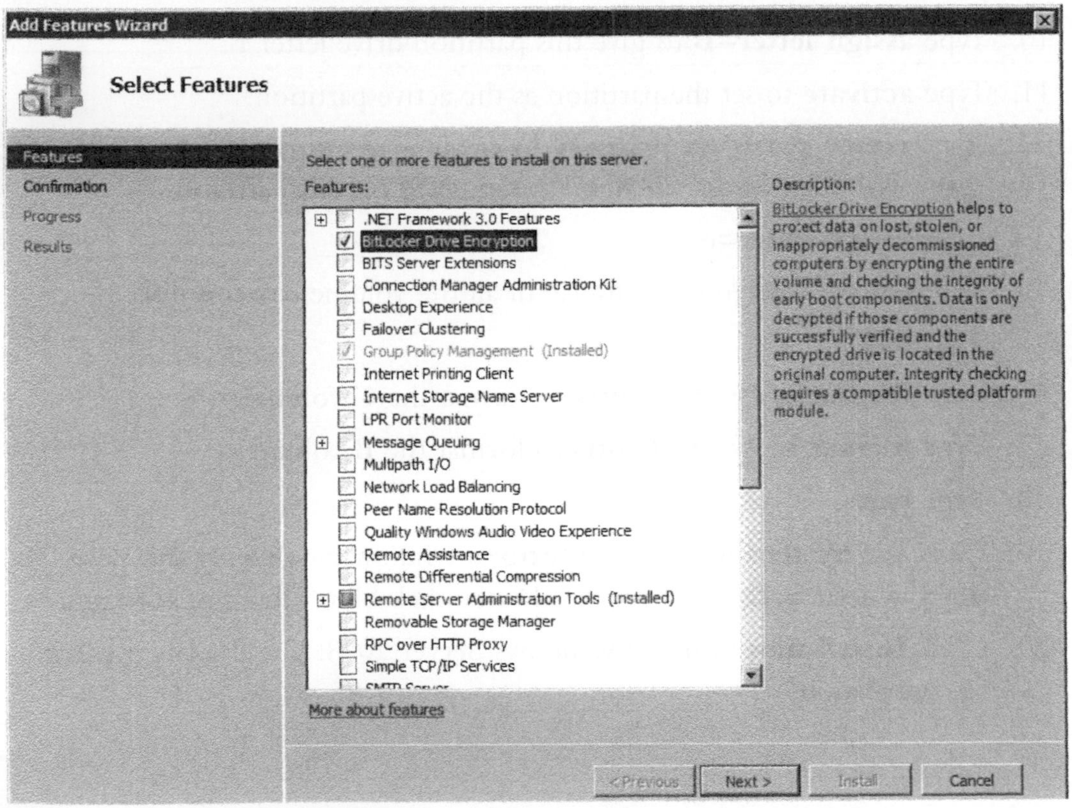

5. On the **Confirm Installation Selections** page, click **Install**.

6. When installation is complete, click **Close**.

7. In the **Do you want to restart** Window click **Yes**.

NOTE

Before you start with BitLocker configuration, make sure that you open Server Manager (in case you selected the **Do not show me this console at next logon** checkbox) and let the Post-Install wizard finish the installation.

Turning on and Configuring BitLocker

After installing the BitLocker Feature on your Server and rebooting the system, you need to turn on BitLocker via a Control Panel applet. Make sure you are logged on as an administrator on the system and you have decided where to store the recovery password. In case your computer does not have a TPM module or the TPM module is not supported, you will receive a warning (see Figure 5.7).

Figure 5.7 Warning That a TPM Is Missing or Incompatible

 A TPM was not found. A TPM is required to turn on BitLocker. If your computer has a TPM, then contact the computer manufacturer for BitLocker-compatible BIOS.

Here are the steps to follow for turning on BitLocker.

1. Log on as an administrator.

2. Click **Start**, click **Control Panel**, and then click **BitLocker Drive Encryption**.

3. On the **BitLocker Drive Encryption** page, click **Turn On BitLocker** on the operating system volume (see Figure 5.8).

Figure 5.8 The Server Is Ready to Turn on BitLocker

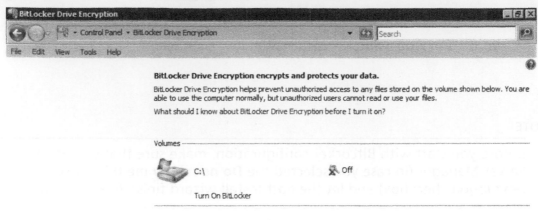

4. On the **BitLocker Drive Encryption Platform Check** dialog box click **Continue with BitLocker Drive Encryption**.

5. If your TPM is not initialized already, you will see the **Initialize TPM Security Hardware** screen.

6. On the **Save the recovery password** page, click **Save the password on a USB drive** (see Figure 5.9).

Figure 5.9 Saving the BitLocker Password

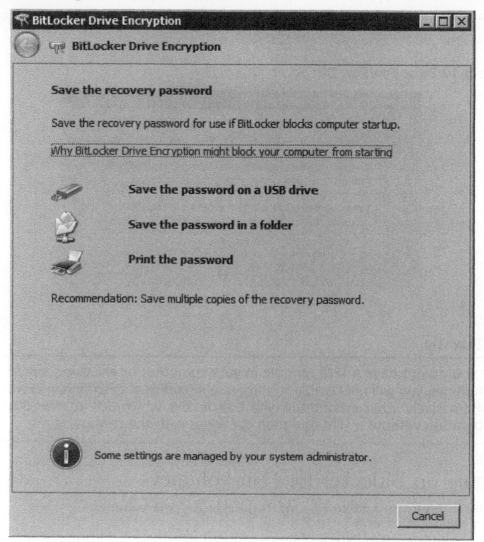

7. On the **Save a Recovery Password to a USB Drive** box, select your USB drive and click **Save**.

8. On the **Encrypt the selected disk volume** page, confirm that the **Run BitLocker System Check** checkbox is selected, and then click **Continue**.

9. Confirm that you want to reboot.

During the reboot phase, BitLocker verifies the system and makes sure it is ready for encryption. After rebooting the system, you should log back on to the system and verify that the **Encryption in Progress** status bar is displayed in the BitLocker Control Panel applet. In case your system cannot be enabled for BitLocker, an error message pops up during logon (see Figure 5.10).

Figure 5.10 Error Enabling BitLocker

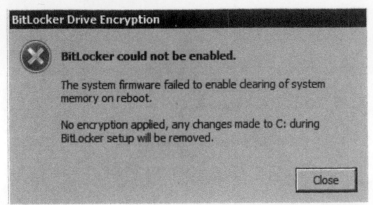

TEST DAY TIP

If you do not have a TPM module in your computer or are using virtual machines, you will not be able to configure BitLocker as described in Exercise 6.3. Alternatively, you can continue with Exercise 6.5, which first enables BitLocker operation without a TPM and then continues with the configuration.

Turning on Bitlocker for Data Volumes

Now we'll show you how to turn on BitLocker for data volumes.

1. Log on as an administrator.

2. Click **Start**, click **All Programs**, click **Accessories**, and then click **Command Prompt**.

3. At the command prompt type **manage-bde –on <volume>: -rp –rk F:**. This will encrypt the named volume, generate a recovery password, and store a recovery key on drive F:\ (which is the USB drive, in this example). Don't forget to record the recovery password!

4. At the command prompt type **manage-bde –autounlock –enable <volume>:** to enable automatic unlocking of the volume. The key to

automatically unlock the volume on each restart is stored on the operating system volume, which must be fully encrypted before this command is issued.

NOTE

Windows Server 2008 mounts a protected data volume as normal. The keys for protecting a data volume are independent of the keys used to protect the operating system volume. The key-chain protecting the data volume is also stored on the encrypted boot volume, therefore allowing the boot volume to automatically mount any data volume after system restart.

Configuring BitLocker for TPM-Less Operation

The following steps configure your computer's Group Policy settings to turn on BitLocker on systems without a TPM.

1. Logon as an administrator.

2. Click **Start**, click **Run**, type **gpedit.msc** in the open box, and then click **OK**.

3. In the **Local Group Policy Editor** console tree, click **Local Computer Policy**, click **Administrative Templates**, click **Windows Components**, and then click **BitLocker Drive Encryption**.

4. Double-click the setting **Control Panel Setup: Enable Advanced Startup Options**.

5. Select the **Enabled** option, select the **Allow BitLocker without a compatible TPM** check box, and then click **OK** (see Figure 5.11).

Figure 5.11 Enabling TPM-less Operation in the Local Group Policy

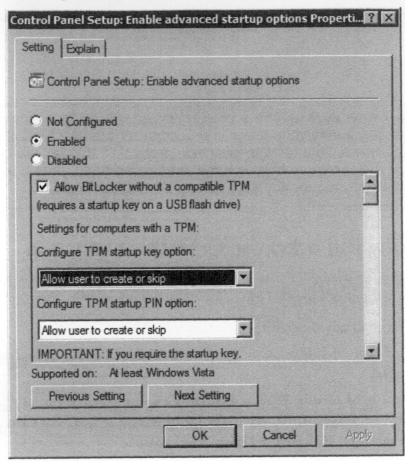

Turning on BitLocker on Systems without a TPM

Turning on BitLocker on systems without a TPM is similar to the normal activation process. Make sure you have a USB flash drive available to store the startup key.

1. Log on as an administrator.

2. Click **Start**, click **Control Panel**, and then click **BitLocker Drive Encryption**.

3. On the **BitLocker Drive Encryption** page, click **Turn On BitLocker** on the operating system volume.

4. On the **BitLocker Drive Encryption Platform Check** dialog box click **Continue with BitLocker Drive Encryption**.

5. On the **Set BitLocker startup preferences** page select **Require Startup USB key at every startup** (see Figure 5.12).

Figure 5.12 USB Startup Key Selection Screen

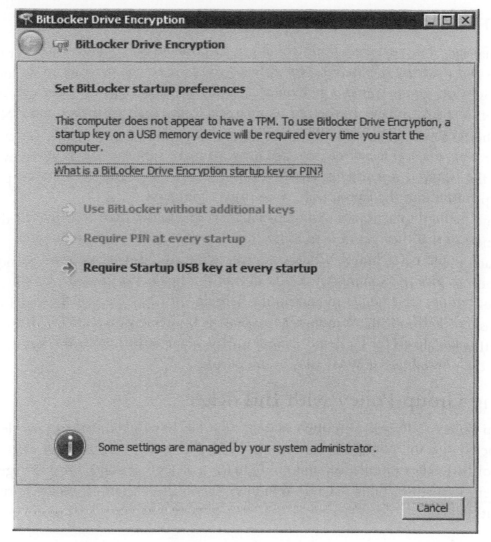

6. On the **Save your Startup Key** page select your USB drive from the list and click **Next**.

7. On the **Save the recovery password** page, click **Save the password on a USB drive**.

8. On the **Save a Recovery Password to a USB Drive** Box, select your USB drive and click **Save**.

9. On the **Encrypt the selected disk volume** page, confirm that the **Run BitLocker System Check** checkbox is selected, and then click **Continue**.

10. Confirm that you want to reboot.

Administration of BitLocker

In a managed Enterprise environment, it can be problematic to allow each user to enable BitLocker by themselves. Not only do you have to add the user to the local administrators group, you also give out the management of recovery passwords and/or PINs and startup keys. In the real world, users forget their passwords and PINs. So why should this be different with BitLocker recovery information? Here's an example: A user with a laptop decides to use BitLocker to make sure the data is secure even when the laptop is stolen. After enabling BitLocker, the user puts the recovery password printout into the laptop bag... A security nightmare!

One method to act upon such deficiencies is to educate users and increase their awareness so that they get more sensitive for security-related matters. Another approach might be technical. Windows Server 2008 extends well-known techniques and tools to give the administrator control over the BitLocker lifecycle. Group Policies settings were added to control the behavior of BitLocker on client and server systems. Furthermore, the Windows Management Instrumentation (WMI) Interface for BitLocker allows for local and remote management of BitLocker. We will talk about the possibilities of WMI later in this chapter.

Using Group Policy with BitLocker

Group Policy (GPO) in Windows Server 2008 has been extended to provide BitLocker-specific configuration settings. With GPO, the administrator can control BitLocker installation and configuration as well as centralized storage of recovery passwords. Table 5.1 lists Windows Server 2008's Group Policy settings for BitLocker.

Table 5.1 Overview of Windows Server 2008 BitLocker Group Policy Settings

Policy	Policy Path	Scope	Description
Configure encryption method	Windows Components\ BitLocker Drive Encryption	Machine	This policy setting allows you to configure the algorithm and key size used by BitLocker Drive Encryption.
Configure TPM platform validation profile	Windows Components\ BitLocker Drive Encryption	Machine	This policy setting allows you to configure how the computer's Trusted Platform Module (TPM) security hardware secures the BitLocker encryption key. This policy setting does not apply if the computer does not have a compatible TPM or if BitLocker has already been turned on with TPM protection.
Control Panel Setup: Configure recovery folder	Windows Components\ BitLocker Drive Encryption	Machine	This policy setting allows you to specify the default path that is displayed when the BitLocker Drive Encryption setup wizard prompts the user to enter the location of a folder in which to save the recovery password.
Control Panel Setup: Configure recovery options	Windows Components\ BitLocker Drive Encryption	Machine	This policy setting allows you to configure whether the BitLocker Drive Encryption setup wizard will ask the user to save BitLocker recovery options.
Control Panel Setup: Enable advanced startup options	Windows Components\ BitLocker Drive Encryption	Machine	This policy setting allows you to configure whether the BitLocker Drive Encryption setup wizard will ask the user to set up an additional authentication that is requested each time the computer starts. You can further configure setting options for computers with and without a TPM.

Continued

Table 5.1 Continued. Overview of Windows Server 2008 BitLocker Group
Policy Settings

Policy	Policy Path	Scope	Description
Prevent memory overwrite on restart	Windows Components\ BitLocker Drive Encryption	Machine	This policy setting controls computer restart performance at the risk of exposing BitLocker secrets. BitLocker secrets include key material used to encrypt data.
Turn on BitLocker backup to Active Directory Domain Services	Windows Components\ BitLocker Drive Encryption	Machine	This policy setting allows you to manage the Active Directory Domain Services (AD DS) backup of BitLocker Drive Encryption recovery information.

Storing BitLocker and TPM Recovery Information in Active Directory

In conjunction with Group Policy and a downloadable toolkit, Active Directory can be configured to store backup information for Windows BitLocker and the Trusted Platform Module. Recovery information includes the recovery password, the TPM owner password, and the information required to identify to which computers and volumes the recovery information applies. Optionally, you can also save a package containing the actual keys used to encrypt the data as well as the recovery password required to access those keys.

As a best practice, configure Active Directory integration first and then allow BitLocker usage on clients and servers. If you enable BitLocker on clients first, recovery passwords for those computers are not stored in Active Directory, leading to an inconsistent experience in case you have to recover.

Storage of BitLocker Recovery Information in Active Directory

BitLocker recovery information is stored in Active Directory as a child object to the computer object. That is, the computer object acts as the parent container for a recovery object. Each BitLocker object includes the recovery password as well as other recovery information. Multiple recovery objects can exist under each computer account because there can be more than one recovery password for each protected volume.

BitLocker recovery information is stored in objects from type *msFVE-RecoveryInformation*. These objects are named after the following scheme:

```
<Object Creation Date and Time><Recovery GUID>
```

For example:

```
2008-01-30T08:17:05-09:00{063DC7a8-879D-DE34-FF6F-2417448D55CB}
```

Each msFVE-RecoveryInformation object contains the attributes listed in Table 5.2.

Table 5.2 Attributes Associated with the msFVW-RecoveryInformation Objects

Attribute Name	Description
ms-FVE-RecoveryPassword	Contains the 48-digit recovery password
ms-FVE-RecoveryGuid	Contains the GUID associated with a BitLocker recovery password
ms-FVE-VolumeGuid	Contains the GUID associated with a BitLocker-supported disk volume
ms-FVE-KeyPackage	Contains a volume's BitLocker encryption key

Storage of TPM Information in Active Directory

TPM owner passwords are stored as an attribute of the computer object in Active Directory. During TPM initialization or when the TPM password is changed, the hash of the password is stored in Active Directory in the *ms-TPM-OwnerInformation*.

Prerequisites

Since BitLocker Active Directory backup stores information in Active Directory objects, you need to extend the schema to support the storage of BitLocker-specific data. Schema extensions and scripts for enabling the Active Directory backup functionality are included in a downloadable toolkit from Microsoft. To access the download follow this link: http://go.microsoft.com/fwlink/?LinkId=78953. After extraction, the following sample scripts should help with the implementation:

- Add-TPMSelfWriteACE.vbs
- BitLockerTPMSchemaExtension.ldf
- List-ACEs.vbs
- Get-TPMOwnerInfo.vbs
- Get-BitLockerRecoveryInfo.vbs

> **NOTE**
>
> BitLocker recovery information is stored in Active Directory attributes flagged as confidential. The confidential flag is a feature introduced in Windows Server 2003 Service Pack1 and provides advanced access control for sensitive data. With this feature, only domain administrators and authorized users have read access to those attributes. Therefore Active Directory backup for BitLocker recovery information should be implemented only if your domain controllers are running Windows Server 2003 Service Pack 1, Windows Server 2003 R2, or Windows Server 2008, ensuring backed up BitLocker information is properly protected.

Extending the Schema

The first step in configuring Active Directory BitLocker backup is extending the Active Directory schema to allow storage of BitLocker specific objects (see Figure 5.13). Before you start, extract the toolkit files to a folder named **C:\BitLocker-AD**.

To extend the Active Directory schema:

1. Logon with an account that is a member of the schema admins group.

2. Click **Start**, click **All Programs**, click **Accessories**, and then click **Command Prompt**.

3. At the command prompt, type **cd /d C:\BitLocker-AD**.

4. At the command prompt, type **ldifde -i -v -f BitLockerTPMSchema Extension.ldf -c "DC=X" "distinguished name of your domain" -k -j**. Do not forget the period at the end of the command!

Figure 5.13 Schema Extension Output

```
C:\BitLocker-AD>ldifde -i -v -k -f BitLockerTPMSchemaExtension.ldf -c
"DC=X" "DC=nsoftincad,dc=internal" -j .
Connecting to "Alpha.Nsoftincad.Internal"
Logging in as current user using SSPI
Importing directory from file "BitLockerTPMSchemaExtension.ldf"
Loading entries
1: CN=ms-TPM-OwnerInformation,CN=Schema,CN=Configuration,DC=nsoftincad,dc=internal
Entry already exists, entry skipped
```

```
2: CN=ms-FVE-RecoveryGuid,CN=Schema,CN=Configuration,DC=nsoftincad,dc=internal
Entry already exists, entry skipped

3: CN=ms-FVE-RecoveryPassword,CN=Schema,CN=Configuration,DC=nsoftincad,dc=internal
Entry already exists, entry skipped

4: (null)
Entry modified successfully.

5: CN=ms-FVE-RecoveryInformation,CN=Schema,CN=Configuration,DC=nsoftincad,dc=internal
Entry already exists, entry skipped

6: CN=computer,CN=Schema,CN=Configuration,DC=nsoftincad,dc=internal
Entry modified successfully.

7: (null)
Entry modified successfully.

8: CN=ms-FVE-VolumeGuid,CN=Schema,CN=Configuration,DC=nsoftincad,dc=internal
Entry already exists, entry skipped

9: CN=ms-FVE-KeyPackage,CN=Schema,CN=Configuration,DC=nsoftincad,dc=internal
Entry already exists, entry skipped

10: (null)
Entry modified successfully.

11: CN=ms-FVE-RecoveryInformation,CN=Schema,CN=Configuration,DC=nsoftincad,dc=internal
Entry modified successfully.

12: CN=ms-FVE-RecoveryInformation,CN=Schema,CN=Configuration,DC=nsoftincad,dc=internal
Attribute or value exists, entry skipped.

13: CN=ms-TPM-OwnerInformation,CN=Schema,CN=Configuration,DC=nsoftincad,dc=internal
Entry modified successfully.

14: CN=ms-TPM-OwnerInformation,CN=Schema,CN=Configuration,DC=nsoftincad,dc=internal
Entry modified successfully.

15: CN=ms-FVE-RecoveryGuid,CN=Schema,CN=Configuration,DC=nsoftincad,dc=internal
Entry modified successfully.

16: CN=ms-FVE-RecoveryGuid,CN=Schema,CN=Configuration,DC=nsoftincad,dc=internal
Entry modified successfully.

17: CN=ms-FVE-RecoveryGuid,CN=Schema,CN=Configuration,DC=nsoftincad,dc=internal
Entry modified successfully.

18: CN=ms-FVE-RecoveryGuid,CN=Schema,CN=Configuration,DC=nsoftincad,dc=internal
Entry modified successfully.

19: CN=ms-FVE-RecoveryPassword,CN=Schema,CN=Configuration,DC=nsoftincad,dc=internal
Entry modified successfully.
```

```
20: CN=ms-FVE-RecoveryPassword,CN=Schema,CN=Configuration,DC=nsoftincad,dc=internal
Entry modified successfully.

21: CN=ms-FVE-RecoveryPassword,CN=Schema,CN=Configuration,DC=nsoftincad,dc=internal
Entry modified successfully.

22: (null)
Entry modified successfully.

15 entries modified successfully.
The command has completed successfully
```

Setting Required Permissions for Backing Up TPM Passwords

The second step is to set permission in Active Directory. By default Windows Vista clients can back up BitLocker recovery information in Active Directory. However, to back up the TPM owner password an Access Control Entry (ACE) must be added to the computer object. To add the ACE use the **Add-TPMSelfWriteACE.vbs** script from the toolkit. To add the ACE entry:

1. Log on with a domain administrator account.

2. Click **Start**, click **All Programs**, click **Accessories**, and then click **Command Prompt**.

3. At the command prompt type **cscript Add-TPMSelfWriteACE.vbs**.

The script will add a single ACE to the top-level domain object in your domain. The ACE is inherited by all computer child objects in Active Directory.

Enabling Group Policy Settings for BitLocker and TPM Active Directory Backup

Here are the steps to follow to configure Group Policies for clients and servers to use BitLocker Active Directory Backup.

1. Log on with a domain administrator to any Domain Controller.

2. Click **Start**, click **All Programs**, click **Administrative Tools**, and then click **Group Policy Management**.

3. In the Group Policy Management Console, expand the forest tree down to the domain level.

4. Right-click the **Default Domain Policy** and select **Edit**.

5. In the Group Policy Management Editor, open **Computer Configuration**, open **Administrative Templates**, open **Windows Components**, and then open **BitLocker Drive Encryption**.

6. In the right pane, double-click **Turn on BitLocker backup to Active Directory**.

7. Select the **Enabled** option, select **Require BitLocker backup to AD DS**, and click **OK**.

To further enable storage of TPM recovery information:

8. Open **Computer Configuration**, open **Administrative Templates**, open **System**, and then open **Trusted Platform Module Services**.

9. In the right pane, double-click **Turn on TPM backup to Active Directory**.

10. Select the **Enabled** option, select **Require TPM backup to AD DS**, and click OK.

WARNING

In this example, we use the *Default Domain Policy* to configure Active Directory backup for BitLocker and TPM recovery information. However, in a real-world scenario you would create a new GPO that contains only BitLocker specific settings!

Recovering Data

BitLocker will lock the computer when an encryption key is not available. Likely causes for this can be:

- Inserting the BitLocker-protected drive into a new computer
- Replacing the computer motherboard
- Performing maintenance operation on the TPM (such as clearing or disabling)
- Updating the BIOS
- Upgrading critical early boot components that cause system integrity validation to fail

- Forgetting the PIN when PIN authentication has been enabled

- Losing the USB flash drive containing the startup key when startup key authentication has been enabled

When TPM fails to check the integrity of startup components, it will lock the computer at a very early stage before the operating system starts. When locked, the system enters recovery mode. You can use a USB flash drive with the recovery password stored on it or use the keyboard to enter the recovery password manually. In recovery mode, the keyboard assignment is somewhat different: you use functions keys to enter digits. F1 through F9 represents digits 1 trough 9, F10 represents 0.

Testing Bitlocker Data Recovery

To test BitLocker for data recovery, follow these steps:

1. Log on as an administrator.

2. Click **Start**, click **Run**, type **tpm.msc** in the open box, and click **OK**. The **TPM Management Console** is displayed.

3. Under **Actions**, click **Turn TPM Off**.

4. Provide the TPM owner password, if required.

5. When the **Status** panel in the **TPM Management on Local Computer** task panel reads "Your TPM is off and ownership of the TPM has been taken," close that task panel.

6. Click the **Safely Remove Hardware** icon in the notification area to remove the USB flash drive from the system.

7. **Restart** your computer. When you restart the computer, you will be prompted for the recovery password, because the startup configuration has changed since you encrypted the volume.

8. The **BitLocker Drive Encryption Recovery Console** should appear.

9. **Insert** your USB flash drive and press **ESC**. The computer will restart automatically.

10. The system should boot normally.

TIP

If you do not have a USB flash drive with the recovery password on it, you would press **ENTER** instead of ESC. After pressing **ENTER**, the system prompts you for the recovery password. Input the recovery password and press **ENTER** again.

Disabling BitLocker

If you want to turn off BitLocker, you need to decide if you want to disable BitLocker or decrypt the volume. Disabling BitLocker allows for TPM maintenance while the data is kept encrypted. Decrypting the volume means that the entire volume will be decrypted. Disabling BitLocker is supported only on operating system volumes and not on data volumes.

To turn off BitLocker Drive Encryption:

1. Click **Start**, click **Control Panel**, click **Security**, and then click **BitLocker Drive Encryption**.

2. On the **BitLocker Drive Encryption** page, find the volume on which you want BitLocker Drive Encryption turned off, and click **Turn Off BitLocker Drive Encryption**.

3. From the **What level of decryption do you want** dialog box, click either **Disable BitLocker Drive Encryption** or **Decrypt the volume** as needed.

Active Directory Rights Management Services

Active Directory Rights Management Services (AD RMS) is a format- and application-agnostic service designed to safeguard information by deterring inadvertent sharing of information with unauthorized people. AD RMS protects information when it is connected and when it is not connected to the corporate network. A usage policy is bound to the protected item so that no matter where it travels the rights are enforced to ensure that only the authorized recipient is able to access the contents. The policy can restrict users from actions such as viewing, copying, forwarding, and printing.

Previously shipped as an add-on for Windows Server, AD RMS is now included out-of-the-box as a role in Windows Server 2008. This release delivers a number of enhancements focused on easing administration and opening up cross-organization collaboration.

Active Directory Rights Management Services (AD RMS) includes features not available in Microsoft Windows RMS. Windows RMS was available for Windows Server 2003 and was used to restrict access to rights-protected content to files made by RMS-enabled applications. The added features were incorporated to ease administrative overhead of AD RMS and to extend use outside the organization. New features include:

- AD RMS is now a server role
- Microsoft Management Console (MMC) snap-in
- Integration with AD FS
- Self-enrollment of AD RMS servers
- The ability to delegate responsibility with new AD RMS administrative roles

As shown in Figure 5.14, AD RMS works through a service cluster providing license issuing and validation services to a group of users. As a user accesses AD RMS for the first time through an RMS-enabled application, his machine is enrolled with the RMS cluster and is issued a Client Licensor Certificate (CLC). This certificate is a key component in the protection process. It enables the user to publish content with a specific usage policy assigned. The usage policy is derived from several elements:

- **Actions** Explicitly allowed, denied, or undefined actions that include a default set (view, edit, save, export, print, forward, reply, reply all, extract, allow macros, view rights) and the ability to define new application-specific actions

- **Expiration Policy** Disable the content after a specific date, a duration following the content license being applied, or a duration following the initial opening of the document (akin to a "self-destruct" option)

- **Revocation Policy** Requiring the content to check a revocation list each time the content is accessed to ensure that the user's right to access the content has not been explicitly revoked

- **Extended Policy** Miscellaneous settings including granting the user the ability to view using a browser-based RMS viewer, forcing the user to obtain a new license every time she accesses the content, and adding additional custom attributes

Figure 5.14 AD RMS

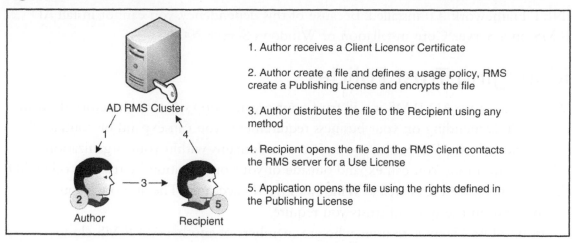

1. Author receives a Client Licensor Certificate

2. Author create a file and defines a usage policy, RMS create a Publishing License and encrypts the file

3. Author distributes the file to the Recipient using any method

4. Recipient opens the file and the RMS client contacts the RMS server for a Use License

5. Application opens the file using the rights defined in the Publishing License

AD RMS Cluster

Author

Recipient

Users can create their own custom policy based on a combination of the above as exposed by the application, or they can use policies defined at the organization level. The organization-defined policies, known as *policy templates*, provide a basis for implementing uniform policies across a large number of users (e.g., "Confidential Company Information Read Only", "For Research and Development Teams Only"). The policy syntax is based on Extensible Rights Markup Language (XrML). It allows third-party developers to RMS-enable their application and extend the AD RMS service to meet their information protection needs. With the policy created the information can be distributed by any means necessary to the authorized recipients.

When the recipients receive the information their RMS-enabled application applies for a Use License. The first time the machine accesses the RMS service a Machine Certificate (MC) is issued to the computer. The RMS client then validates the viewer's identity by creating a Rights Account Certificate (RAC) for the user. With the MC and RAC the RMS client evaluates the usage policy. If everything checks out okay, the user is issued a Use License to access the content and the application enables that access. Microsoft ships two main sets of RMS-enabled applications today in the Office suite and Internet Explorer. For Office, you require the Professional edition or better to author protected content, whereas lower editions are only able to view the content. Internet Explorer acts as a viewer for RMS-protected content through an ActiveX plug-in.

You can deploy AD RMS in either a stand-alone server or a clustered configuration. This gives you the flexibility to get started with a basic configuration and scale up to handle a larger volume of usage or implement redundancy as needed.

Before you install AD RMS on Windows Server 2008, you will need to have the .NET Framework 3.0 installed. Because of this dependency, you cannot install AD RMS on a Server Core installation of Windows Server 2008.

Managing Trust Policies

When you set up AD RMS it will trust your organization's Active Directory domain by default. Depending on your business requirements you can expand or contract the boundaries of your RMS trust to specific user domains within your organization or other organizations. You can expand outside of your organization by trusting other AD RMS clusters, AD FS, as well as Windows Live ID accounts. The approach you take will depend on the types of trusts you require.

Issuing Use Licenses to users who are members of another AD RMS cluster requires that you explicitly trust the other cluster. You do this by adding the external cluster's information into the Trusted User Domain (TUD) section of the Trust Policy. Once you've added it, you can allow or deny specific users or groups of users within the external AD RMS cluster.

Follow along as we extend the Trust Policy to another AD RMS cluster.

1. Open the **Control Panel**, and under **System and Maintenance | Administration Tools** double-click the **Active Directory Rights Management Services** shortcut.

2. In the **Active Directory Rights Management Services** management console, expand the cluster node and **Trust Policie**s node in the left-hand pane, and then click the **Trusted User Domains** node.

3. In the right-hand action pane, click the **Import Trusted User Domain** link.

4. In the **Import Trusted User Domain** dialog, provide the location of the **Trusted User Domain File** given to you by the administrator of the other AD RMS cluster, provide a **Display Name**, and click **Finish**.

To minimize the administrative burden for a small or diverse group of accounts you can use the Windows Live ID service as a source of RACs for users. Before you can do this, you will need to configure your AD RMS cluster to trust the Windows Live ID service. In preparation for this, be sure to enable anonymous access and expose the AD RMS licensing Web service (located at /_wmcs/licensing on your

Web server) for external users to obtain use licenses. Now, we will extend the Trust Policy to Windows Live ID.

1. Open the **Control Panel**, and under System and Maintenance | Administration Tools double-click the **Active Directory Rights Management Services** shortcut.

2. In the **Active Directory Rights Management Services** management console, expand the cluster node and **Trust Policie**s node in the left-hand pane, and then click the **Trusted User Domains** node.

3. In the right-hand action pane, click the **Trust Windows Live ID** link.

AD RMS can also issue Publishing Licenses to users in other AD RMS clusters. This is useful if a trusted external cluster belongs to separate business units within your organization where a fully federated trust cannot be established. This process adds the external cluster's Server Licensor Certificate (SLC) to the Trusted Publishing Domain (TPD) list.

Now let's go through the steps for extending the trust policy to allow external users to receive publishing licenses.

1. Open the **Control Panel**, and under **System and Maintenance | Administration Tools** double-click the **Active Directory Rights Management Services** shortcut.

2. In the **Active Directory Rights Management Services** management console, expand the cluster node and **Trust Policie**s node in the left-hand pane, and then click the **Trusted Publishing Domains** node.

3. In the right-hand action pane, click the **Import Trusted Publishing Domain** link.

4. In the **Import Trusted Publishing Domain** dialog, provide the location of the **Trusted Publishing Domain File** given to you by the administrator of the other AD RMS cluster, provide the **Password** for the file and a **Display Name**, and click **Finish**.

Federated trusts are an alternative to adding trusted organizations to both TUD and TPD lists. It is useful when you have a trusted partner organization with which you are working and sharing information. To protect both parties these trusts are not transitive, meaning that the TUD and TPD lists of one organization do not automatically apply to the other organization. The trust is established at the highest level only. Now, we'll go through the steps to establish a federated trust.

1. Open the **Control Panel**, and under **System and Maintenance | Administration Tools** double-click the **Active Directory Rights Management Services** shortcut.

2. In the **Active Directory Rights Management Services** management console, expand the cluster node and **Trust Policies** node in the left-hand pane, and then click the **Federated Identity Support** node.

3. In the right-hand action pane, click the **Enable Federated Identity Support** link.

4. In the right-hand actions pane. click **Properties**.

5. In the **Federated Identity Support** dialog, on the **Policies** tab, provide the **Federated Identity Certificate Service URL** for the external AD RMS cluster that will be trusted and click **OK**.

Exclusion Policies

In addition to including organizations, you can exclude certain users based on e-mail domains, specific addresses, applications, RMS client version, and Windows operating system version.

When using the Windows Live ID trust you can exclude specific users from obtaining a use certificate by adding them to the exclusion list. This could be useful if there are known users who present a security risk to corporate information. Now, we'll walk through the steps of excluding Windows Live IDs.

1. Open the **Control Panel**, and under **System and Maintenance | Administration Tools** double-click the **Active Directory Rights Management Services** shortcut.

2. In the **Active Directory Rights Management Services** management console, expand the cluster node and **Trust Policies** node in the left-hand pane, and then click the **Trusted User Domains** node.

3. In the middle pane, right-click the **Windows Live ID** row and select **Properties**.

4. In the **Windows Live ID Properties** dialog, click the **Excluded Windows Live IDs** tab, enter the e-mail addresses or domains which you want to exclude, and click **OK**.

You can also exclude specific user accounts from your AD RMS cluster or other trusted clusters using the e-mail address or public key from the user's RAC. By doing this, you will prevent the user from obtaining a new Use License from your AD RMS cluster. Note that this exclusion does not apply to other AD RMS clusters that trust your users.

1. Open the **Control Panel**, and under **System and Maintenance | Administration Tools** double-click the **Active Directory Rights Management Services** shortcut.

2. In the **Active Directory Rights Management Services** management console, expand the cluster node and **Exclusion Policie**s node in the left-hand pane, and then click the **Users** node.

3. In the right action pane, click the **Enable User Exclusion** link.

4. In the right action pane, click the **Exclude User** link.

5. In the **Exclude User** dialog, provide the e-mail address of the user or the public key string and click **Finish**.

If you have an RMS client application which you no longer trust, either because an updated version is available or known defects in the application make it a risky application, you can prevent users from using that application for protected content. This policy will prevent AD RMS from issuing a new Use License to clients who are using the specified version of the software. As with the user exclusion, this will apply only to your AD RMS cluster. Now, we'll walk through the steps of excluding applications.

1. Open the **Control Panel**, and under **System and Maintenance | Administration Tools** double-click the **Active Directory Rights Management Services** shortcut.

2. In the **Active Directory Rights Management Services** management console, expand the cluster node and **Exclusion Policie**s node in the left-hand pane, and then click the **Applications** node.

3. In the right action pane, click the **Enable Application Exclusion** link.

4. In the right action pane, click the **Exclude Application** link.

5. In the **Exclude Application** dialog (see Figure 5.15), provide the filename and version range to be excluded and click **Finish**.

Figure 5.15 The Exclude Application Dialog

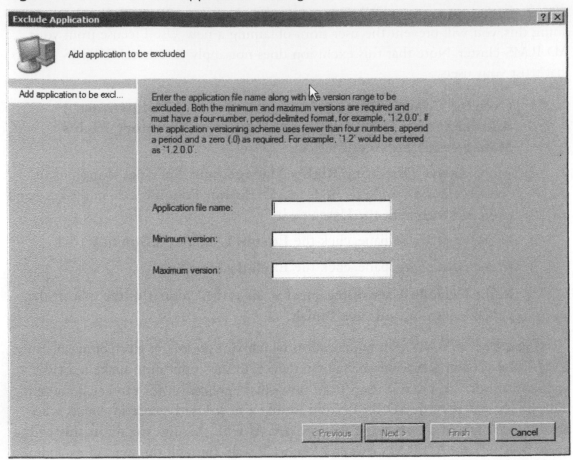

You can perform two other types of exclusions with AD RMS: client and operating system version exclusions. The lockbox is the RMS client component that stores a user's private key. With continued security research there is a possibility that vulnerabilities are found in a particular release of the RMS client. To mitigate the risks associated with older versions you can specify the minimum RMS client lockbox component version for which Use Licenses will be issued by the AD RMS cluster. Microsoft posts the latest released version of this component on its Web site located at http://go.microsoft.com/fwlink/?LinkID=12995.

Finally, you can restrict older versions of the RMS client running on either Microsoft Windows 98 Second Edition or Windows Millennium Edition. These operating systems do not support a number of critical security features available in later releases. Restricting them from accessing RMS content will ensure that your content is protected using the best measures available. As with all other exclusions, you will need to enable the Windows Version exclusion on each individual AD RMS cluster.

Configuring Policy Templates

Rights policy templates provide a set of predefined rules for users to leverage in their RMS-enabled applications when making decisions regarding how to protect information. These templates form a basis for implementing uniform policies across a large number of users (e.g., "Confidential Company Information Read Only", "For Research and Development Teams Only"). They provide administrators the ability to define the information sharing parameters, and later revoke the content as a whole when the template is deleted. Let's now create a policy template.

1. Open the **Control Panel**, and under **System and Maintenance | Administration Tools** double-click the **Active Directory Rights Management Services** shortcut.

2. In the **Active Directory Rights Management Services** management console, expand the cluster node in the left-hand pane, and then click the **Rights Policy Template** node.

3. In the right action pane, click the **Create Distributed Rights Policy Template** link.

4. In the **Create Distributed Rights Policy Template** dialog, on the **Add Template Identification Information** step, click the **Add** button, provide the **Name** and **Description** of the template, and click **Next**.

5. On the **Add User Rights** step, click the **Add** button and type in the e-mail address of the user or group, or select **Anyone** to apply this policy to everyone. Then select the **Rights** from the list and click **Next**.

6. On the **Specify Expiration Policy** step, set the appropriate **Content** and **Use License** expiration and click **Next**.

7. On the **Specify Extended Policy** step, review the options and click **Next**.

8. On the **Specify Revocation Policy** step, review the options and click **Finish**.

When you are finished with a policy template it is recommended that you archive the template instead of deleting it. This will allow AD RMS to continue to issue Use Licenses for content protected with the particular template. When you do finally delete a policy template it is recommended that you back up the configuration database before doing so to enable you to recover rights-protected content if necessary. We'll now archive a policy template.

1. Open the **Control Panel**, and under **System and Maintenance | Administration Tools** double-click the **Active Directory Rights Management Services** shortcut.

2. In the **Active Directory Rights Management Services** management console, expand the cluster node in the left-hand pane, and then click the **Rights Policy Template** node.

3. In the middle pane, select the policy to be archived.

4. In the right action pane, click the **Archive this Rights Policy Template** link.

5. On the warning dialog, click **Yes**.

Managing Your AD RMS Cluster

Now let's discuss ways to manage your AD RMS cluster.

Super User

The Super User group is an administrative group whose members can decrypt any protected content, and subsequently remove the content protection from the file. By default, this group is disabled and contains no members. To enable it you will need to assign an Active Directory Universal Group to represent the AD RMS super group. Here are the steps to follow:

1. Open the **Control Panel**, and under **System and Maintenance | Administration Tools** double-click the **Active Directory Rights Management Services** shortcut.

2. In the **Active Directory Rights Management Services** management console, expand the cluster node and **Security Policie**s node in the left-hand pane, and then click the **Super Users** node.

3. In the right-hand action pane, click the **Enable Super Users** link.

4. In the middle pane, click the **Change Super User Group** link.

5. In the **Super Users** dialog, click the **Browse** button and locate a Universal Group in Active Directory to represent the **Super Users Group**; then click **OK**.

Removing AD RMS

With usage over time, AD RMS has become a critical component of your business infrastructure. A number of items have been protected and removing AD RMS from the environment may cause those items to become inaccessible. To prevent the loss of information you should properly decommission the AD RMS environment. This changes the behavior of the AD RMS cluster to provide a decryption key for all rights-protected content which had been published using its licenses. This will give your organization and its users a chance to save their content without the content protection features and the system administrators a chance to remove all AD RMS clients from the environment. Upon decommissioning an AD RMS cluster, you will no longer be able to administer the environment. Ensure that you have adequately backed up the system before performing this step. Now, we'll walk through the steps of decommissioning a server.

WARNING

Removing AD RMS without first decommissioning it will leave all protected content inaccessible for any scenario that requires a new Use License.

1. Open **Windows Explorer** and locate the **Decommissioning.asmx** file (typically found in %SYSTEMDRIVE%\inetpub\wwwroot_wmcs\ decommission); then grant the Everyone group Read & Execute permissions.

2. Open the **Control Panel**, and under **System and Maintenance | Administration Tools** double-click the **Active Directory Rights Management Services** shortcut.

3. In the **Active Directory Rights Management Services** management console, expand the cluster node and **Security Policie**s node in the left-hand pane, and then click the **Decommissioning** node.

4. In the right-hand action pane, click the **Enable Decommissioning** link.

5. In the middle pane, click the **Decommission** button.

6. When prompted with a warning about decommissioning, click **Yes**.

7. Repeat these steps for the rest of the servers in the AD RMS cluster.

Reporting

AD RMS provides some basic usage reporting that will give you a view into who is using the rights protection services in your organization. There are three main reports:

- **Statistics Report** This report provides the number of RACs issued by the AD RMS cluster. It is mainly used for licensing purposes.

- **System Health** This provides two views—request type and performance—of the activity on a system:

  - **Request Type Summary** Outlines the number of success, failure, and total requests by request type, including a drill-down to the specific user

  - **Request Performance Report** Provides an average duration and total number of requests by type

- **Troubleshooting Report** This displays the number of success, failure, and total requests by request type for a specific user. The report is useful for determining which server responded and the details behind the request and response.

These reports are available in the AD RMS management console under Reports (see Figure 5.16).

Figure 5.16 The User Request Analysis Report

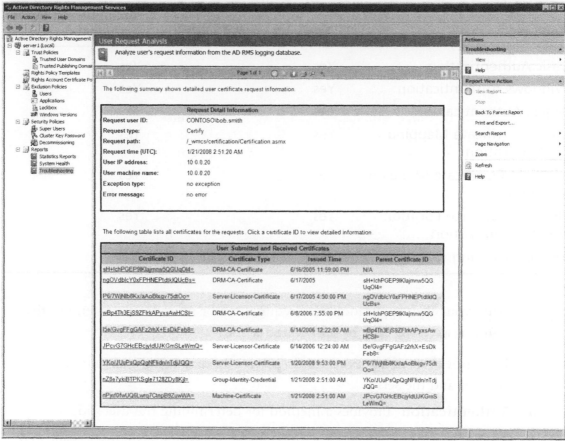

In the last three releases it would be hard to dismiss the incredible growth and maturing of the Windows Server Web application services offerings. From what was an add-on option pack item to a key component that businesses have come to rely on, you can bet that this release is nothing short of impressive. While carrying on the mandate to ship a secure, scalable solution for Web applications and services, the product group has managed to deliver an impressive foundation for Web-based solutions.

Table 5.3 is an overview of the security features available across Windows Server 2008, both Full and Server Core installations.

Table 5.3 Security Features Available for Windows Server 2008

Feature	Available on Full Install	Available on Server Core Install
Basic Authentication	Yes	Yes
Windows Authentication	Yes	Yes
Digest Authentication	Yes	Yes
Client Certificate Mapping Authentication	Yes	Yes
IIS Client Certificate Mapping Authentication	Yes	Yes
Uniform Resource Location (URL) Authorization	Yes	Yes
Request Filtering	Yes	Yes

Protecting your Web application may require one or more tactics to ensure that the application is accessed only by authorized users:

- **Transport Security** Focused on privacy of data being transmitted between the user and the server

- **Authentication** Provides a method for determining the user's identity

- **Authorization** Evaluates a set of rules to determine if the user is allowed to make the request

This section will take you further into each tactic and the details behind them. There have been few key changes that support more secure communication, authentication, and authorization:

- **IIS_IUSRS Group** Replaces the IIS_WPG group from previous releases to service as a security group to which permissions are assigned that will be required by all the application pool identities.

- **Built-in IUSR Account** Replaces the IUSR_MachineName from previous releases with a built-in account that uses a constant security identifier (SID) across servers that helps to maintain consistent access control lists (ACL). Use of the built-in account eliminates the need to have a password assigned to this account as well. For IIS installations on domain controllers it will prevent the IUSR account from becoming a user-accessible domain account.

- **Inheritance and Merging of IP Restriction Rules** Allows more flexible ways to apply authorization rules based on a single computer, group of computers, a domain, all IP addresses, and/or any unlisted entries.

- **Request Filtering** The URLScan tool, which previously shipped as an add-on tool, is now incorporated in the HTTP protocol handler.

- **Native URL Authorization** A more efficient, globally accessible way to secure specific files and paths without having to rely on third-party tools or ASP.NET.

Transport Security

Protecting the privacy of the data being transmitted is the primary focus of transport security. There are a number of options within the Windows Server 2008 infrastructure to protect the privacy. You may want to wrap all data being transmitted, for example, through a virtual private network or IPSec tunnel. With this as the extreme at one end, IIS provides a more moderate and widely used method for protecting data using Secure Socket Layers (SSL) and Transport Layer Security (TLS). TLS is the more commonly deployed standard today and provides the ability to fall back to SSL 3.0 if the client does not support TLS. SSL/TLS uses digital certificates to encrypt the communication. At a high level the process works as follows:

1. The client makes a request to the Web server for a secure connection.

2. The server sends back its public encryption key.

3. The client checks the key to ensure:

    - The name of the host being requested matches the key.

    - The key is within the valid date range.

    - The key's issuer is trusted by the client.

4. If the client determines that it can trust the server's public key it will send its public key to the server.

5. The server will generate a password and encrypt it using both the client's public key and the server's private key, and send it back to the client.

6. The client will decrypt the password as evidence that the server is the one who sent the password, thereby establishing that only the server and the

client will be the only other party capable of reading the encrypted information.

7. The client will send the request to the server encrypted with the password that the server sent to it.

This process has been well established for quite some time and works with all major browsers. IIS fully supports using SSL/TLS certificates to encrypt communication between the server and users. Under the covers, IIS 7 now handles SSL/TLS requests in the kernel by default (it was available in IIS 6, but not enabled by default). This provides a big boost to the performance of secure requests.

Notes from the Underground…

Host Headers and SSL

As mentioned earlier in the chapter, host headers enable you to share an IP address among multiple sites. A call to www.contoso.com will result in Host: www.contoso.com:80 being passed in the header of the request. This allows the HTTP protocol handler to hand the request off to the appropriate Web site. For connections that use secure socket layer (SSL) the ability to use host headers was first introduced in Windows Server 2003 Service Pack 1.

Before you get too excited there are some restrictions that you will need to take into account. The first is that the SSL certificate must contain all the common names of the sites. For example, if you are binding www.contoso.com and store.contoso.com to the same IP address, your SSL certificate will need to contain both host names in the common name field. The most secure approach is to use multiple common names using the subjectAltName property, but it is also the most difficult to obtain as it is not commonly available through certificate authorities (CA). Most certificate authorities promote the use of wildcard certificates instead. A wildcard certificate enables you to use the certificate for all subdomains (e.g., *.contoso.com would work for www.contoso.com, store. contoso.com, foo.contoso.com, bar.contoso.com, foo.bar.contoso.com). Consult your preferred certificate authority on the cost of a wildcard or subjectAltName certificate as they are not usually supported by the typical offering.

With your new certificate in hand you need to bind the certificate to a Web site. Under the covers IIS does not bind it to the Web site, but the IP address

Continued

being used. The reason for this is simple; the HTTP header value that contains the host name is encrypted at the time that the HTTP protocol handler needs to make the decision of which certificate to use. This means that you can have only one SSL certificate per IP address and that explains why you need a wildcard certificate or one with the subjectAltName properties included. To see a list of certificates and their corresponding IP address bindings use the following NetSh command:

```
NetSh.exe HTTP Show SSLCert
```

Adding an SSL binding with host header support currently is not supported through the graphical user interface. You will need to use the AppCmd tool, programmatically, or edit the ApplicationHost.config to add the binding. Here is the AppCmd syntax for adding the binding:

```
AppCmd.exe Set Site /Site.Name:"Contoso Store" /+Bindings.[Protocol="HTTPS",
BindingInformation="*:443:store.contoso.com"]
```

With that in place you can now access both of your sites using SSL.

IIS 7 also introduces a new management interface for security certificates. This new interface gives you a single point to review all the certificates installed on your server along with exposing the ability to generate a self-signed certificate from within the interface. Previously self-signed certificates were available only through the command-line SelfSSL tool that shipped with the IIS 6.0 Resource Kit tools (see Figure 5.17).

Figure 5.17 Server Certificates Module Configuration

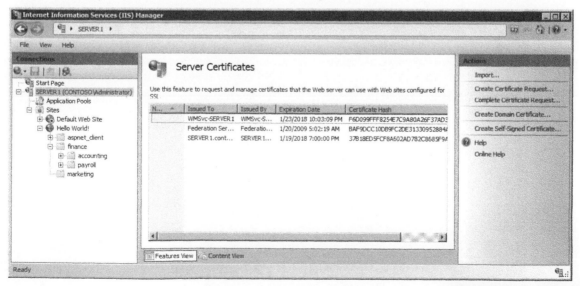

The first step to enabling a secure site is to import or create a new certificate into the server. When creating a certificate you can create one from an online connected certificate authority (CA) like the Certificate Services role that ships with Windows Server 2008, a third-party CA (e.g., Comodo, Thwarte, Verisign), or generate a self-signed certificate. Whichever path you choose the one thing to remember is that the client will need to trust the certificate's issuer in order to trust the certificate. When using a self-signed certificate no one will trust it unless they take steps to specifically add it to their trusted certificates list.

Adding a New Security Certificate

1. Open **Control Panel** and under **System and Maintenance | Administration Tools**, double-click the **Internet Information Services (IIS) Manager** shortcut.

2. In the **Internet Information Services (IIS) Manager** management console click the server node, in the middle pane click **Server Certificates**.

3. In the right-hand **Actions** pane click **Create Certificate Request**.

4. In the **Request Certificate** dialog on the **Distinguished Name Properties** page (see Figure 5.18) provide the host name that will be used to access your site (e.g., www.contoso.com) along with your company information and click **Next**.

Figure 5.18 Distinguished Name Properties Page

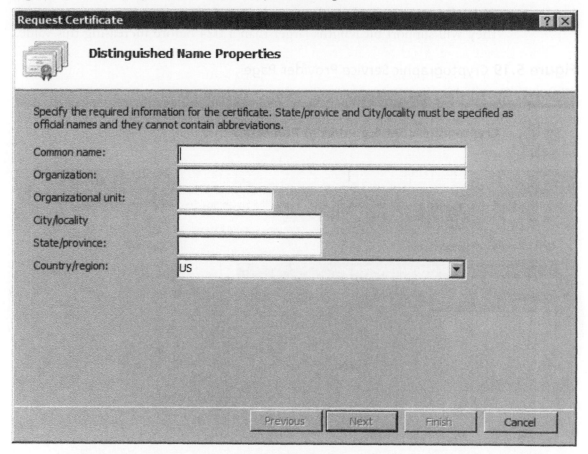

5. On the **Cryptographic Service Provider Properties** page choose a **Cryptographic Server Provider**, a minimum of 1,024 **Bit Length** for the key, and click **Next** (see Figure 5.19).

- **RSA SChannel Cryptographic Provider** Uses an MD5 hash with an SHA hash, signed with an RSA private key. It supports SSL2, PCT1, SSL3, and TLS1 protocols.

- **DH SChannel Cryptographic Provider** Uses the Diffie-Hellman algorithm and supports SSL3 and TLS1 protocols. Use this algorithm when you must exchange a secret key over an insecure network without prior communication with the client.

- **Bit Length** The default length supported by most browsers and certificate authorities is 1,024 bits. With processors becoming more powerful, expect to see a move toward 2,048 bit length certificates past the year 2010. Be sure to check with your chosen certificate authority to ensure they will support bit lengths larger than 1,024 before increasing this value.

Figure 5.19 Cryptographic Service Provider Page

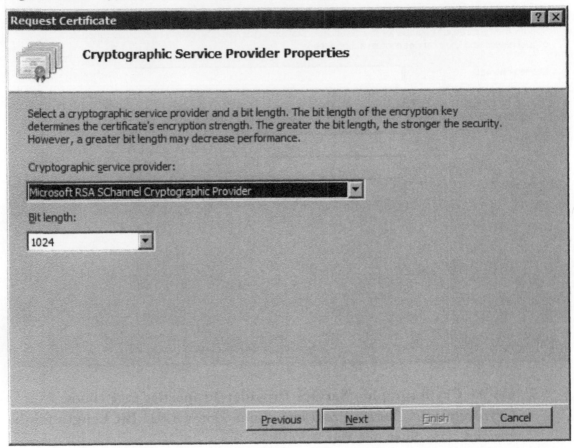

6. On the **File Name** page provide a path and name of a file where to sort the certificate request and click **Next**.

7. Contact your preferred certificate authority to obtain the response file for your request.

   ■ If you are looking to test out the SSL functionality there are a number of providers that will give you a free trial SSL certificate that lasts for anywhere from 15 to 60 days. This is handy because they have all the trust features of regular certificates with no cost.

8. When you obtain the response file, open **IIS Manager** and return to the **Server Certificates** section.

9. In the right-hand actions pane click **Complete Certificate Request**.

10. In the **Complete Certificate Request** dialog on the **Specify Certificate Authority Response** page, locate the **Certificate Authority's Response** file, provide a **Friendly Name** for the certificate, and click **Next** to complete the process.

Configuring & Implementing…

The Real Differences between SSL Certificates

When you are out shopping for an SSL certificate it can get quite confusing as to what the differences are between the various offerings. For the most part you are buying trust in that the certificate you will be issued is trusted by the client. Under the covers the technical differences boil down to these:

- **Standard Certificate** A basic security certificate that will suit most users and will work for 40-bit encryption up to 256-bit encryption in most modern browsers

- **Server Gated Certificate** Before the United States dropped its cryptography export laws in January of 2000 these certificates added a step in the security handshake to see whether the client could support stronger cryptographic algorithms (ciphers). This allowed older browsers an opportunity to step-up their level of encryption if they did not use 128-bit or higher encryption by default.

- **Extended Validation Certificate** From a technical perspective these certificates are no different than a standard certificate with the exception that they have some additional metadata attached to the certificate. This metadata is used by browsers that are capable of reading it to determine if they should identify for the user (e.g., turn the address bar green) that the site has gone through extra validation steps. The validation steps and data included are available in the extended validation certificate guidelines at www.cabforum.org.

Continued

With the data in hand modern browsers will signal to the user through actions like turning the address bar green as shown in Figure 5.20. This feature of popular browsers like Internet Explorer 7 is meant to help users identify the site authenticity.

- **Wildcard Certificate** One of the three preceding certificates, but using an asterisk (*) somewhere in the domain name to signify a wildcard value. This is generally considered a premium service and commercial providers reflect this fact in their pricing model.

When choosing certificates remember that the level of encryption used in most cases is decided on as a mutual agreement between the client and the server. Both parties can choose to use a minimum level of encryption. With IIS this value is represented by a single check box to force clients to use a minimum of 128-bit encryption or have IIS refuse the connection request. Other advertised features have no impact on the security provided by the SSL-enabled session.

Figure 5.20 Internet Explorer Address Bar of a Site Using Extended Validation Certificate

With the certificate in place you can now bind the certificate to your Web site. Under the covers the security certificate is bound to an IP address since the request header information is encrypted when the server needs to determine which certificate

to use. Once the certificate is bound you can choose to force the use of SSL on all or part of the site.

To enable secure communication on your Web site, follow these steps:

1. Open **Control Panel** and under **System and Maintenance | Administration Tools**, double-click the **Internet Information Services (IIS) Manager** shortcut.

2. In the **Internet Information Services (IIS) Manager** management console expand the server node, right-click your site, and select **Edit Bindings**.

3. In the **Site Bindings** dialog click **Add**.

4. In the **Add Site Binding** dialog set the Type to **HTTPS**. From the **SSL Certificate** list choose your certificate and click **OK** (see Figure 5.21).

Figure 5.21 Add Site Binding Dialog

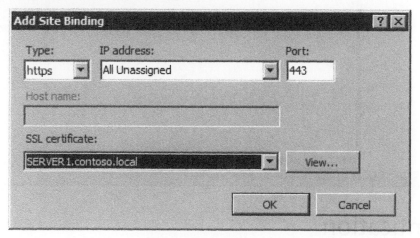

5. In the **Site Bindings** dialog click **Close**.

6. Expand your site node, locate and click a folder (or select the site to enforce SSL on the site as a whole) that you wish to secure.

7. In the middle pane under **Features View**, double-click **SSL Settings**.

8. In the **SSL Settings** module check **Require SSL**, **Require 128-bit SSL**, and in the right-hand Actions pane click **Apply** (see Figure 5.22).

   - Most modern Web browsers support 128-bit SSL. This option was put in place because up until 2000 the United State government restricted the export of certain cryptographic algorithms, which left a good portion of the world stuck with 40- or 56-bit sessions, which provided a lesser degree of security.

Figure 5.22 SSL Settings Module Configuration

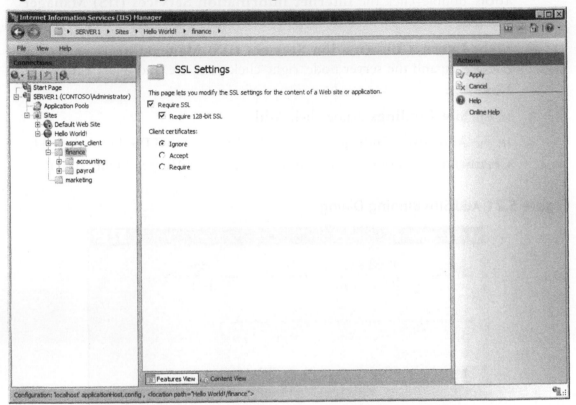

Authentication

Authentication is the process of asserting the identity of the user making a request to the Web server. With this identity we can track who is doing what and evaluate rules to determine if they are authorized to perform specific actions. IIS ships with several types of authentication modules that can be used to determine a user's identity:

- **Anonymous** Enabled by default to allow any user to access public content with a username and password.

- **Basic** Requires the user to provide a username and password. This authentication protocol is a standard across all platforms. It does not perform any sort of encryption with the information provided by the user. As such you should use it with SSL to ensure that the credentials are sent over a secure connection.

- **Digest** Similar to basic authentication but instead of sending the password in clear text it sends an MD5 hash across the wire, which is verified by the server. One of the disadvantages to this method is that it requires that the password be stored using reversible encryption. It is also vulnerable to man-in-the-middle attacks.

WARNING

The RFC-standard Digest authentication requires HTTP 1.1, and the password must be stored in reversible encryption within the security data store (Active Directory, local SAM). Advanced Digest gets around the reversible encryption by storing the hash in Active Directory, but it works only on Internet Explorer 5.0 or later.

- **Windows** Used mainly in intranet scenarios, it allows browsers to use the current user's Windows domain credentials to authenticate the connection. Under the covers it uses NTLM or Kerberos to handle the authentication.
- **Client Certificates** Users provide a digital certificate that is mapped to a user account.

With the exception of client certificates, enabling these authentication modules usually requires nothing more than toggling of their state to enabled. The options for most of the modules are limited to either identity impersonation options or default realms for authentication.

Follow these steps to enable basic authentication on a folder:

1. Open **Control Panel** and under **System and Maintenance | Administration Tools**, double-click the **Internet Information Services (IIS) Manager** shortcut.

2. In the **Internet Information Services (IIS) Manager** management console expand the server, site node, and locate a folder to secure (or choose the site as a whole) and click your selection.

3. In the middle pane under **Features View** double-click **Authentication**.

4. Right-click the **Basic Authentication** module and select **Enable** (see Figure 5.23).

Figure 5.23 Authentication Module Configuration

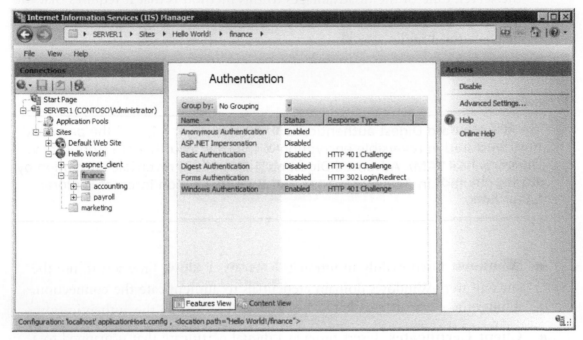

If you are using an ASP.NET runtime environment you have two other authentication modules that are specific to ASP.NET-based Web applications:

- **Forms** Enables you to provide a rich Web-based authentication and user registration experience.

- **ASP.NET Impersonation** Enables you to use a specific account, or the account specified by another IIS authentication module, to execute the application as opposed to the application pool identity.

These authentication modules have been available in ASP.NET since the 1.1 release of the .NET Framework. The IIS Manager exposes a number of the configuration options that traditionally have been managed through the ASP.NET tab in the previous release of IIS or directly in the web.config (see Figure 5.24).

Figure 5.24 Edit Forms Authentication Settings Dialog

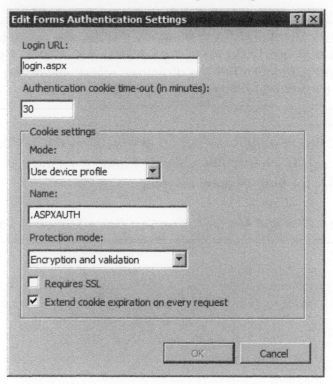

Considerations When Using Client Certificates

In the previous section you may have noticed some options around whether or not to ignore, accept, or require client certificates. These options are contained within the SSL Settings because the client certificate submission process is a part of the SSL module. This also means that you will need SSL enabled on sites and folders where you want to use client certificate mapping. When a client certificate is received it can be mapped back to a user account in one of three ways:

- **Active Directory Client Certificate Mapping** Looks to the local Active Directory domain to locate a match for the client certificate that was applied. Note that using this option requires that it be used across all sites on the server.

- **One-to-One Mapping** Allows you to specify through the configuration the identity to be used for the user with whom the certificate matches.

- **Many-to-One Mapping** Like one-to-one mapping it allows you to control through the configuration the user identity used when the certificate is matched. This method allows you to map multiple users to a single identity.

> **WARNING**
>
> Active Directory Client Certificate Mapping disables the ability to use one-to-one and many-to-one certificate mapping because it is able to resolve back to both users and groups within the directory, effectively doing the same thing as both one-to-one and many-to-one certificate mapping.

At the time of this writing there was no graphical interface to the one-to-one and many-to-one certificate mapping controls. Listing 5.1 shows an example of the configuration values for both of these mapping methods.

Listing 5.1 One-to-One and Many-to-One Certificate Mapping Configuration

```
<configuration>
...
<system.webServer>
  ...
  <security>
    ...
    <authentication>
      <iisClientCertificateMappingAuthentication enabled="true">
        <manyToOneMappings>
          <add name="FinanceUsers" description="Finance Users"
               enabled="true" permissionMode="Allow"
               userName="CONTOSO\FinanceDelegate" password="DF923uD@#2">
            <rules>
              <add certificateField="Subject"
                matchCriteria="john@contoso.com" />
              <add certificateField="Subject"
                matchCriteria="jane@contoso.com" />
              <add certificateField="Subject"
                matchCriteria="sam@contoso.com" />
              <add certificateField="Subject"
                matchCriteria="sally*@contoso.com" />
            </rules>
          </add>
        </manyToOneMappings>
        <oneToOneMappings>
          <add enabled="true" certificate="-----BEGIN CERTIFICATE-----
```

```
MIIBqDCCARECAQAwaTELMAkGA1UEBhMCVVMxDjAMBgNVBAgTBVRleGFzMRMwEQYD
VQQHEwpMYXNDb2xpbmFzMRIwEAYDVQQKEwlNaWNyb3NvZnQxDjAMBgNVBAsTBU10
ZWFtMREwDwYDVQQDFAhOVFZPT0RPTzCBnjANBgkqhkiG9w0BAQEFAAOBjAAwgYgC
gYBxmmAWKbLJHg5TuVyjgzWW0JsY5Shaqd7BDWtqhzy4HfRTW22f31rlm8NeSXHn
EhLiwsGgNzWHJ8no1QIYzAgpDR79oqxvgrY4WS3PXT7OLwIDAQABoAAwDQYJKoZI
hvcNAQEEBQADgYEAVcyI4jtnnV6kMiByiq4Xg99yL0U7bIpEwAf3MIZHS7wuNqfY
acfhbRj6VFHT8ObprKGPmqXJvwrBmPrEuCs4Ik6PidAAeEfoaa3naIbM73tTvKN+
WD301AfGBr8SZixLep4pMIN/wO0eu6f30cBuoPtDnDulNT8AuQHjkJIc8Qc=
-----END CERTIFICATE-----"
                userName="CONTOSO\FinanceDelegate" password="DF923uD@#2"
            </oneToOneMappings>
        </iisClientCertificateMappingAuthentication>
      </authentication>
      ...
    </security>
   ...
  </system.webServer>
 ...
</configuration>
```

Unlike the other two methods, enabling Active Directory Client Certificate is exposed through the graphical interface. The option is exposed at the server node level, and when it is set, it disables the ability to use one-to-one and many-to-one mappings on the server. To learn how to associate a certificate with an Active Directory user account refer to the Windows Server 2008 documentation around public key infrastructure.

Follow these steps to enable Active Directory Client Certificate mapping:

1. Open **Control Panel** and under **System and Maintenance | Administration Tools**, double-click the **Internet Information Services (IIS) Manager** shortcut,

2. In the **Internet Information Services (IIS) Manager** management console click the server node,

3. In the middle pane under **Features View** double-click **Authentication**.

4. Right-click the Active Directory Client Certificate Mapping module and select **Enable**.

Authorization

With the user's identity established the next step is to determine if the user can perform the action that is being requested. Authorization encompasses a set of rules that are evaluated based on a number of conditions, which could include the user's identity, to provide a decision as to whether or not to allow the user's request to be acted upon. IIS provides three core modules focused on authorization and supporting services—URL authorization, IP authorization, and request filtering.

URL Authorization

Originally brought into the IIS environment by ASP.NET, the URL Authorization module has been rewritten as a native IIS module to allow everyone to take advantage of an easy way of restricting access to specific folders and files. This module allows Web content managers the ability to control access in a manner similar to the use of NTFS permissions. Unlike NTFS permissions, you do not need file system access to the server to apply permissions since everything is managed through the web.config file stored at the root of the site or within a given folder. As well, this allows you to easily carry the permissions with the site as it moves environments. In the following steps, we'll show you how to restrict access to a folder:

1. Open **Control Panel** and under **System and Maintenance | Administration Tools,** double-click the **Internet Information Services (IIS) Manager** shortcut.

2. In the **Internet Information Services (IIS) Manager** management console expand the server, site node, and locate a folder to secure (or choose the site as a whole) and click your selection.

3. In the middle pane under **Features View** double-click **Authentication**.

4. On the **Authentication** page ensure that the **Anonymous Authentication** module is **Disabled**, select one of the other authentication modules, and click **Enable** in the right-hand **Actions** pane.

5. Click the Back arrow in the top left-hand corner.

6. On the folder page in the middle pane under **Features View**, double-click **Authorization Rules**.

7. On the **Authorization Rules** page click the **Add Allow Rule** in the right-hand action page.

8. Select the **Specified Users** radio button, provide a username, and click **OK** (see Figure 5.25).

Figure 5.25 Add Allow Authorization Rule Dialog

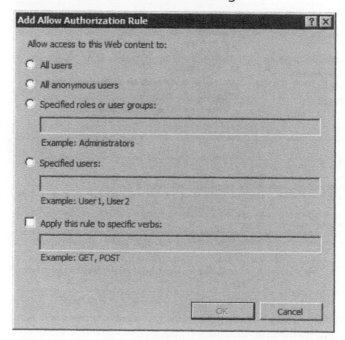

When users attempt to access a page to which they have been denied, they will receive a 401.2 unauthorized error. With the addition of detailed error requests the server-side error message gives you a number of useful elements to help you troubleshoot access denied issues being caused by URL authorization. As shown in Figure 5.26, you can see that we are dealing with the URL Authorization Module, that the file is a static file, along with the logon method and user account being used to access the URL.

Figure 5.26 Server-Side Version of Unauthorized Page Access Error Message

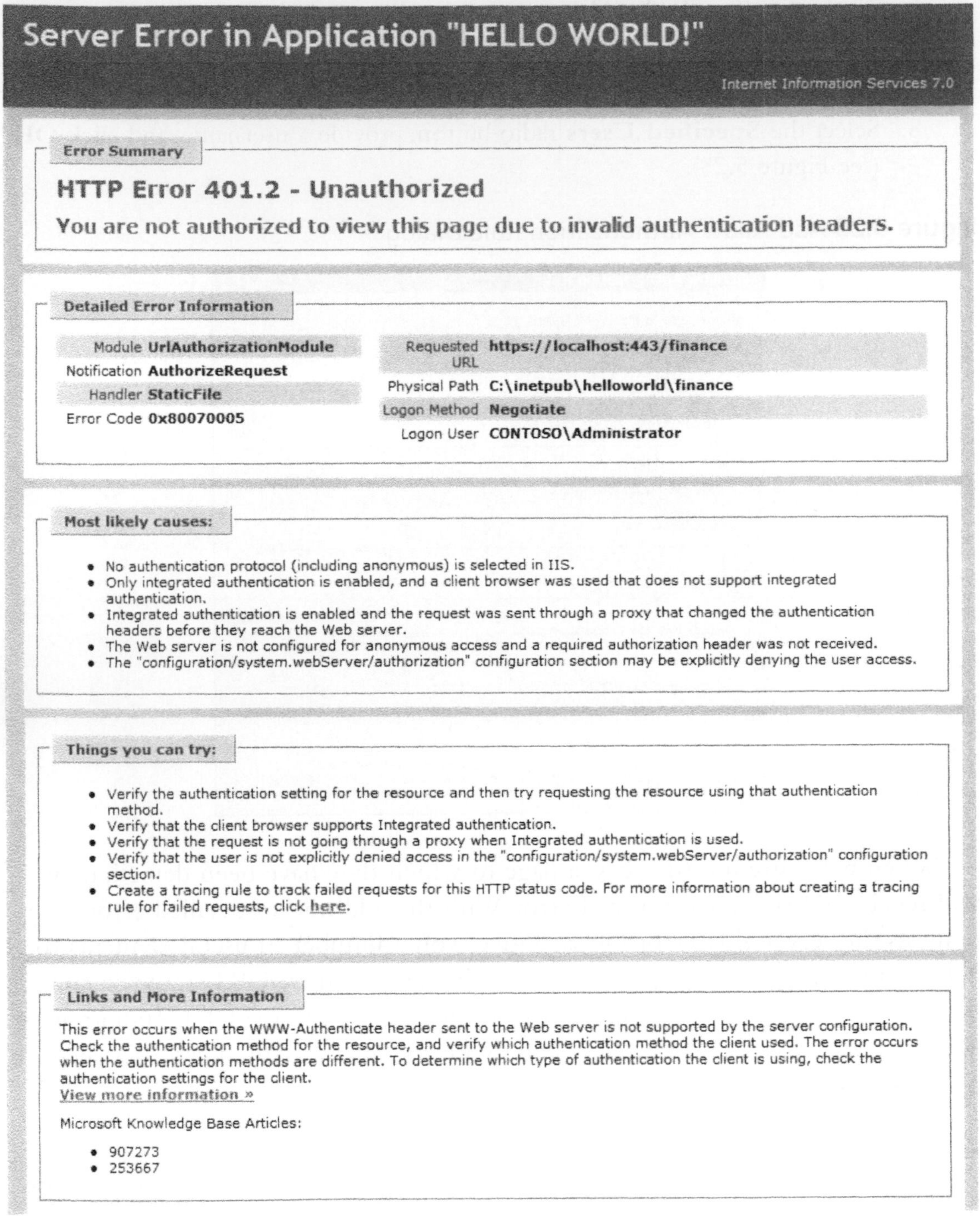

IP Authorization

The ability to restrict access to specific IP addresses has existed for quite some time across both servers and networking devices such as firewalls. In the past this function, like file permissions, was available only through IIS Manager and was tough to replicate across to other servers as it was stored in the metabase. This setting, along with all other configuration options, has been moved to the new XML-based configuration files. This allows you to centralize, copy, and manipulate the settings using new programming interfaces and command-line tools as well as the traditional graphical user interface.

Here are the steps to follow for restricting access to users based on their IP addresses.

1. Open **Control Panel** and under **System and Maintenance | Administration Tools**, double-click the **Internet Information Services (IIS) Manager** shortcut.

2. In the **Internet Information Services (IIS) Manager** management console expand the server, site node, and locate a folder to secure (or choose the site as a whole) and click your selection.

3. In the middle pane under **Features View**, double-click **IPv4 Address and Domain Restrictions**,

4. In the right-hand actions pane click **Add Deny Entry**.

5. In the **Add Deny Restriction Rule** dialog, select the **Specific IPv4 Address** radio button, provide an IP address (e.g. 127.0.0.1 if you want to test http://localhost) and click **OK**.

When users attempt to access a page to which they have been denied, they will receive a 403.6 forbidden error. Another option is to restrict users based on their domain names (see Figure 5.27). You will need to enable this through the Edit Feature Settings link in the module page on IIS. Be aware that the added overhead of DNS resolution for each IP address could negatively affect the performance of your application.

Figure 5.27 Add Allow Restriction Rule Dialog with Domain Restrictions Enabled

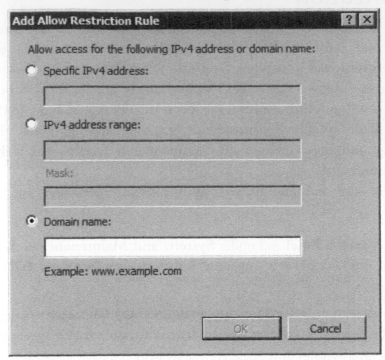

Configuring & Implementing...

Authorization Manager

You can use Authorization Manager in applications that require role-based authorization, such as ASP.NET Web applications, ASP.NET Web services, and client/server systems based on .NET Remoting. Windows Server 2008's enhanced version of Authorization Manager includes support for custom object pickers and business rule groups. Authorization Manager is also now capable of storing authorization stores in AD, SQL, or XML.

Request Filtering

Previously available through an add-on known as URLScan, the request filtering features provide an additional layer of security by inspecting incoming requests for seven different characteristics that might indicate a malformed or malicious attack:

- **Double-Encoded Requests** Attackers may encode a request twice to get around a first layer of filtering. This filter will detect it, reject the request, and log a 404.11 error.

- **High Bit Characters** You may choose to not want to accept non-ASCII characters (e.g., Unicode characters) because your application has not been tested or does not support it. This filter will detect the non-ASCII characters, reject the request, and log a 404.12 error.

- **File Extensions** Your Web application may contain certain files that you do not want anyone to download in any case (e.g., a DLL file in an ASP.NET application). You can add a list of allowed and denied extensions, which will cause IIS to reject the request and log a 404.7 error.

- **Request Limits** This filter will look at how long the content is in the request, the length of the URL, and more specifically the length of the query string. If any of those measurements exceed the maximum values provided this filter will reject the request and log a 404.13, 404.14, or 404.15, respectively.

- **Verbs** There are different types of requests that are identified using verbs (e.g., PUT, GET, and POST). If your application uses only specific types you can tell IIS to reject the request for other types and log a 404.6 error.

- **URL Sequences** There are certain character sequences that you may wish to never have in your request (e.g., a double period "…" often signifies someone trying to relatively traverse your folder structure). This filter will reject requests that match the sequences and log a 404.5 error.

- **Hidden Segments** This filter will enable you to reject requests for content from certain segments. Listing 4.7 contains an example where the bin folder has been specified causing IIS to reject requests that contains the bin folder in the URL. Note that the filter is able to distinguish between a request for http://contoso.com/bin/somefile.dll and http://contoso.com/binary/somefile.zip. The latter request would be allowed through because the filter looks at the URL segment as a whole. It will reject the first request and log a 404.8 error.

Unfortunately IIS Manager does not expose these configuration values. If you want to enable request filtering and tune it to your environment you will need to do it directly in the configuration file or through one of the programmatic APIs. Listing 5.2 shows a sample excerpt of the configuration settings.

Listing 5.2 Request Filtering Configuration Example

```
<configuration>
  ...
  <system.webServer>
    ...
    <security>
      ...
      <requestFiltering allowDoubleEscaping="false"
                        allowHighBitCharacters="true"
                        maxAllowedContentLength="1024768"
                        maxQueryString="64"
                        maxUrl="260">
        <denyUrlSequences>
          <add sequence=".."/>
        </denyUrlSequences>
        <fileExtensions allowUnlisted="true" >
          <add fileExtension=".dll" allowed="false"/>
          <add fileExtension=".xml" allowed="false"/>
        </fileExtensions>
        <hiddenSegments>
          <add segment="BIN"/>
        </hiddenSegments>
        <verbs allowUnlisted="false">
          <add verb="GET" allowed="true" />
          <add verb="PUT" allowed="false" />
        </verbs>
      </requestFiltering>
      ...
    </security>
    ...
  </system.webServer>
  ...
</configuration>
```

Even though you may have to work with the application developer to gain necessary input, this module in particular is extremely useful in reducing the attack surface of your Web application. It is recommended that you take the time to take full advantage of the filters offered by this module.

.NET Trust Levels

With a number of new IIS features based around the .NET Framework it is important to understand how .NET Trust Levels impact your Web applications and IIS itself. A trust level conveys a policy of permissions that an application is allowed to perform. Each trust level has a different set of permissions applied. By default the policies build upon one another from Minimal, which can do very few things to Full, which can perform a number of things:

- **Full Trust** The application is able to execute anything with the security bounds granted to the process identity.

- **High Trust** Restricts applications from calling unmanaged code (e.g., Windows APIs, COM objects, etc.), writing to the event log, message queues, or databases.

- **Medium Trust** Restricts the application from navigating any part of the file system except its own application directory, accessing the registry, or making network and Web service calls.

- **Low Trust** Restricts the application from writing to the file system.

- **Minimal** Restricts the code to doing basic algorithmic work.

If the out-of-the-box trust levels do not suffice application developers can define a custom trust policy based on a series of intrinsic and custom permissions. For a complete list of permissions see the .NET Framework Developer's Guide at http://msdn2.microsoft.com/en-us/library/5ba4k1c5.aspx.

WARNING

The trust levels and permissions system, known as Code Access Security, is confusing to many developers as well as administrators. Think of the policies as another type of access control list (ACL) with individual access control entries (ACE) that allow or deny you from performing an action on a resource. The resources can vary from external services, such as databases and Web services, to internal Windows subsystems, such as the registry, event log, and file system.

The trust level that you chose for an application should be sufficient for it to function, but like all good security practices, not excessive beyond the needs of the application. In most environments application developers will communicate the level of trust their application needs. As IT professionals understanding what that means helps us understand the boundaries in which the application can function in the server environment. The trust levels can be set at the site and folder level. It is most practical, however, to set it at the level a Web application is defined or the root of the site.

Summary

Protecting data is extremely important for companies in the global marketplace today, and many of these companies' networks are based on Microsoft infrastructure. A Windows server provides a number of useful functions in a company's network infrastructure. BitLocker is Microsoft's answer to providing better security by encrypting the data stored on the drive's operating system volume, and is available only in the Enterprise and Ultimate versions of Vista. This new security feature goes a long way toward helping users and organizations protect their data.

AD RMS protects information when it is connected and when it is not connected to the corporate network. A usage policy is bound to the protected item so that no matter where it travels the rights are enforced to ensure that only the authorized recipient is able to access the contents. The policy can restrict users from actions such as viewing, copying, forwarding, and printing.

Authorization encompasses a set of rules that are evaluated based on a number of conditions, which could include the user's identity, to provide a decision as to whether or not to allow the user's request to be acted upon. IIS provides three core modules focused on authorization and supporting services—URL authorization, IP authorization, and request filtering.

Solutions Fast Track

BitLocker

☑ BitLocker is Microsoft's answer to providing better security by encrypting the data stored on the drive's operating system volume

☑ You can set up BitLocker in three configurations: TPM only, TPM and USB flash drive, and TPM and PIN.

☑ To use a BitLocker-enabled system, the key must be stored in RAM while the system is up and running. Universities have found that when a system is shut down, it's possible to retrieve the key from RAM for up to several minutes, giving a hacker complete control over the entire system and all files stored on the drive. The main way to avoid this, of course, is to never leave a system unattended in an unsecured area in the first place. The next step is to completely shut down the system so that the RAM can be allowed to fully discharge.

Active Directory Rights Management Services

☑ Previously shipped as an add-on for Windows Server, AD RMS is now included out-of-the-box as a role in Windows Server 2008.

☑ AD RMS is a format- and application-agnostic service designed to safeguard information by deterring inadvertent sharing of information with unauthorized people.

☑ When you set up AD RMS it will trust your organization's Active Directory domain by default. Depending on your business requirements you can expand or contract the boundaries of your RMS trust to specific user domains within your organization or other organizations.

Authorization

☑ Authorization encompasses a set of rules that are evaluated based on a number of conditions, which could include the user's identity, to provide a decision as to whether or not to allow the user's request to be acted upon.

☑ IIS provides three core modules focused on authorization and supporting services—URL authorization, IP authorization, and request filtering.

☑ Previously available through an add-on known as URLScan, the request filtering module provides an additional layer of security by inspecting incoming requests for seven different characteristics that might indicate a malformed or malicious attack.

Frequently Asked Questions

Q: I want to use BitLocker but my motherboard doesn't have a TPM. Is it still possible to enable BitLocker?

A: Yes. The default BitLocker configurations will have to be modified to use a USB flash drive.

Q: I have a media file that uses Digital Rights Management. How can I remove the DRM protection from the file?

A: It's impossible to remove the DRM protection from any file that has been created with it.

Q: Does Rights Management work with mobile devices?

A: Yes, there is a mobile module for Rights Management Services. However, only Windows Mobile devices are supported with Rights Management. Check with your wireless vendor or mobile manufacturer for support and availability on particular models.

Chapter 6

Microsoft Windows Server 2008: Networking Essentials

Solutions in this chapter:

- Not Your Father's TCP/IP Stack
- The Network and Sharing Center
- Network Map

☑ Summary

☑ Solutions Fast Track

☑ Frequently Asked Questions

Introduction

In this chapter, we'll look at how IP addressing is configured in the Windows Server 2008 environment, and we'll also explore the related IP services. In addition we discuss using the Network and Sharing Center and Network Map.

Not Your Father's TCP/IP Stack

Before TCP/IP there was the 1822 Protocol, which was developed in 1969 for the Advanced Research Projects Agency (ARPA) of the U.S. Department of Defense. In 1973 Vint Cerf and Bob Kahn took the existing protocols and rebuilt them into what we now know as TCP/IP version 4. These protocols became the foundation of what we now use on the Internet.

In TCP/IP version 4 (IPv4) we had a 32-bit address space that would support approximately 4.9 billion addresses. This was more than enough for the ARPA network (ARPANET) that they were working on. In the early days of the APRANET one computer was added every 20 days. In the 70's and 80's there was no question of running out of addresses on this private network used by the government and university research facilities to share data. In 1990 the responsibility for the network was transferred to the National Science Foundation and became the NSFNET. Although government and universities still shared the network, National Science Foundation added six supercomputers, and opened up its use to high-tech companies as well.

In 1995 the National Science Foundation offered the backbone of the network to a communications company, who would then have control of the NSFNET and thereby make it a for-profit network. The company purchased part of the backbone and other companies were able to purchase pieces, thus creating the Internet as we know it today.

Once the Internet became a for-profit network of interconnected networks, it became apparent that the public address space of IPv4 was not sufficient to meet the demands of a global network. The use of standards like network address translation (NAT) bought time while a new standard was developed. This new standard became IPv6, the next generation of Internet Protocol addressing.

Notes from the Underground...

TCP/IP: The Next Generation

Windows Server 2008 includes the following new features:

- A dual-layer IP architecture for IPv6
- Support for a strong host model and for scaling on multiprocessor computers
- New packet filtering and security for APIs
- Support for a kernel-mode programming interface, called Winsock Kernel, which was designed to replace the transport driver interface (TDI) in Windows XP and Windows Server 2003
- Routing compartments and new mechanisms for protocol stack overloads

For a full discussion of the changes to the TCP/IP implementation in Windows Server 2008 read Microsoft's TechNet article located at www.microsoft.com/technet/community/columns/cableguy/cg0905.mspx.

Introduction of IPv6 and Dual Stack

The dual-stack architecture of IPv6 allows for the running of IPv6 and IPv4 at the same time. If both endpoints are capable of communicating on IPv6, they will. If either of the endpoints cannot use IPv6, they will fall back to IPv4. This makes the transition to IPv6 smoother as both endpoints do not have to be native IPv6 all at once.

IPv6 Addressing Conventions

IPv6 uses a 128-bit address space. The first 64 bits are the network portion and the remaining 64bits are the host portion of the address. The first 16 bits will determine the address type.

The main types of addresses are unicast, multicast, and anycast.

Unicast addresses are used for endpoint-to-endpoint communications and can be site local, link local or globally routable address. If communication between endpoints is internal and access to the Internet is not required, then site or link local addresses can be used. If connection to the Internet is required, then globally routable address are to be used.

IPv6 Assigned Unicast Routable Address Prefixes

Here is a list of IPv6 assigned Unicast routable address prefixes.

- **Prefix (Hex)** Description
- **2001::/16** IPv6 Internet
- **2002::/16** IPv6 to IPv4 transition mechanisms
- **2003::/16 3FFD::/16** Unassigned (for future use)
- **3FFE::/16** 6Bone

As you can see there is a tremendous address space. Anycast addressing became the replacement for broadcast. Broadcast packets were a misnomer under IPv4 as the destination address 255.255.255.255, the universal broadcast, was never truly a broadcast to all stations on all networks. Routers in each network stop the passing of broadcast packets, keeping them on the network that they originated on. These packets were really only able to talk to "any device" on my network, so they renamed them anycast.

There are some special addresses reserved for specific uses on networks—for example, loopback, internal-only networks, and so on.

A few of the special addresses include the following:

- **::1/128 (or just ::1)** Local loopback address, refers to the local computer.
- **::FFFF:0:0/96** Prefix used for IPv4 mapped addresses.
- **::0/128** Used to point to the default gateway for your system.
- **FE80::/64** A local-link address. Seeing this address assigned to an interface indicates there was no DHCPv6 server available.

IPv6 Auto-Configuration Options

Depending on how your IPv6 routers are set up, auto-configuration of an IPv6 client can happen in three ways: stateless, stateful, or both. In *stateless* mode, an IPv6 client configures its own IPv6 address by using IPv6 router advertisements. In *stateful* mode, an IPv6 client will get its addressing information from a Dynamic Host Conversion Protocol version 6 (DHCPv6) server when it receives router advertisement messages with no prefix options (and when certain other conditions are met). This also occurs if no IPv6 routers are available. The *both* option uses stateful and stateless together. The most common example of this is an IPv6 client using stateless auto-configuration to obtain an IPv6 address and using stateful auto-configuration to get DNS and other IP configuration information from a DHCPv6 server.

In addition, addresses can be nontemporary (the equivalent of static IP addresses in IPv4) or temporary. Routers, gateways, and other devices may need these types of addresses and, just as with IPv4, you can allow a host to auto-configure or you can manually set up the IPv6 addressing.

IPv6 Transition Technologies

Because the transition to IPv6 won't happen overnight (or even anytime soon), there are numerous ways companies can transition to IPv6. Some options are provided in the list below. For more information, you can visit the Microsoft Web site and query for the title "IPv6 Transition Technologies." The following list includes some options for transitioning to IPv6:

- **Dual IP Layer architecture** Allows computers to communicate using both IPv6 and IPv4. This is required for ISATAP and Teredo hosts, and for 6to4 routers.

- **IPv6 over IPv4 tunneling** Places IPv6 packet data inside an IPv4 header with an IP value of 41. This tunneling technique is used with either ISATAP or 6to4.

- **Intra-Site Automatic Tunnel Addressing Protocol (ISATAP)** Allows IPv6 hosts to use IPv6 over IPv4 tunneling to communicate on intranets.

- **6to4** Allows IPv6 hosts to communicate with the IPv6-based Internet. A 6to4 router with a public IPv4 address is required.

- **Teredo** Allows IPv4/IPv6 hosts to communicate with the IPv6-based Internet even if they are behind a network address translator (NAT).

Configuring IPv6 Settings

The first time you log on to a Windows 2008 server you will get the server manager screen shown in Figure 6.1.

Figure 6.1 Server Manager on Windows Server 2008

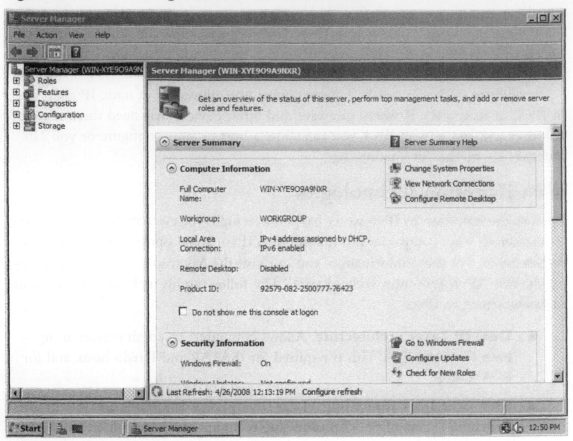

You can go directly to the Network Connections Control Panel Page (see Figure 6.2) using the Computer Information Section of the Server Summary.

Figure 6.2 The Network Connections Control Panel

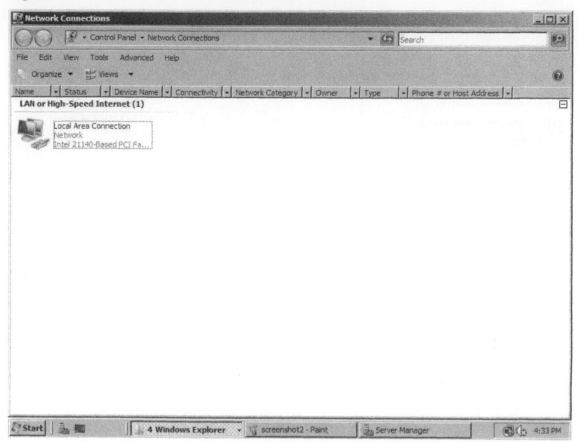

In the Network Connections Control Panel you will find your Ethernet and Wireless network connections. Right-click on the connection you wish to work with and select **Properties** from the pop-up menu (see Figure 6.3).

Figure 6.3 Selecting a Connection

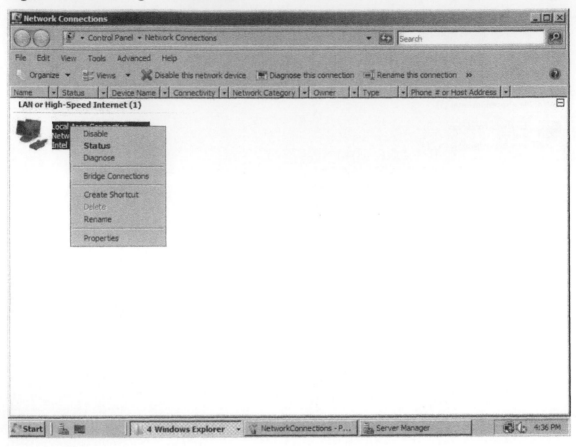

Once you have selected Properties, the screen shown in Figure 6.4 will appear.

Figure 6.4 Local Area Connection Properties

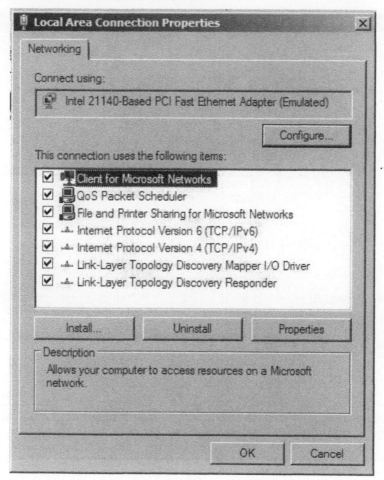

From the Networking tab you can set the options for IPv6 (see Figure 6.5).

Figure 6.5 IPv6 Properties

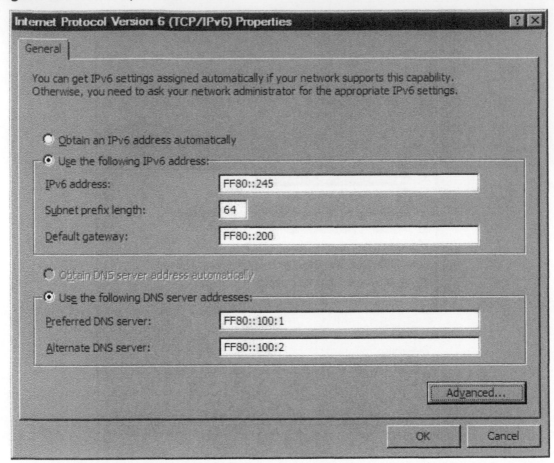

As with IPv4, you would typically allow host computers to obtain an IPv6 address automatically from the DHCP server. However, since this computer is a server, you may want to assign a nontemporary IP address to it. (Recall that nontemporary is the IPv6 equivalent of a static IP address in IPv4.) If you choose to use a nontemporary address, you could click the radio button next to the **Use the following IPv6 address** option and enter the specifics. Also remember that if you set a nontemporary IP address here, you should create a reservation for this address in the DHCP server so that this address does not get assigned to another computer on the network. Best practices typically include creating your DHCP server scope and reservations before activating the DHCP server, then activating the DHCP server and assigning nontemporary (and static) IP addresses. This helps avoid potential problems with IP address assignments.

Using the Network and Sharing Center

The network section of Windows Server 2008 has been completely revamped. Network settings in Windows Server 2008 are now managed in the Network and Sharing Center (see Figure 6.6). In previous Microsoft operating systems such as Windows 2000, XP, and 2003, network settings were configured in My Network Places. The Network and Sharing Center has many new features not available in My Network Places.

Figure 6.6 The Network and Sharing Center

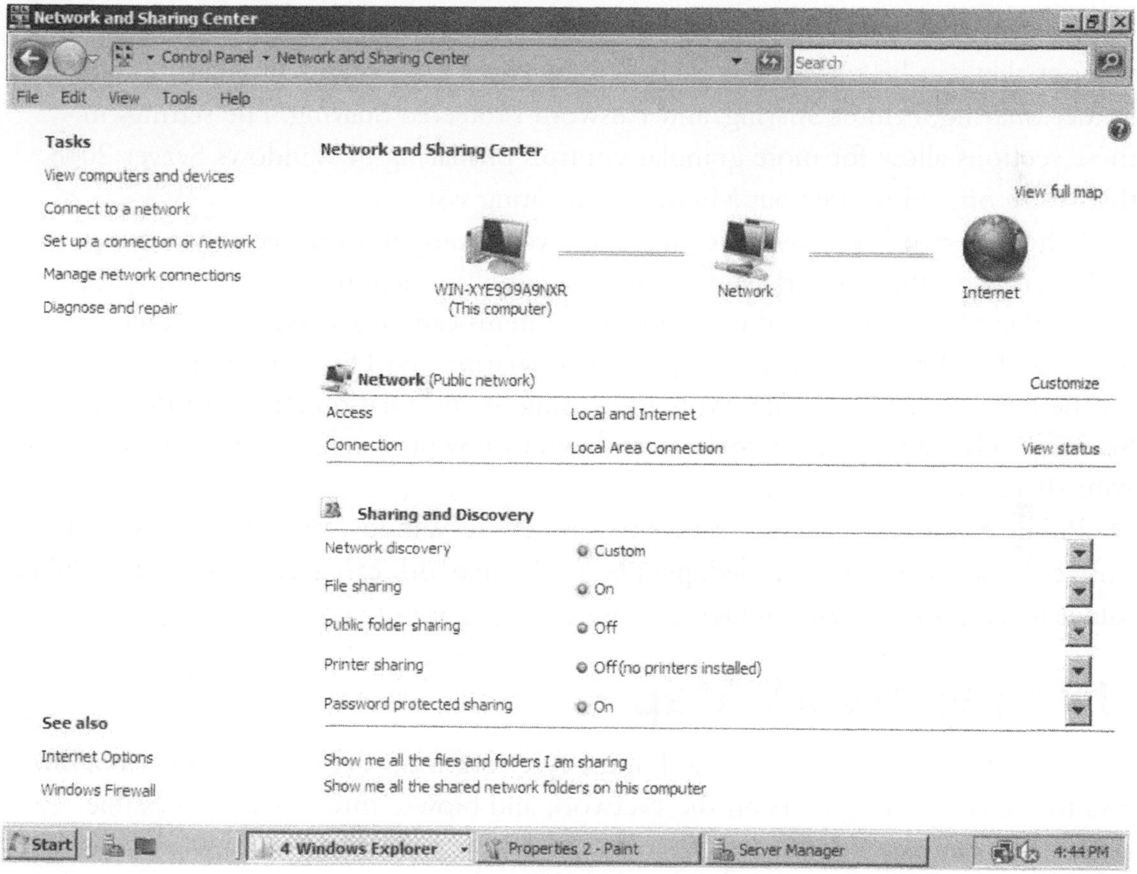

Are You Owned?

Security and Shared Folders

One feature of the Network and Sharing Center is the "Show me all the files and folders I am sharing". This feature will display any shared information from your server that will be available to users on the network. You should run this occasionally to make sure you are not vulnerable due to improper sharing properties and permissions.

The Sharing and Discovery section of the Network and Sharing Center has five sections that can be configured, including Network Discovery, File Sharing, Public Folder Sharing, Printer Sharing, and Password Protected Sharing. The settings in these sections allow for more granular controls of sharing in Windows Server 2008 than were offered in previous Microsoft operating systems.

When Network Discovery is turned on, your computer can see other computers and devices on the network, and those devices will be able to see your computer. When File Sharing is turned on, your shared items can be accessed by people on the network. The Printer Sharing component of Sharing and Discovery will allow people on the network to use printers you are sharing. If you turn on Password Protected Sharing, only people with a computer account on your system will be able to access your shares and shared devices.

Public Folder Sharing is a feature that is new to Windows Server 2008. When Public Folder Sharing is enabled, people on the network can access files in the Public folder located in the Users folder.

Using Network Map

The View Computers and Devices link in Network Map (see Figure 6.6) will allow you to see other computers on the Network and browse through any accessible shares. You can also use this link to add a printer or a wireless device to your network, as well as reaccess the Network and Sharing Center. Double-clicking on a computer will display any shares available to you on that device (see Figure 6.7).

Figure 6.7 Shares Available on a Computer Device

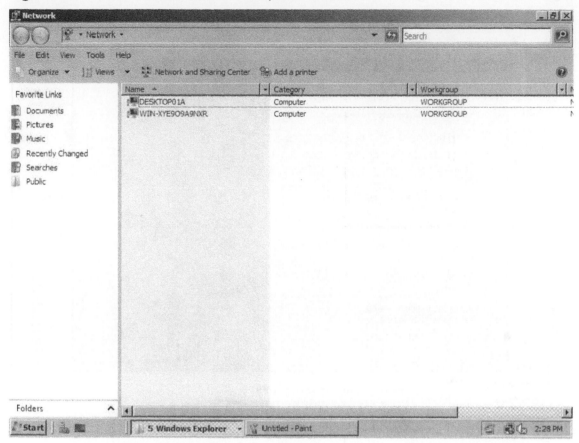

Connect to a Network

If you select Connect to a network from the Network and Sharing Center and you have not created any other networks or connections, the screen shown in Figure 6.8 will appear.

Figure 6.8 Connecting to a Network

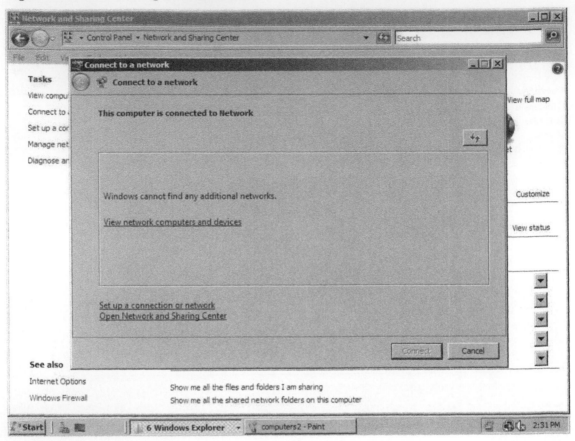

From this screen you can view the network map (see Figure 6.8) or you can set up a VPN, wireless, or dial-up network connection.

Select the type of network connection you wish to set up and follow the prompts. For example, to set up a VPN connection to the workplace, click on **Connect to a workplace** and click **Next** (see Figure 6.9).

Figure 6.9 Selecting a Type of Network Connection

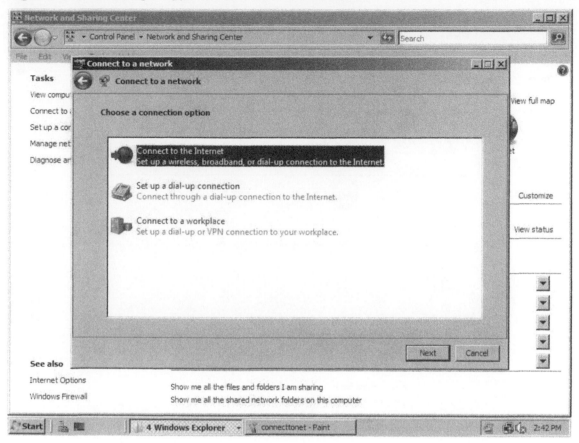

The Connect to a network dialog box gives you the option of using your existing Internet connection to create the VPN or dialing directly to the remote facility (see Figure 6.10).

Figure 6.10 Options for a VPN Connection

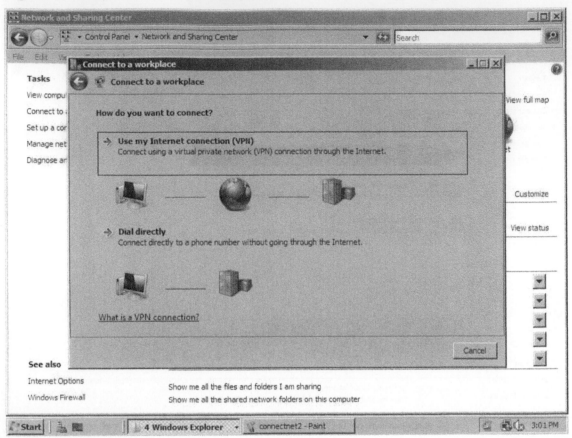

Use my Internet connection is the default option. On the next screen you can enter the address of the destination (see Figure 6.11). You have three options to entering the destination:

- **Fully Qualified Domain Name** vpn.syngress.com
- **IPv4 IP Address** 192.168.21.4
- **IPv6 IP Address** 2001::2041:1284:99af

Figure 6.11 Entering the Address of Your Destination

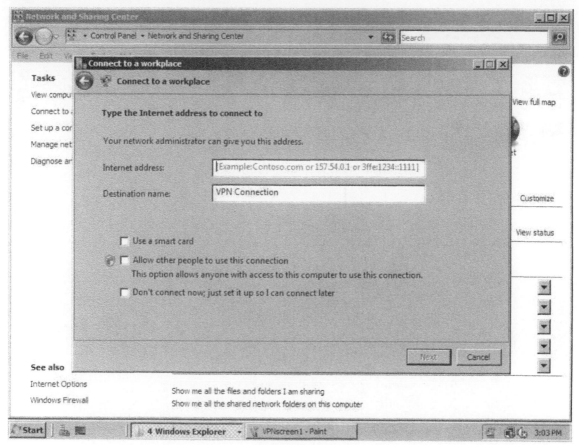

Also, if your company uses Smart Card technology, you can select that here in the **Connect to a workplace** dialog box. The **Set up a connection or network** will take you to the aforementioned options as well.

Manage Network Connections

From the Network Connections screen, shown in Figure 6.12, you can work with network hardware settings such as network cards, wireless adapters, and other connections you have created on the system.

You can also modify VPN connections from this screen if you have configured any VPN connections.

Figure 6.12 Working with Network Hardware Settings

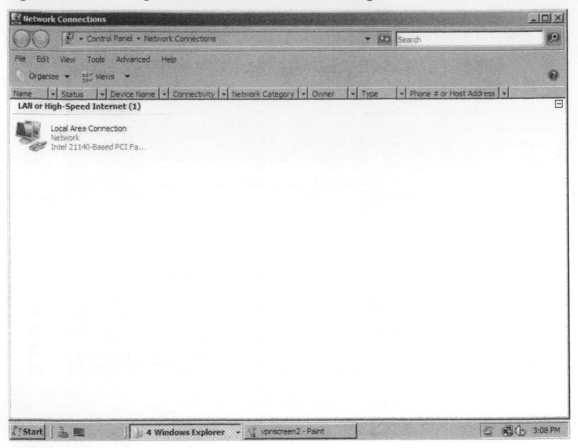

Diagnose and Repair

The Diagnose and Repair link will attempt a probe to see if you are able to connect to the Internet. If Windows is able to connect to the Internet without any problem, Diagnose and Repair will inform you that Windows did not find any problems with your Internet Connection, as seen in Figure 6.12. If a problem is found, Diagnose and Repair will inform you that the computer is unable to communicate with the Microsoft Web site. The Windows Network Diagnostics message will then give suggestions to try to fix the problem (see Figure 6.13).

Figure 6.13 The Diagnose and Repair Link

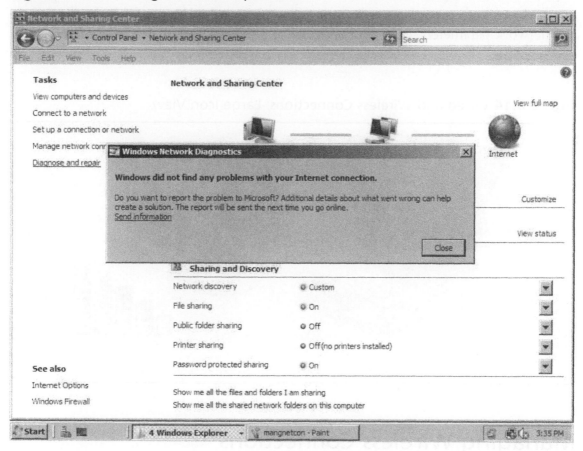

In summary, the Network and Sharing Center is a redesigned feature for Windows Server 2008 that allows users to easily manage their network settings from one convenient location. Networking is playing a more vital role in home networks today. The Network and Sharing Center simplifies network administration of computers. As more devices start to become networked with our home computer systems, such as videogame consoles, simplifying the way devices can be networked together is even more important to the consumer.

Managing Wired Connections

Managing Ethernet connections in Windows Server 2008 is similar to managing wired connections in Windows XP and Windows Server 2003. Start by clicking on the **Network and Sharing Center** in the Control Panel. Click the **Manage Network Connections** link from the list in the task pane. All Ethernet network connections are displayed with an RJ-45 connection at the bottom. In contrast, wireless connections are displayed with green bars, indicating signal strength (see Figure 6.14). To check any network parameters, click on the device and select **Change settings of this connection**.

Figure 6.14 Wired and Wireless Connections: Large Icon View

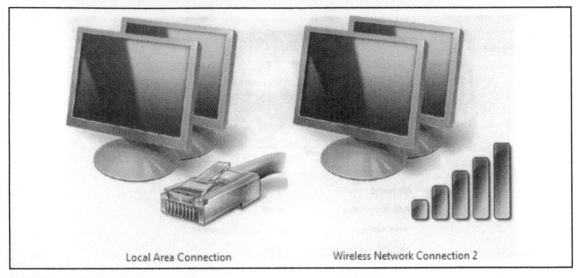

Local Area Connection   Wireless Network Connection 2

Managing Wireless Connections

One major improvement of Windows Server 2008 over Windows XP and Windows Server 2003 is more control over your wireless settings. There were two major security issues with wireless on previous Microsoft operating systems. One issue was connecting to unsecured networks automatically, and the other issue was firewall settings that might leave a user vulnerable in a hotspot. Windows XP systems have a bad habit of automatically connecting to wireless networks within their range. Although the default wireless settings of XP can be changed, the fact that it connects to unsecured networks by default is somewhat disturbing. Another limitation of XP (and 2003) is the fact that your firewall settings will remain the same when migrating from your home network to a hotspot. This is extremely alarming if the user happens to have open shares with sensitive documents. While this example may seem far-fetched, it is very common for users to have open shares on their system at work or home, and then migrate to a hotspot. A malicious user at the hotspot could access files in any of your shares.

And, if there is no password on the administrative account, that malicious user may even be able to access the administrative shares.

To manage wireless connections in Windows Server 2008, open **Network and Sharing Center** in the Control Panel. Click on the **Manage Wireless Networks** link from the list in the task pane. Clicking the **Add** button will give you a menu of three items, including **Add a network that is in range of the computer**, **Manually create a network profile**, and **Create an ad-hoc network**.

The **Add a network that is in range** option in Manage Wireless Connections will display a list of networks that are broadcasting their Security Set Identifier (SSID). Along with each network displayed will be information about whether the network has security enabled or if it is unsecured. Windows Server 2008 will warn you that your information may be visible to others if you connect to an unsecured network. Unless you are on a secure site, people using sniffing tools such as Wireshark will be able to capture all of your plain text data. Microsoft recommends using WPA2 if your equipment will support it. There is a list of other wireless recommendations made by Microsoft in a TechNet article, located at http://technet.microsoft.com/en-us/library/bb727047.aspx. It is common knowledge among wireless security experts that WiFi Protected Access version 2 (WPA2) with Advanced Encryption Standard (AES) encryption and a very difficult passphrase should be used on wireless networks. While Wired Equivalent Privacy (WEP) or WPA with Temporal Key Integrity Protocol (TKIP) is better than nothing, these security mechanisms can be defeated.

The **Manually create a network profile** option in Manage Wireless Networks can be utilized if a network is not broadcasting its SSID. Turning off the broadcast of the SSID will help to prevent people from connecting to your network. If you are not broadcasting the SSID of your access point, users will not see the network in their list of available networks to connect to in Windows XP or Windows Server 2008. While turning off the broadcast of the SSID will help increase the security of your wireless, it will not prevent hackers with the right tools from getting the information. Even if the access point is not broadcasting the SSID, security measures such as the use of WPA2 with AES encryption and a strong passphrase should also be utilized.

The **Create an ad-hoc network** is the final option when adding a network in Manage Wireless Networks. The ad hoc network will allow a group of computers to network without an available access point. In Windows Server 2008, you can set up an ad hoc network with no encryption, WEP, or WPA2, as seen in Figure 6.12. WPA2 is recommended, and your WPA2 passphrase can be from 8 to 63 characters long. Numbers, symbols, and uppercase and lowercase letters can all be utilized in the passphrase. Note: It can be up to 64 characters long if you only use the numeric characters 0 to 9 and letters A to F. The characters can be displayed for you in plain text if you check the **Display characters** check box, as seen in Figure 6.15.

Figure 6.15 WPA2 Passphrase for an Ad Hoc Network Set Up in Windows Server 2008

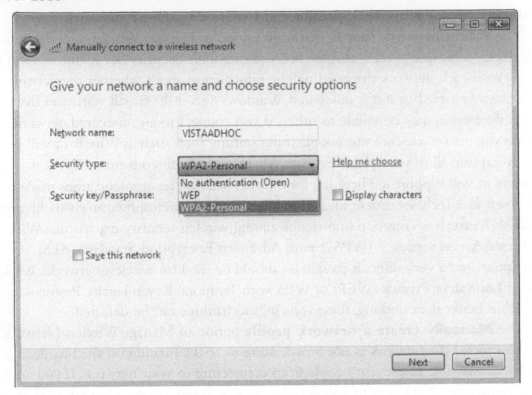

With Windows Server 2008, there is a strange option that is displayed after you set up an ad hoc network. After users finish setting up an ad hoc network, they are asked if they wish to set up Internet Connection Sharing, as seen in Figure 6.16.

TIP

The Windows Server 2008 operating system supports open, WEP, and WPA2 encryption schemes. WPA2 is the strongest encryption method to use. Microsoft does not recommend connecting to open wireless networks in Windows Server 2008.

Figure 6.16 Internet Connection Sharing with Ad Hoc Network Set Up

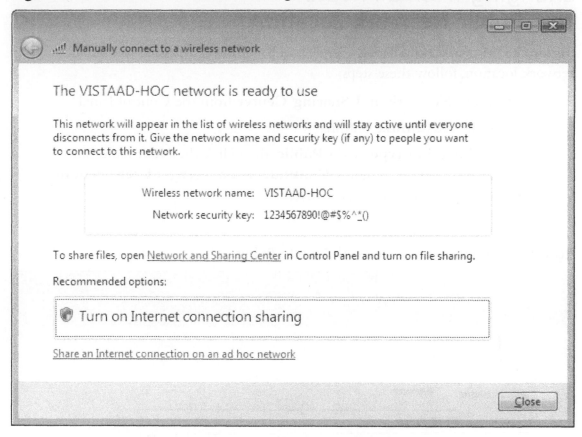

The reason that this is most likely recommended by Microsoft, as seen in Figure 6.16, is that users connecting to this network will receive an IP address of 192.168.0.X from the DHCP service that coincides with enabling Internet Connection Sharing (ICS). If ICS were not enabled, users would receive an Automatic Private IP Address, or APIPA. Automatic Private IP Addresses are in the 169.254.X.X range. Normally, users do not have Internet access when they are setting up an ad hoc network. However, if a user has more than one network card in their system, it could be possible. The danger here, however, is if the user provides a gateway to the Internet for other users, the person could potentially be providing illegal Internet services for others connecting to the wireless network.

Changing from a Private to a Public Network Location

To use the Network and Sharing Center to change from a private to a public network location, follow these steps:

1. Open the **Network and Sharing Center** from the Control Panel.

2. Click the **Customize** button.

3. Under **Location type**, select **Public**, then click the **Next** radio button, as seen in Figure 6.17. Click **Continue** if you receive a **User account Control** pop-up box. Click **Close**.

Figure 6.17 Changing the Network Type to Public

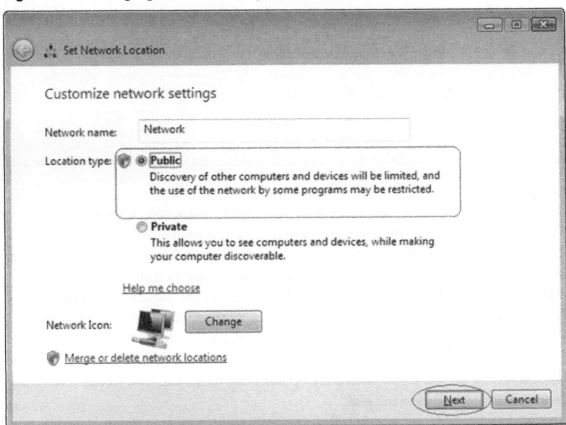

Other Troubleshooting Methods

If the Windows Network Diagnostics does not report any problems, your computer should be able to connect to the Internet without a problem. If you receive a report, try all of the suggested steps to see if the problem can be fixed. Those steps include unplugging your cable modem and waiting for it to come back online.

If you are connected to a gateway, try to ping the gateway. Use the network map to find the IP address of the gateway on your network. Open a command prompt by typing **cmd** in the start search box. Then type **ping** followed by the IP address of the gateway. An example would be **ping 192.168.1.1**. If you cannot ping the gateway, check the settings of your network interface in Windows Server 2008 and on the router. If you can ping the gateway, try pinging www.yahoo.com. If you are able to ping www.yahoo.com, your settings should be good and you should be able to access the Internet. If you are getting a message that the name cannot be resolved, it is most likely an issue with DNS. Check the DNS settings of your network interface in Windows Server 2008 and on the router. If all else fails, try rebooting the system.

Summary

In this chapter we reviewed IPv6 addressing capabilities. We also looked at the Server Manager in Windows Server 2008 and its abilities to work with network configuration. We toured the Network and Sharing Center, where we saw how to set up a VPN connection, how to see what files and folders were shared, as well as how to diagnose and troubleshoot network problems.

We then looked at wireless networking options and how to safely use 802.11 wireless networking in our network. And lastly, we looked at general network troubleshooting and diagnostic solutions.

Solutions Fast Track

Not Your Father's TCP/IP Stack

☑ In TCP/IP version 4 (IPv4) we had a 32-bit address space that would support approximately 4.9 billion addresses.

☑ The dual stack architecture of IPv6 allows for the running of IPv6 and IPv4 at the same time.

☑ IPv6 uses a 128-bit address space. The first 64 bits are the network portion and the remaining 64 bits are the host portion of the address.

The Network and Sharing Center

☑ The Network section of Windows Server 2008 has been completely revamped. Network settings in Windows Server 2008 are now managed in the Network and Sharing Center.

☑ The Sharing and Discovery section of the Network and Sharing Center has five sections that can be configured: Network Discovery, File Sharing, Public Folder Sharing, Printer Sharing, and Password Protected Sharing.

☑ Public Folder Sharing is a feature that is new to Windows Server 2008. When Public Folder Sharing is enabled, people on the network can access files in the Public folder located in the Users folder.

Network Map

☑ The View Computers and Devices link in Network Map will allow you to see other computers on the network and browse through any accessible shares.

☑ The View Computers and Devices link also enables you to add a printer or a wireless device to your network, as well as reaccess the Network and Sharing Center.

☑ With Network Map, you can work with network hardware settings, like network cards, wireless adapters, and other connections you have created on the system.

Frequently Asked Questions

Q: Are the networking features in Windows Server 2003 more secure than previous operating systems?

A: Yes, Microsoft has included new security features including native support for Ipv6, which can use IPSec encryption between endpoints.

Q: Is wireless support more secure in Windows Server 2008 than in previous operating systems?

A: Yes, with the support for WPA2 encryption you can make your wireless more secure.

Q: Are the networking features of Windows Server 2008 easier to configure and troubleshoot?

A: Yes, with the Network and Sharing Center you have an easier interface to work with all aspects of networking. Also, with the Diagnose and Troubleshoot Wizard it is easier to solve basic networking problems.

Chapter 7

Microsoft Windows Server 2008: Server Core

Solutions in this chapter:

- Server Core Features
- Server Core Components
- Server Core Best Practices
- Server Core Administration

☑ Summary

☑ Solutions Fast Track

☑ Frequently Asked Questions

Introduction

What is Server Core, you ask? It's the "just the facts, ma'am" version of Windows 2008. Microsoft defines Server Core as "a minimal server installation option for Windows Server 2008 that contains a subset of executable files, DLLs and services, and nine server roles." Server Core provides only the binaries needed to support the roles and the base operating system. By default, fewer processes are generally running.

Server Core is so drastically different from what we have come to know with Windows Server NT, Windows Server 2000, or even Windows Server 2003 over the past decade-plus that it looks more like MS-DOS than anything else (see Figure 7.1). Within Server Core, you won't find Windows Explorer, Internet Explorer, a Start menu, or even a clock!

Figure 7.1 The Server Core Console

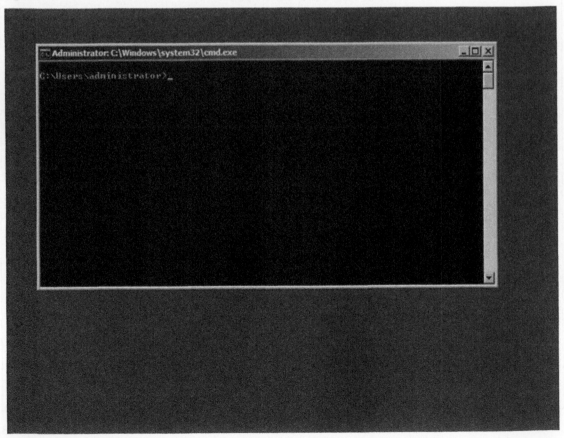

Becoming familiar with Server Core will take some time. In fact, most administrators will likely need a cheat sheet for a while. To help with it all, you can find some very useful tools on Microsoft TechNet at http://technet2.microsoft.com/windowsserver2008/en/library/47a23a74-e13c-46de-8d30-ad0afb1eaffc1033.mspx?mfr=true. This link provides command and syntax lists that can be used on Server Core. The good news is, for those of you who want the security and features of Server Core with the ease-of-use of a graphical user interface (GUI), you have the ability to manage a Server Core installation using remote administration tools.

Server Core Features

For years, Microsoft engineers have been told that Windows would never stand up to Linux in terms of security simply because it was too darn "heavy" (too much) code, loaded too many modules (services, startup applications, and so on), and was generally too GUI-heavy. With Windows Server 2008, Microsoft engineers can stand tall, thanks to the introduction of Server Core.

The concept behind the design of Server Core is to truly provide a minimal server installation. The belief is that rather than installing all the application, components, services, and features by default, it is up to the implementer to determine what will be turned on or off.

The installation of Windows 2008 Server Core is fairly simple. During the installation process, you have the option of performing a standard installation or a Server Core installation. Once you have selected the hard drive configuration, license key activation, and end-user license agreement (EULA), you simply let the automatic installation continue to take place. When installation is done and the system has rebooted, you will be prompted with the traditional Windows challenge/response screen, and the Server Core console will appear.

When you install Windows Server 2008 without the extra overhead, it limits the number of roles and features that can be used by your server. So why should you install a Server Core in your organization? For the following benefits:

- Minimal attack vector opportunities
- Requires less software maintenance
- Uses less disk space for installation

Server Core Has Minimal Attack Vector Opportunities

Server Core is a bare installation of Windows Server 2008. A machine provisioned with Server Core has fewer binaries installed, which as a result have a reduced attack interface. With less binary available on the system, the change of vulnerable DLLs is decreased. This will force an attacker to expend more effort in finding a security flaw in one of the Windows DLLs.

If we look at the number of services installed by default on a Server Core machine and those on a regular Windows 2008 installation, we see a big difference. I did a comparison on two of my test machines. I executed the command *sc query | find "SERVICE_NAME:" /c* (see Figure 7.2) on the Server Core machine, as well as on my normal Windows 2008 machine. This command counts the number of services installed on a machine. The Server Core had 38 services installed, while the normal Windows 2008 installation had 49 services installed. I did this quick check directly after the initial installation. This means no additional roles were installed. Fewer services installed and running means greater security. By the way, this check was performed between Windows Server 2008 Enterprise (Server Core Installation) and Windows Server 2008 Enterprise (Full Installation).

Figure 7.2 Counting the Number of Services on a Server Core Machine

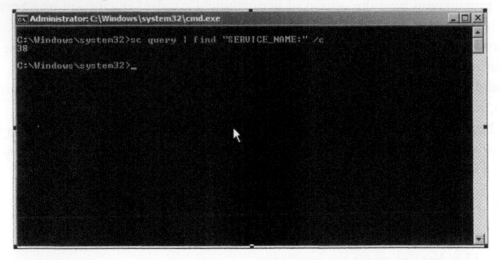

Microsoft has also removed the most insecure programs like Internet Explorer, Windows Media Player, Windows Messenger, Outlook Express, and so on. Much deeper underlying dependencies are also removed—for example, .NET Framework.

Because .NET Framework is missing, there is no PowerShell, Servermanagercmd.exe, or ASP.Net either. But Microsoft is working on a slimmed-down version of the .NET Framework for a future release. Because fewer applications and services are installed, we can say that the attack surface is far smaller than a regular Windows Server product.

Server Core Requires Less Software Maintenance

We all know the term *Patch Tuesday*, and we all know that some admins don't like rebooting their most important servers to take care of the companies' core business on those occasions. Well, for those admins, there is hope. Microsoft believes that because of the slim version of Server Core, the number of patches required for this Windows version will be reduced by 60 percent, compared with a regular Windows Server 2008 machine. This will dramatically decrease the patch management cycle.

The Server Core machine only does what it has to do. Why should you install a combined DHCP/DNS server on a full Windows installation (which has a lot of additional services and components installed that aren't be used) just to fulfill these two roles? You can better install it on Server Core because this only provides the key network infrastructure roles without all the superfluous DLLs and services.

· Last year, I attended a live demo session from Marcus Murray at Tech-Ed Orlando. The session title was *Why I Can Hack Your Network in a Day*. According to Marcus, 95 percent of the software running within a company isn't properly patched, and most of the security flaws are caused by this un-patched software. If we look at Server Core, not much software will be installed besides the antivirus and backup software. And maybe you want to keep it this way. Server Core isn't designed to serve as an application platform.

TIP

In the later section "Server Core – Administration," you will learn how you can enable Windows Update for Server Core. If you want to see a list of installed patches, type the following command:

wmic qfe list

If you want to manually install a patch, use the following command:

Wusa.exe <patchname>.msu /quiet

For more information, type **wusa.exe /?** at the command prompt.

Server Core Uses Less Disk Space for Installation

A Server Core installation requires about 1 gigabyte (GB) of disk space, and for paging, another 512 (MB) is needed. In total, approximately 2GB is required for operations. If we take a look at the official installation requirements, Microsoft minimum installation needs 10GB of disk space; however; 40GB or greater is recommended. Servers with more than 16GB of internal memory require more disk space for paging and dump files.

The advantage of the reduced disk footprint expresses itself in quicker unattended installs and faster booting. Disk costs aren't that expensive anymore. Nevertheless the reduced disk footprint can be a big pro for large datacenters. Imagine having a big datacenter with hundreds of Web-farm front-end servers installed on Server Core, and you are responsible of provisioning them. Imaging these servers with a small cloned image or an unattended installation would be a piece of cake.

Server Core Components

Microsoft has built a new type of operating system (OS) with fewer capabilities, which means less code, so the change of an exploit should be minimal. But what are the consequences of stripping an OS so drastically? One thing's for sure. Server Core can't easily be used as an application server. The strength of Server Core is to fulfill the key functions of a Windows infrastructure. Think about DHCP, DNS, Active Directory Domain Services, and so on. We don't have balloon notifications, but who will miss them. Wait a minute, though… isn't a password expiration a balloon notification? Ok, Microsoft missed that one. Also vendors of antivirus, backup, or other agents have some work to do. Agents installed on Server Core cannot have shell or GUI dependencies and may not require managed code. Many of you may be wondering which components are actually there and which components are missing. The following paragraphs will provide you with the answers to these two questions.

What Is There?

First of all, we have the command prompt. Many DOS commands we know from the past still work for Server Core. So do *fc*, *label*, *defrag*, *ftp*, *diskcomp*, and so on still work? Yes. A good start is the A–Z command line reference. See the link: http://technet2.microsoft.com/windowsserver/en/library/552ed70a-208d-48c4-8da8-2e27b530eac71033.mspx?mfr=true. There is a little GUI support, but most of the installing and configuring have to be done using the command line. This means that deploying and managing Server Core installations requires a little more knowledge than a normal installation does. This has an advantage in that system administrators have to think about their design and not just click around till it works. However, not all configurations can be done with the standard DOS commands, and this is where *scregedit.wsf* comes in.

scregedit.wsf is a script that helps you edit the Registry easily without opening it. With *scregedit.wsf*, you can enable remote desktop for administration, enable automatic updates, configure the pagefile, enable error reporting, and so on. For more info on how to use this command, see the later section "Server Core – Administration."

Of course, we also have the kernel and the Hardware Abstraction Layer (HAL). But the number of device drivers is limited. Fortunately, you have the opportunity to install additional drivers after the initial installation.

The core subsystem takes care of the security (logon scenarios), file systems, RPC, winlogon, networking, and so on. Some infrastructure features are also crucial to let Windows Core work properly. These features include (as mentioned before) the command shell, but also: domain join, event log, performance counters, http support, and the WMI infrastructure.

TIP

Much of the device drivers in Server Core aren't installed. To get a list of all installed drivers, type:

Sc query type= driver

If you want to determine the version of a particular file—for example, the hal.DLL—type the following command:

wmic datafile where name="c:\\windows\\system32\\hal.dll" get version

If you want to install a driver that is not available on the Server Core machine, you must copy the driver to a location on the Server Core machine. If you're finished copying, you can execute the following command:

Pnputil –i –a <path>\<driver>.inf

The Server Core architecture is shell-less, but not completely GUI-less. Two Control Panel applets are available. The *regional and language options* applet and the *date and time* applet. Many Technology Adoption Program (TAP) customers have been complaining about the lack of a text editor in the early developing days of Server Core. The only way to open log files, scripts, and so on was remotely. That's why, since the release of the Beta 2 version of Server Core, Notepad is added (see Figure 7.3).

Figure 7.3 Notepad on a Server Core Machine

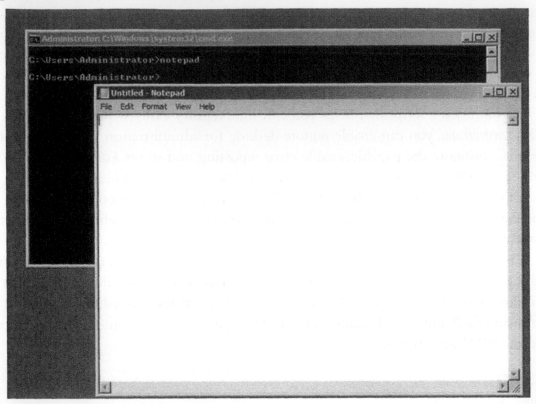

Another GUI-tool is regedit. Because not all modifications on the system can be made by the command prompt, it's sometimes necessary to edit the Registry. In other words, if you want to make an advanced modification, *regedit* rules.

Besides *regedit*, you can also use the key combination **Ctrl + Shift + Esc**. After pressing these keys, the task manager will appear, letting you see which applications, processes, and services are running. Using task manager, you can also take a quick look at the current load of the server and/or see what the network throughputs are.

Last but not least is the logon screen. These GUI applications are installed by default on Server Core. Firstly, you can add some extra tools or applications like *Mark Russinovich's Sysinternals* for troubleshooting purposes. If you want to install an application on Server Core, read the installation instructions carefully to be sure the application is supported. Many applications you may want to install won't detail possible complications as long they don't depend on DLLs (which aren't available on Server Core).

Server Core also includes the Windows Management Instrumentation (WMI). This is a standardized infrastructure environment that makes it easy to manage servers running Windows operating systems. The command-line version of WMI is the Windows Management Instrumentation Command (WMIC) line. WMIC isn't new, but it can come in handy when administering Server Core. WMIC is more intuitive than WMI because it uses aliases. Later on, we'll see how WMIC can be used to change the computer name or change the pagefile of a Windows Core operating system.

Other good tools are available to remotely administer Server Core. As in the past, we can connect to a server Core Machine with remote desktop. If we have installed the Remote Server Administration Tools (RSAT) on Windows Vista SP1, we can administer Server Core from there. It's obvious we can do our management tasks from a GUI-based Windows 2008 server with Microsoft Management Console (MMC). If we want to connect remotely using remote command capabilities, we can use WS-Management—better known as WINRM/WINRS (Windows Remote Management/Windows Remote Shell). These tools provide more security than others because they operate as a Web services-based mechanism that runs on port 80 or 443. If you must traverse firewalls, WINRM/WINRS lets you open just a single port and even run it encrypted because it supports Secure Sockets Layer (SSL). WINRM/WINRS is not new. It was first introduced with the R2 version of Windows Server 2003. It's also possible to configure this tool in a manner in which remote command capabilities are only possible from a particular subnet. In this way, we can configure WINRM/WINRS to allow only administrators' management workstations to connect to the Server Core machines.

WARNING

If you want to configure WINRM/WINRS to support SSL communication, you must require a valid certificate with server authentication capability and a matching CN. Self-signed certificates don't work.

Which Roles Can Be Installed?

Administrators think of servers in terms of roles. That's our fileserver, that's the DNS server, and so on. A server always fulfills a particular role. For this reason, Microsoft has changed its approach for installing software. A server role provides the key functionality of a particular server. Add/Remove Programs doesn't exist anymore and has been replaced by Server Manager. If you want to add a role or feature, the Server Manager is the place to do it. But Server Manager doesn't work in Server Core because it uses managed code. So should we use the command-line version *servermanagercmd.exe*? No. Servermanagercmd.exe uses .NET Framework, which isn't modular enough to break it down and let it fit within Server Core. So we use a replacement command called *ocsetup*. With the command *ocsetup*, you can install roles and features on Server Core. One Server Core role you can't install with the *ocsetup* is Active Directory Domain Services (AD DS). In the later section, "Server Core – Administration," you will learn how to use the *ocsetup* and how to install AD DS on Server Core.

The following roles can be installed on Server Core:

- Active Directory Domain Services
- Active Directory Lightweight Directory Services (AD LDS)
- DHCP Server
- DNS Server
- File Services
- Print Server
- Web Server (IIS) (ASP.net is not available for Server Core)
- Hyper-V (This role is not available by default)
- Streaming Media Services (This role is not available by default)

A feature is a functionality that is designed to support the main server roles. The features that Server Core supports are outlined next.

The following features can be installed on Server Core:

- Failover Clustering
- Network Load Balancing
- Subsystem for Unix-based applications
- Backup
- MultipathIo
- Removable Storage Management
- BitLocker Drive Encryption

NOTE

BitLocker Drive Encryption is an integral new security feature in Windows Server 2008 that protects servers at locations such as branch offices, as well as mobile computers (for all those roaming users out there). BitLocker provides offline data and operating system protection by ensuring that data stored on the computer is not revealed if the machine is tampered with when the installed operating system is offline.

To see which roles and features are installed on Server Core, use the command *oclist.exe*. The result of executing the *oclist* command on a Server Core machine is shown next. The following output is modified. The subcomponents from the roles and features are not displayed because it generates six pages of output.

Use the listed update names with Ocsetup.exe to install/uninstall a server role or optional feature.

Adding or removing the Active Directory role with OCSetup.exe is not supported. It can leave your server in an unstable state. Always use DCPromo to install or uninstall Active Directory.

Microsoft-Windows-ServerCore-Package
Not Installed:BitLocker
Not Installed:BitLocker-RemoteAdminTool
Not Installed:ClientForNFS-Base
Not Installed:DFSN-Server
Not Installed:DFSR-Infrastructure-ServerEdition
Not Installed:DHCPServerCore
Not Installed:DirectoryServices-ADAM-ServerCore
Not Installed:DirectoryServices-DomainController-ServerFoundation
Not Installed:DNS-Server-Core-Role
Not Installed:FailoverCluster-Core
Not Installed:FRS-Infrastructure
Not Installed:IIS-WebServerRole
Not Installed:Microsoft-Windows-RemovableStorageManagementCore
Not Installed:MultipathIo
Not Installed:NetworkLoadBalancingHeadlessServer

Not Installed:Printing-ServerCore-Role
Not Installed:QWAVE
Not Installed:ServerForNFS-Base
Not Installed:SNMP-SC
Not Installed:SUACore
Not Installed:TelnetClient
Not Installed:WAS-WindowsActivationService
Not Installed:WindowsServerBackup
Not Installed:WINS-SC

If you want to install a role, you can type **start /w ocsetup DNS-Server-Core-Role** to install DNS. If you want to install DHCP, use the command **start /w ocsetup DHCPServerCore**. Remember, the commands are case-sensitive. Make sure to supply the correct role or feature name after the command *start /w ocsetup* because the role names are not consistently used. Some roles are written with a hyphen, while others aren't. If you want to de-install a role, first stop the role service with **NET STOP**, and then type **start /w ocsetup serverrolename /uninstall** to uninstall the filled-in role.

What Is Missing?

In my opinion, the biggest disadvantages of Server Core are that PowerShell and ASP.net on IIS don't work on Server Core because they both depend on .NET Framework. Ok, that's said. If it makes you happy, PHP is supported. But let's go further. We all know Vista and that WOW feeling—and one thing's for sure, that WOW feeling is definitely missing. We don't have glassy windows and flip 3D; we don't even have a Desktop, Start Menu, Control Panel, Explorer, Windows Media Player, and the rest. But the big question is, do we need all this on a server? If we take the roles and features that can be installed on Server Core and compare this with the roles and features that can be installed on a regular Windows Server 2008 machine, we get the list shown in Table 7.1.

Table 7.1 Available and Unavailable Roles and Features on Server Core

Roles	Availablility
Active Directory Certificate Services	No
Active Directory Domain Services	Yes
Active Directory Federation Services	No
Active Directory Lightweight Directory Services (AD LDS)	Yes
Active Directory Rights Management Services (AD RMS)	No
Application Server	No
DHCP Server	Yes
DNS Server	Yes
Fax Server	No
File Services	Yes
Print Server	Yes
Streaming Media Server	Yes
Hyper-V	Yes
Network Policy and Access Services	No
Terminal Services	No
Universal Description, Discovery, and Integration Services	No
Web Server (IIS)	Yes
Windows Deployment Services	No
Windows Sharepoint Services	No
Features	**Availability**
BitLocker	Yes
BitLocker Remote Administration Tool	Yes
BITS Server Extensions	No
Connection Manager Administration Kit	No
Desktop Experience	No
Failover Cluster	Yes
Group Policy Management	No
Internet Printing Client	No

Continued

Table 7.1 Continued. Available and Unavailable Roles and Features on Server Core

Roles	Availablility
Internet Storage Name Server	No
LPR Port Monitor	No
Message Queuing	No
Microsoft .NET Framework 3.0 Features	No
Multipathlo	Yes
NLB	Yes
Peer Name Resolution Protocol	No
Quality Windows Audio Video Experience	Yes
Remote Assistance	No
Remote Differential Compression	No
Remote Server Administration Tools	No
Removable Storage Management	Yes
RPC over HTTP Proxy	No
Services for NFS	No
Simple TCP/IP Services	No
SMTP Server	No
SNMP Services	
Storage Manager for Storage Area Networks	No
Subsystem for Unix-based applications	Yes
Telnet Client	
Telnet Server	No
Trivial File Transfer Protocol Client	No
WAS (WindowsActivationService)	Yes
Windows Internal Database	No
Windows Internet Name Service (WINS)	
Windows PowerShell	No
Windows Process Activation Service	No
Windows Server Backup Features	
Windows System Resource Manager	No
Wireless LAN Service	No

Server Core Best Practices

If you work as a field engineer and must install Server Core at various customer locations, wouldn't it be nice to have some kind of manual that summarizes some of the best practices? Some documentation exists in books and on the Internet, but the neater tricks are hard to find, or can't be found at all. Working as a consultant, I collected some of these tricks and bunched them together. Some made me think, "Hey, why didn't I think of that?" Other tricks (I think) are pretty cool, like *"enabling remote cmd.exe with terminal services."* In the paragraphs that follow, you'll find some practical tips that will come in handy when implementing Server Core.

Installing Software

Just to be sure… you do have backup clients and antivirus engines running on your servers, don't you? Thankfully, it's possible to install antivirus software like Microsoft's ForeFront and backup agents such as Symantec Backup Exec 12 on Windows 2008 Server Core. But how do you arrange this if you don't have *Add/Remove Programs* or even a GUI? Well, you still have msiexec.exe and the normal executable files. If you want to install an application with *msiexec*, just type **msiexec /i productname .msi/**. See Table 7.2 for some of the most oft-used command-line switches for *msiexec*. If you want to see the full list, use the link: http://support.microsoft.com/kb/227091. You may get the feeling that without a GUI nothing can happen with your Server Core installation. With fewer DLLs, the attack surface may be reduced, but it's still advisable to install antivirus and backup agents on the machine. Maybe it's better to say that Server Core is shell-less and a little bit GUI-less. If you want, you can still install lots of software, as long as the software doesn't need DLLs (which are aren't available on Server Core). It's even possible to install a browser like Mozilla Firefox on Server Core. But it's strongly recommended you only install supported software on Server Core.

Table 7.2 *msiexec* Command-Line Parameters

Switch	Parameters	Description
/i	Package|ProductCode	Installs or configures a product
/f	[p|o|e|d|c|a|u|m|s|v] Package|ProductCode	Repairs a product
		p - Reinstalls a product only if a file is missing
		o - Reinstalls a product if a file is missing or if an older version of a file is installed
		e - Reinstalls a product if a file is missing or an equal or older version of a file is installed
		d - Reinstalls a product if a file is missing or a different version of a file is installed
		c - Reinstalls a product if a file is missing or the stored checksum value does not match the calculated value
		a - Forces all files to be reinstalled
		u - Rewrites all required user-specific Registry entries
		m - Rewrites all required computer-specific Registry entries
		s - Overwrites all existing shortcuts
		v - Runs from the source file and re-caches the local package
/a	Package	Administrative installation option; installs a product on the network
/x	Package|ProductCode	Uninstalls a product

Changing Background Settings and More

Imagine you are a system administrator and working in a server park with approximately 200 Core Servers. Ten of them are very important because these are installed with IIS and take care of the companies' core business. You surely don't want to mess up these servers. So you are looking for a manner to distinguish these servers from the others.

Well let's use the old fashioned way. We can change the background color to (for instance) red. Type *regedit* in the console, browse to the key **HKEY_CURRENT_ USER\Control Panel\Colors\Background**, and change the value to **255 0 0**. Don't forget to log off and log on again so your Registry changes are applied. The default background is now changed to red.

If you want to disable the screensaver, again type *regedit* at the command prompt and go to **HKEY_CURRENT_USER\Control Panel\Desktop\ScreenSaveActive**. Then, change the value from **1** to **0**. But maybe you want to do the opposite and add a screensaver with a warning text that says *Don't touch my Web server!* The Web servers are still your companies' core business, right? The screensaver we're taking about is called Marquee and the screensaver file is not available on Server Core by default, so we have to copy it. Locate the file *ssmarque.scr* (c:\windows\system32\) on an XP machine and copy it to the same location on a Server Core machine. On the Core Machine, open the Registry with *regedit.exe* and browse to **HKEY_CURRENT_ USER\Control Panel\Desktop**. Change the value *SCRNSAVE.EXE* to *C:\WINDOWS\system32\ssmarque.scr* and you're almost done. If you want to change the default screensaver timeout of ten minutes, change the value *ScreenSaveTimeOut* from *600* seconds to a value better suited to your needs. The last thing we must do is change the default text from the screensaver. To arrange this, type the command *c:\ windows\system32\ssmarque.scr* in the command prompt and change the text in the box. (See Figure 7.4.)

Figure 7.4 Changing the Screensaver in Server Core

Tools & Traps...

Changing Your Display Resolution

You can increase or decrease your display resolution by editing the Registry. First, make a Registry export using the following key: *HKLM\SYSTEM\CurrentControlSet\Control\Video*. Now you can safely edit the Registry because you have a backup. Browse to the key *HKLM\SYSTEM\CurrentControlSet\Control\Video*. Beneath this key are a couple of GUIDS. You have to "play" with it a little to find out which of the GUIDS belongs to your video card. Under the key *video\GUID\0000* should be two *Dword* values: *defaultsettings.xresolution* and *defaultsettings.yresolution*. After editing these settings so they correspond with your display resolution, don't forget to reboot. Remember, modifying the Registry can be dangerous.

If you want to set your display settings during an unattended install, use the following tags:

```
<Display>
    <HorizontalResolution>1024</HorizontalResolution>
    <VerticalResolution>768</VerticalResolution>
    <ColorDepth>16</ColorDepth>
</Display>
```

The following link displays a complete unattended sample file: http://technet2.microsoft.com/windowsserver2008/en/library/47a23a74-e13c-46de-8d30-ad0afb1eaffc1033.mspx?mfr=true.

Enabling *remote cmd.exe* with Terminal Services

Imagine you are still working on that company that has approximately 200 Core Servers, and you are looking for a way to remotely administer them. You are in possession of one GUI-based Server 2008 machine. The following steps should be performed to get remote cmd.exe working as a Terminal Services Remote Program. This "cool" function is similar to administering Server Core with *mstsc.exe /v server name*. The only difference is that you don't use the full-sized remote desktop functionality anymore, only a "published" remote application. The protocol used is still RDP.

1. Enable Remote Desktop on the Server Core computer by typing the command prompt *cscript c:\windows\system32\scregedit.wsf /ar 0*.

2. Install the role *Terminal Server* on the GUI Server 2008 machine with Server
    Manager or by typing **servermanagercmd.exe –install TS-Terminal-Server** at the
    command prompt. Don't forget to reboot after installation. (See Figure 7.5.)

Figure 7.5 Installing Terminal Services on a Full Windows 2008 Installation

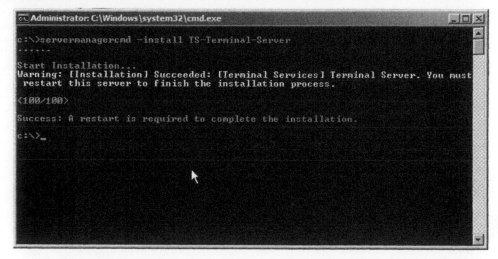

3. After the reboot, open the MMC **TS RemoteAPP Manager** you just
    installed. Remember, you must open TS RemoteAPP Manager with MMC
    because Server Manager doesn't let you make connections with other servers.

4. Instead of a local computer, select the IP address or hostname of the Core
    Server. (See Figure 7.6.)

5. Click **Add RemoteApps** in the upper right corner, and then click **Next**.

6. Click **Browse** and type ***servercorename*\c$\system32\cmd.exe**, and then
    click **Open | Next | Finish**.

7. cmd.exe will be added to the list of remote programs.

8. In the **RemoteApps** pane, you should see the application you just created.
    Right-click the application and select **create .rdp File**.

9. Save the RDP file to the location of your choice.

10. If you open the RDP file, a remote command session will start to the Server
    Core machine.

Figure 7.6 Remotely Connected to a Server Core Machine with TS RemoteApp Manager

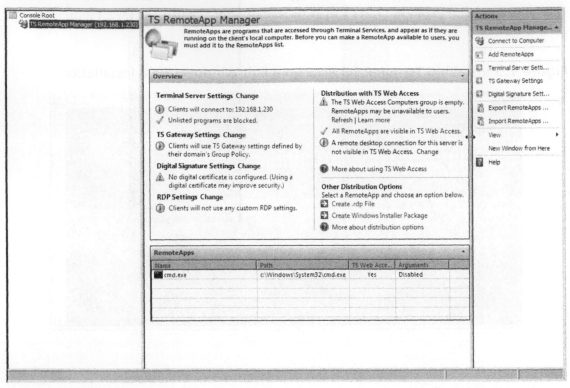

If you walked through the preceding steps, you just administered Server Core with *remoteAPPS*. Why should you open the full screen RDP version with *mstsc* if you only need the command prompt window? This is an excellent way to administer your Server Core machines. After opening the RDP file, you'll see a normal DOS box like any other DOS box on your local machine. Keep in mind, however, that every command you're executing will be executed on the remote machine, not the local. Especially when connecting to multiple remote Server Core machines, you probably don't remember anymore which DOS box is for which server. To help with this, the next paragraph offers a solution to this dilemma.

Changing the Command Prompt

Maybe you didn't notice it, but there is no time indication on a Server Core machine. After you execute the command ***prompt [$t]$ssp$g***, your command prompt will look like that shown in Figure 7.7, letting you know exactly when it's lunchtime.

Figure 7.7 Changing the Look of the Command Prompt

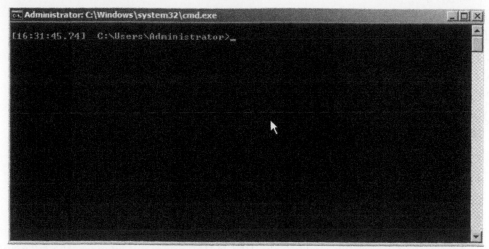

If we analyze the command, we see that *[$t]* is the variable that shows the time, *$s* is a space, *$p* shows the current drive and path, and *$g* shows the greater than sign >. If you perform remote administration on more than one machine, it's a best practice to change the default prompt in such a way as to distinguish the command prompts from each other. The variable *%computername%* can help you with this. After executing the command **prompt [$t]$s[%computername%]sp$g**, your prompt will look like the following:

```
[16:46:42.65] [CORE] C:\Users\Administrator>
```

where *Core* is the computer name of the Server Core machine. Unfortunately, when you log off, your settings are lost. If you wish to save your changes permanently, use the Registry. Type **Regedit** at the command prompt. Locate the key **HKLM\System\CurrentControlSet\Control\Session Manager\Environment**. Create an expandable string value with the name **prompt**. The value of the string can be the same as the prompt commands we used earlier—for example, *[$t]$s[%computername%]sp$g*. Type **prompt /?** to see what methods are available to change the command prompt.

Prompt can be made up of normal characters and the following special codes:

$A & (Ampersand)
$B | (Pipe)
$C ((Left parenthesis)
$D Current date
$E Escape code (ASCII code 27)

$F) (Right parenthesis)

$G > (Greater-than sign)

$H Backspace (erases previous character)

$L < (less-than sign)

$N Current drive

$P Current drive and path

$Q = (Equal sign)

$S (Space)

$T Current time

$V Windows version number

$_ Carriage return and linefeed

$$ $ (Dollar sign)

If Command Extensions are enabled, the PROMPT command supports the following additional formatting characters:

$+ zero or more plus sign (+) characters depending upon the depth of the PUSHD directory stack, one character for each level pushed.

$M Displays the remote name associated with the current drive letter or the empty string if current drive is not a network drive.

Administrating Server Core with RDP

Every system administrator knows the command *mstsc /v servername /console*. With this command, we start a Remote Desktop session to another machine. If we want to connect to a Server Core machine, we must first enable Remote Desktop on this particular server. With the GUI versions of Windows, we right-clicked **Computer** to open Properties, afterwards selected the tab **Remote**, and then marked the checkbox **Enable Remote Desktop on this Computer**. In Server Core, we can't do this anymore. But don't worry… we can execute the command *cscript c:\windows\system32\ screedit.wsf /ar 0* to enable Remote Desktop. This command will also create an exception rule in Windows Firewall. With the command *cscript c:\windows\system32\scregedit. wsf /ar 1*, we can disable it again. If we want to see the current settings, we use the command *cscript c:\windows\system32\scregedit.wsf /ar /v*. If you have problems connecting to Server Core with Windows XP, execute the command *cscript c:\windows\system32\ scregedit.wsf /cs 0*. This disables some enhanced security settings that are implemented by Server 2008 and Vista.

Tools & Traps...

Administering Terminal Server Sessions

They aren't often used by administrators, but certain command-line syntaxes can be employed to administer terminal server sessions. For reference, see: http://technet2.microsoft.com/windowsserver/en/library/1db49727-f587-424d-8d98-bb51630d13a01033.mspx?mfr=true. The following command queries all the processes on a server with IP address 192.168.1.230.

    query process * /server:192.168.1.230

USERNAME	SESSIONNAME	ID	PID	IMAGE
(unknown)	services	0	4	system
system	services	0	308	smss.exe
system	services	0	376	csrss.exe
system	services	0	420	wininit.exe
system	services	0	504	services.exe
system	services	0	516	lsass.exe
system	services	0	524	lsm.exe
system	services	0	688	svchost.exe
network service	services	0	740	svchost.exe
local service	services	0	780	svchost.exe
system	services	0	872	svchost.exe
network service	services	0	888	slsvc.exe
local service	services	0	952	svchost.exe
network service	services	0	1048	svchost.exe
local service	services	0	1160	svchost.exe
system	services	0	1308	taskeng.exe
system	services	0	1376	frameworkser...
system	services	0	1500	mcshield.exe
system	services	0	1528	vstskmgr.exe
system	services	0	1556	naprdmgr.exe
network service	services	0	1580	svchost.exe
local service	services	0	1612	svchost.exe
network service	services	0	1652	svchost.exe
system	services	0	1976	svchost.exe
network service	services	0	1664	msdtc.exe
system	console	1	2788	csrss.exe

Continued

system	console	1	2828	winlogon.exe
(unknown)	console	1	1324	taskeng.exe
(unknown)	console	1	1432	taskmgr.exe
(unknown)	console	1	3472	cmd.exe
(unknown)	console	1	2540	rundll32.exe
(unknown)	console	1	2648	notepad.exe

The following command kills the process with Process ID Number (PID) 2648. In this case, it's Notepad.

tskill /server:192.168.1.230 2648

Creating Batch Menus

Maybe you remember the good old *choice.exe* from the Windows NT and Windows 2000 resource kits. Choice.exe allows users to select one item from a list of choices and returns the index of the selected choice. The resource kit tool is so often used that it became a built-in command in Windows 2003. Unfortunately, the Server Core version of Windows 2008 doesn't have a choice.exe or a replacement command. Instead of typing long commands—for example, to disable or enable the Windows firewall—you can use choice.exe to create a batch file menu that represents the shortcuts of the long commands. You can download choice.exe from the following location.ftp://ftp.micro-soft.com/Services/TechNet/samples/PS/Win98/Reskit/SCRPTING/CHOICE.EXE. Look at the batch file that follows. This simple batch file gives you an idea how choice. exe can be used. Download choice.exe from the location just mentioned and place it somewhere in the Path—for instance, %systemroot%\system32. Copy and paste the following text in a text file and save it with the extension **.bat**. If you execute the batch file, your screen should show what's displayed in Figure 7.8.

```
@ECHO OFF
REM - Script written by Remco Wisselink
:BEGIN
CLS
```

```
ECHO Press (1) To Change the date/time or timezone
ECHO Press (2) To Change the regional settings
ECHO Press (3) To enable the firewall
ECHO Press (4) To disable the firewall
CHOICE /N /C:1234 PICK A NUMBER (1, 2, 3 or 4)%1
IF ERRORLEVEL ==4 GOTO Four
IF ERRORLEVEL ==3 GOTO THREE
IF ERRORLEVEL ==2 GOTO TWO
IF ERRORLEVEL ==1 GOTO ONE
GOTO END
:Four
ECHO You pressed (4)
netsh firewall set opmode mode=disable
GOTO END
:THREE
ECHO You Pressed (3)
netsh firewall set opmode mode=enable
GOTO END
:TWO
ECHO You Pressed (2)
control intl.cpl
GOTO END
:ONE
ECHO You Pressed (1)
control timedate.cpl.
:END
```

Figure 7.8 What's Displayed in a Batch File

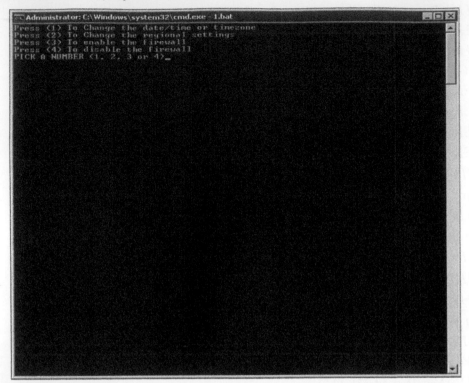

Combining Server Core,
Read-Only Domain Controller, and BitLocker

Branch offices are often badly secured. If a branch office's domain controller gets stolen, it's wise to reset all your passwords. Not only must the user account passwords be reset but also the passwords from administrative and service accounts. Why? Because the passwords are locally cached on the domain controller. You don't have to be a rocket scientist to crack all the domain passwords with password cracking tools like lovecrack. Windows 2008 has a new infrastructure solution called Read-Only Domain Controller (RODC). The advantage of an RODC is that you can define which passwords should be cached on the server. For this reason, the RODC is a perfect solution for Branch Offices. If you implement this solution, it's a good thing to only replicate and cache the passwords from normal user accounts that have low level privileges. And it's obvious that you replicate and cache only passwords from accounts that actually reside at the branch office. In the event of a stolen RODC, you only have to reset the accounts whose passwords are cached on the domain controller.

Another security measure we can take is to encrypt the disk with Windows Server 2008's BitLocker. BitLocker is a security feature that protects the operating systems disks by doing a full drive encryption. If you have to design a solution for branch offices, think about the perfect combination: Server Core, RODC, and BitLocker.

Server Core Administration

If we want to describe the ways to administer Server Core, we can divide this into three sections. The first section is called *Installing Server Core*. After the installation part, we do some initial configuration, like setting IP addresses and joining the domain. This section is called *Configuring Server Core*. Personally, I think this part is the most fun because of all the command-line stuff. After the configuration part, we can reach the Server Core machine with remote tools like MMC, Remote Administration Tools (RSAT), or WS-Management (Web-Services Management). We will cover these tools in the final section of this chapter, "Administrating Server Core."

Installing Server Core

If you want to install Server Core, you must begin from scratch. You can't upgrade from legacy Windows versions to Server Core, you can't upgrade from a full Windows 2008 installation to Windows Server Core, and you can't upgrade from Windows Server Core to a full Windows 2008 installation either.

The following versions of Server Core are available:

- Standard Version
- Enterprise Version
- Datacenter Version

Windows Server Core is available for 32- and 64-bit architecture. The installation of Server Core is not difficult. At the beginning of the installation process, you can choose to install the full server version or the stripped version, which is Server Core. Another way to install Server Core is unattended. An unattended installation is a way of automating the Server Core installation process. By installing Server Core unattended, you can quickly deploy multiple servers and be confident they are identical.

Steps for a Normal Installation

Perform the following steps to install Server Core with a graphical user interface (GUI). (See Figure 7.9.)

1. Insert the Windows Server 2008 installation media into your DVD drive.

2. When the auto-run dialog box appears, click **Install Now**.

3. Follow the instructions on the screen to complete Setup.

4. After Setup completes, press **Ctrl + Alt + Del**, click **Other User**, type **Administrator** with a blank password, and then press **Enter**. You will be prompted to set a password for the Administrator account.

Figure 7.9 Installation Options for Server Core

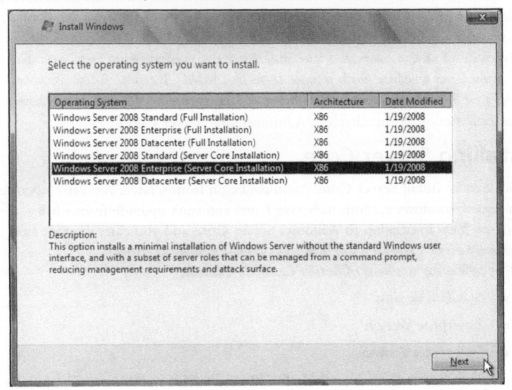

Steps for an Unattended Installation

If you want to install Server Core without user intervention, perform the following steps.

1. Use a text editor to create an .xml file titled **unattend.xml**.

2. Copy the unattend.xml file to a local drive, USB stick, floppy, or shared network resource.

3. Boot the server to Windows Preinstallation Environment (Windows PE).

4. Insert the Windows Server 2008 DVD into your DVD drive.

5. At a command prompt, change to the drive that contains the Windows Server 2008 DVD.

6. Type the following **setup /unattend:<path>\unattend.xml**.

7. Complete the setup.

Configuring Server Core

In the following paragraphs, we will learn how we do the initial configuration of a Server Core machine. Because there is no GUI, practically all configuring must be done through the command line. (I hope the Unix and Linux guys like this part.) You can use this chapter as a reference while you're configuring your Server Core machine. When you're finished with the initial configuration, most of the managing stuff can be done remotely with GUI tools.

Configuring the IPV4 IP-Stack

When the installation is done and the system has rebooted, you will be prompted with the traditional Windows command prompt. Since don't have a graphical user interface, how you do configure, for example, IP addresses? Well, the answer isn't that difficult. We can use the command *netsh*. This command isn't new, and was used in previous versions of Windows, like Windows 2000, Windows 2003, and Windows XP. netsh is not very familiar to GUI-admins either. Nevertheless, it is a powerful command-line utility and we must use it if we want to configure the network configuration on a Server Core machine. The following steps show how to configure the IPv4-stack command line.

1. Identify the network adapter. To do this, in the console window type **netsh interface ipv4 show interfaces** and record the number shown under the Idx column.

2. Set the IP address, subnet mask, and default gateway for the server. To do so, type **netsh interface ipv4 set address name=<ID> source=static address=<StaticIP> mask=<SubnetMask> gateway=<DefaultGateway>**. *<ID>* represents the identification of the networking interface for which you want to change the address. The *<ID>* is identified in step 1, *<StaticIP>* represents the IP address we will assign, *<SubnetMask>* represents the subnet mask, and *<Default Gateway>* represents the IP address of the server's default gateway. See Figure 7.10 for our sample configuration.

Figure 7.10 Configuring IP Addressing on Server Core

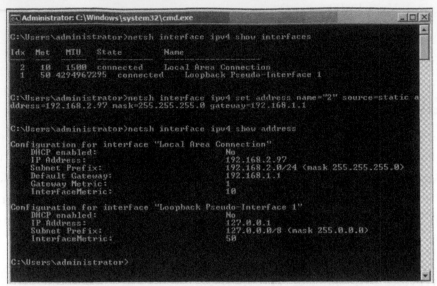

3. Assign the IP address of the DNS server. From the console, type ***netsh inter-face ipv4 add dnsserver name=\<ID> address=\<DNSIP> index=1***. *\<ID>* represents the number from step 1, and *\<DNSIP>* represents the IP address of the DNS server; *index=1* positions the DNS server as primary DNS server, while index=2 positions the DNS server as an alternate DNS server.

4. Assign the IP address of a WINS server. From the console, type ***netsh interface ipv4 add winsserver name=\<ID> address=\<WINSIP> index=1***. *\<ID>* represents the number from step 1, and *\<WINSIP>* represents the IP-address of the WINS server; *index=1* positions the WINS server as primary WINS server, while *index=2* positions the WINS server as an alternate WINS server.

5. Unfortunately, you can't change the DNS suffix using the *netsh* command, so you must use regedit or group policy. If your server will become a member server, then in most circumstances you won't have to configure the DNS suffix because it will automatically get the suffix from the domain to which it belongs. If you want to change the DNS suffix, use the command ***Regedit***, localize **HKLM\SYSTEM\CurrentControlSet\Services\Tcpip\ Parameters**, and change the values for *Domain (REG_SZ)* and SearchList *(REG_SZ)*. If you are not sure how to do this, try it on a normal GUI-based Windows machine and export/import the Registry value.

6. If you want to change the default value for *NetBIOS over TCP/IP* from Enable to Disable, you must use the command *regedit*. It is not possible to configure *NetBIOS over TCP/IP* settings with the command *netsh* or with group policy. After starting **regedit** from the command prompt, localize the key **HKLM\SYSTEM\CurrentControlSet\Services\NetBT\Parameters\Interfaces**. Each network interface card is represented with a subkey *Tcpip_{NETWORKCARDGUID}* below its location. Each subkey has a DWORD value *NetbiosOptions* with a default value of 2. If you change this value to 0, then *NetBIOS over TCP/IP* is disabled.

Configuring Windows Firewall

The Windows Firewall is turned on by default on a Windows Server 2008 machine. You can turn it off with the command *netsh firewall set opmode mode=disable*. However, this should only be done in a test environment, not in a production environment. If you want to enable the Windows Firewall, use the same syntax but substitute *mode=disable* with *mode=enable*. If you install a particular role on a Server Core machine, then the required ports to fulfill the role service will be opened. To enable Remote Administration in Windows Firewall, use the command *netsh advfirewall firewall set rule group="Remote Administration" new enable=yes*. This will enable remote management for any MMC snap-in. In some situations, it may be more appropriate to limit the number of MMCs that can connect. This is where Rule Groups come in. Windows Firewall has some default Rule Groups that correspond to MMCs. If you enable a particular Rule Group, then the corresponding firewall rule will be added to the firewall configuration. Table 7.3 shows the Rule Groups defined within Server 2008.

Table 7.3 MMC Snap-ins and the Corresponding Firewall Rule Groups

MMC Snap-in	Rule Group
Event Viewer	Remote Event Log Management
Services	Remote Service Management
Shared Folders	File and Printer Sharing
Task Scheduler	Remote Scheduled Tasks Management
Reliability and Performance	"Performance Logs and Alerts" and "File and Printer Sharing"
Disk Management	Remote Volume Management
Windows Firewall with Advanced Security	Windows Firewall Remote Management

If you want to allow only specific MMC snap-ins to connect, type *netsh advfirewall firewall set rule group="<rulegroup>" new enable=yes* at the command prompt. Replace *<rulegroup>* with one of the values mentioned in Table 7.3. If you, for example, want to allow other computers or servers to connect to a Server Core machine with *eventviewer execute*, type in the following command at the command prompt: *netsh advfirewall firewall set rule group=" Remote Event Log Management" new enable=yes*.

Configuring Windows Firewall through the command line can prove quite complex in some situations. It's much easier to use the Windows Firewall snap-in from a computer running Windows Vista or Windows Server 2008, and then remotely manage the firewall on a server running a Server Core installation. To accomplish this, first execute the command *netsh advfirewall set currentprofile settings remotemanagement enable*. After executing this command, you're allowed to connect to the Server Core machine with the Windows Firewall MMC. In Figure 7.11, you can see a regular Windows 2008 server connected to a Server Core machine with IP address 10.0.0.1.

Figure 7.11 Configuring Windows Firewall on Server Core from a Regular Windows 2008 Server

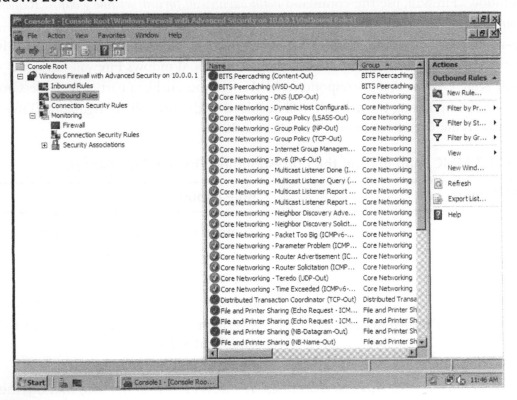

Changing the Hostname

After the initial setup, Server Core has a default random configured hostname. To determine the hostname, use the command *hostname* or *ipconfig /all*. The syntax to change the hostname is *netdom renamecomputer <ComputerName> /NewName:<New ComputerName>*. If you changed the hostname, you have to reboot the machine. You can reboot the machine with the command *shutdown /r /t 0*. After the reboot, you can check to see if the hostname is changed by again typing the command *hostname*. If you want to change the hostname with WMI, use the command *wmic.exe ComputerSystem Where Name="%ComputerName%" Rename Name="NewComputerName"*.

Joining a Domain

You need administrative credentials to join a computer to a domain. To accomplish this, use the following command: *netdom join <ComputerName> /domain:<DomainName> /userd:<UserName> /password:*******. *<ComputerName>* represents the hostname of the machine that is running the Server Core installation, *<DomainName>* is the name of the domain to join, and *<UserName>* is a user account that has permission to join the domain.

Activating the Server

To activate Windows Core Server, you must use a built-in script. The script is named *slmgr.vbs* and can be found in *%windir%\system32*. This script is also used in Windows Vista. If you type the command **cscript c:\windows\system32\slmgr.vbs –ato**, the product will be activated. With the command **cscript c:\windows\system32\slmgr.vbs –xpr**, you can check the expiration date for the current license, and with the command **cscript c:\windows\system32\slmgr.vbs –dlv**, you get the detailed license information. The following are all the command-line options for slmgr.vbs.

> *Microsoft (R) Windows Script Host Version 5.7*
> *Copyright (C) Microsoft Corporation. All rights reserved.*
>
> *Unrecognized option: /?*
> *Windows Software Licensing Management Tool*
> *Usage: slmgr.vbs [MachineName [User Password]] [<Option>]*
>   *MachineName: Name of remote machine (default is local machine)*
>   *User: Account with required privilege on remote machine*
>   *Password: password for the previous account*

Global Options:

-ipk <Product Key>

   Install product key (replaces existing key)

-ato

   Activate Windows

-dli [Activation ID | All]

   Display license information (default: current license)

-dlv [Activation ID | All]

   Display detailed license information (default: current license)

-xpr

   Expiration date for current license state

Advanced Options:

-cpky

   Clear product key from the registry (prevents disclosure attacks)

-ilc <License file>

   Install license

-rilc

   Re-install system license files

-rearm

   Reset the licensing status of the machine

-upk

   Uninstall product key

Volume Licensing: Key Management Service (KMS) Client Options:

-skms <Name[:Port] | :Port>

   Set the name and/or the port for the KMS computer this machine will use

-ckms

   Clear name of KMS computer used (sets the port to the default)

Enabling Automatic Updates

Of course, it's important to patch the Server Core machine. Microsoft claims that the number of patches is decreased by 60 percent, compared to a full Windows Server 2008 version. Nevertheless, it is advisable to enable automatic updates. If you want to configure automatic updates, use the following commands. To enable automatic updates, type **cscript C:\Windows\System32\Scregedit.wsf /au /4**. To disable automatic updates, type **cscript C:\Windows\System32\Scregedit.wsf /au /1**. To view your current settings, type **cscript C:\Windows\System32\Scregedit.**

wsf /au /v. If you want to configure WSUS, use Group Policy or edit the Registry with the command **regedit**.

TIP

If you easily forget commands, try to at least remember this one *Cscript c:\ windows\system32\scregedit.wsf /cli*. It displays some of the most frequently used commands on a Server Core machine.

Microsoft (R) Windows Script Host Version 5.7
Copyright (C) Microsoft Corporation. All rights reserved.

To activate:
   Cscript slmgr.vbs –ato

To use KMS volume licensing for activation:
   Configure KMS volume licensing:
       cscript slmgr.vbs -ipk [volume license key]
   Activate KMS licensing
       cscript slmgr.vbs -ato
   Set KMS DNS SRV record
       cscript slmgr.vbs -skma [KMS FQDN]

Determine the computer name with any of the following:
   Set c
   Ipconfig /all
   Systeminfo
Rename the Server Core computer:
   Domain joined:
       *Netdom renamecomputer %computername% /NewName:new-name / UserD:domain-username /PasswordD:**
Not domain joined:
       Netdom renamecomputer %computername% /NewName:new-name

Changing workgroups:
   Wmic computersystem where name="%computername%" call joindomainorworkgroup name="[new workgroup name]"

Install a role or optional feature:
   Start /w Ocsetup [packagename]
   Note: For Active Directory, run Dcpromo with an answer file.

View role and optional feature package names and current installation state:
   oclist

Start task manager hotkey:
  Ctrl + Shift + Esc

Log off of a Terminal Services session:
  Logoff

To set the pagefile size:
  Disable system pagefile management:
    wmic computersystem where name="%computername%" set
  AutomaticManagedPagefile=False
  Configure the pagefile:
    wmic pagefileset where name="C:\\pagefile.sys" set
  InitialSize=500,MaximumSize=1000

Configure the timezone, date, or time:
  control timedate.cpl

Configure regional and language options:
  control intl.cpl

Manually install a management tool or agent:
  Msiexec.exe /i [msipackage]

List installed msi applications:
  Wmic product

Uninstall msi applications:
  Wmic product get name /value
  Wmic product where name="[name]" call uninstall

To list installed drivers:
  Sc query type= driver

Install a driver that is not included:
  Copy the driver files to Server Core
  Pnputil –i –a [path]\[driver].inf

Determine a file's version:
  wmic datafile where name="d:\\windows\\system32\\ntdll.dll" get version

List of installed patches:
  wmic qfe list

Install a patch:
Wusa.exe [patchame].msu /quiet

Configure a proxy:
Netsh win http proxy set [proxy_name]:[port]

Add, delete, or query a Registry value:
reg.exe add /?
reg.exe delete /?
reg.exe query /?

Swapping Mouse Buttons

Without the windows you probably don't do a lot of mouse clicking in Server Core. But in the event that you're the only left-handed system administrator in a large server park, you may want to switch the left and right mouse button. After executing the command ***RunDll32.exe USER32.DLL,SwapMouseButton*** at the command prompt, the primary and secondary mouse buttons are switched.

Changing the Regional Settings

You can change the regional settings by specifying the settings in an answer file during an unattended setup, or you can set it manually. If you run the command **control intl. cpl**, you will notice that Server Core is not completely GUI-less (see Figure 7.12). After typing the previous command, the Control Panel applet *regional and language options* will appear. Because of some dependencies on a few low-level GUI DLLs, it is not yet possible to use a complete command-line version of this applet. Of course, it's also possible to edit the Registry with *regedit*, but why should you use it if a GUI is available?

Figure 7.12 Changing the Regional and Language Options

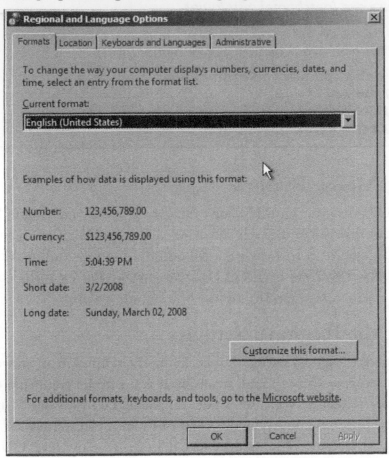

TIP

If you want to change the default numlock behavior, you can enable numlock with the command *reg add HKCU\Control Panel\Keyboard /v InitialKeyboardIndicators /t REG_SZ /d 2*, and disable it with the command *reg add HKCU\Control Panel\Keyboard /v InitialKeyboardIndicators /t REG_SZ /d 0*.

Changing the Date/Time or Timezone

To change the date or time on a Server Core machine, you can respectively use the "old" DOS commands *date* or *time*. If you prefer to use a GUI, you can type **control**

timedate.cpl at the command prompt. After typing this command, the corresponding Control Panel applet will appear. The Control Panel applet *date and time properties* uses the same low-level DLLs as the *regional and language options* applet. For this reason, this applet is still functioning. Microsoft is working on removing these dependencies so these applets probably won't be working in a future release of Server 2008. In the meantime, system administrators can easily manage their servers by using the *intl.cpl* en *timedate.cpl* applets.

Changing the Administrator Password

One of the reasons to install Server Core is because of the reduced attack surface. Fewer binaries are installed, meaning that less software updates are required for the Core Server. Thus, you can conclude that Server Core is more secure. If a security flaw is discovered in a file and the file isn't installed on the system, there won't be a security issue. So why does the installation routine of Server Core allow a blank password? I don't know, but maybe it's better to change this. You can change the password in two ways. The first method is to press **Ctrl + Alt + Del** after the setup completes, then type **Administrator** for the user with a blank password, and press **Enter**. You'll get a prompt to set the password for the Administrator account. But shouldn't we change the password command line since we are administering a Server Core machine? The syntax for this command is easy. *Net user administrator ** . After executing this command, you will get a prompt to change your password. (See Figure 7.13.)

Figure 7.13 Changing the Regional and Language Options

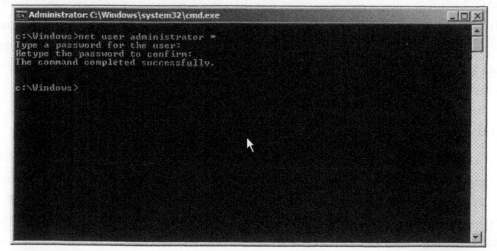

Adding Users to the Local Administrator Group

In some situations, you might want to add users to the local administrators group on a server. The following command adds a user to the local administrator group.

net localgroup Administrators /add <domain>\<username>

If you want to add the user rwisselink sitting in the domain wisselink.local, the command would be:

net localgroup Administators /add wisselink\rwisselink

If you want to delete the user, use the command shown next:

net localgroup Administrators /delete <domain\username>

net localgroup Administators /delete wisselink\rwisselink

Setting the Pagefile

After adding memory to your Server Core machine, it's likely you will want to change the pagefile. Even though you don't have a GUI, it's still possible to change the page-file. By default, the pagefile is configured by the Windows System. If you want to see the current settings, type ***wmic.exe pagefile list /format:list***. If you want a manually configured pagefile, you must first disable the system-managed pagefile with the command ***wmic.exe computersystem where name="%computername%" set Automatic ManagedPagefile=False***. After executing the previous command, you can manually set the pagefile. It's recommended that you give the initial size and the maximum size the same value. In this example, we set the minimum and maximum pagefile size to 1024MB. Use the command ***wmic.exe pagefileset where name="C:\\pagefile.sys" set initialsize=1024,maximumsize=1024***. After you change the pagefile setting, you must reboot your computer. Use the command ***shutdown /r /t 0***. If you prefer the interactive mode, use ***shutdown /i***. Of course, you'll want to make sure the settings were successful. To check this, use the command ***wmic.exe pagefileset list /format:list***.

Installing Server Core Roles

We can't use Server Manager because it has .NET Framework dependencies, and we can't use the command *servermanagercmd.exe* either for the same reason. If we want to install roles or features on Server Core, we need the command *ocsetup.exe*. *ocsetup* is often used to perform scripted installations of Windows components, and substitutes the Sysocmgr.exe tool that we know from previous Windows versions. *ocsetup* has one disadvantage when compared with Server Manager. Server Manager carefully checks dependencies when installing roles or features, while *ocsetup* doesn't. This means you have to install or de-install all the roles and features in the correct order. *ocsetup* installs the following file types.

- Microsoft System Installer (MSI) files (Windows Installer service, msiexec.exe)
- Component-Based Servicing (CBS) components (Package Manager)
- MSI or CBS packages that have an associated custom installer .exe file

The full command-line options for ocsetup are ocsetup.exe [/?] [/h] [/help] component [/log:file] [/norestart] [/passive] [/quiet] [/unattendfile:file] [/uninstall] [/x: parameter]. For the full explanation of the flags see Table 7.4.

Table 7.4 Command-Line Options for *ocsetup.exe*

Parameter	Description
/?, /h, /help	Displays help for all options when run with or without options.
Component	The name of the component to be installed or uninstalled. The component name is case-sensitive.
/log:file	Specifies a non-default log file location.
/norestart	The computer is not rebooted even if required after component installation.
/passive	Unattended mode. Progress only.
/quiet	Quiet mode. No user interaction.
/unattendfile:file	The file contains overrides or additions to default configuration settings. Implies passive mode.
/uninstall	Uninstalls the component. Installation is default.
/x: parameter	Additional configuration parameters to be applied when installing a component that requires a custom installer. *ocsetup* will pass these parameters to the custom installer.

To install a role, type the command **start /w ocsetup <serverrole-name>**. The following examples show the installation commands for all the roles that can be installed on Server Core.

- Active Directory Lightweight Directory Services (AD LDS), *start /w ocsetup DirectoryServices-ADAM-ServerCore.*

- DHCP Server, *start /w ocsetup DHCPServerCore.*

- DNS Server, *start /w ocsetup DNS-Server-Core-Role.*

- File Services:

  - For File Replication service, type *start /w ocsetup FRS-Infrastructure.*

  - For Distributed File System service, type *start /w ocsetup DFSN-Server.*

  - For Distributed File System Replication, type *start /w ocsetup DFSR-Infrastructure-ServerEdition.*

  - For Network File System, type *start /w ocsetup ServerForNFS-Base* and *start /w ocsetup ClientForNFS-Base.*

- Print Services, *start /w ocsetup Printing-ServerCore-Role.*

- Streaming Media Server, *start /w ocsetup MediaServer.* First, you have to copy the appropriate Microsoft Update Standalone package (MSU) to your Server Core installation, and then run the corresponding .MSU files.

- Web Server, *start /w pkgmgr /iu:IIS-WebServerRole;WAS-WindowsActivationService; WAS-ProcessModel.*

- Hyper-V (only available for X64), type *start /w ocsetup Microsoft-Hyper-V.*

- Active Directory Domain Services (AD DS), *dcpromo /unattend:<unattendfile. xml>.* (See the section titled "Installing Active Directory Domain Services on Server Core.")

Notes from the Underground...

Full IIS Installation

If you want to install all available options from Internet Information Services, copy the following command and paste it into the command prompt in Server Core.

start /w pkgmgr /iu:IIS-WebServerRole;IIS-WebServer;IIS-CommonHttp Features;IIS-StaticContent;IIS-DefaultDocument;IIS-DirectoryBrowsing; IIS-HttpErrors;IIS-HttpRedirect;IIS-ApplicationDevelopment;IIS-ASP;IIS-CGI; IIS-ISAPIExtensions;IIS-ISAPIFilter;IIS-ServerSideIncludes;IIS-HealthAnd Diagnostics;IIS-HttpLogging;IIS-LoggingLibra-ries;IIS-RequestMonitor;IIS-Http Tracing;IIS-CustomLogging;IIS-ODBCLogging;IIS-Security;IIS-BasicAuthentication; IIS-WindowsAuthentication;IIS-DigestAuthentication;IIS-ClientCertificateMap pingAuthentication;IIS-IISCertificateMappingAuthentication;IIS-URL Authorization;IIS-RequestFiltering;IIS-IPSecurity;IIS-Performance;IIS-HttpComp ressionStatic;IIS-HttpCompressionDynamic;IIS-WebServerManagementTools; IIS-ManagementScriptingTools;IIS-IIS6ManagementCompatibility; IIS-Metabase;IIS-WMICompatibility;IIS-LegacyScripts;IIS-FTPPublishingService; IIS-FTPServer;WAS-WindowsActivationService;WAS-ProcessModel

If you want to install a feature, type **oclist** to find the required feature name. If you execute this command, you will see a list with all the roles and features that can be installed on Server Core, and whether they are installed or not. The command can't make a distinction between a role or feature. The reason for this is that *oclist* uses a lower-level API, which has no hardcode logic in it. Microsoft wants to keep the command flexible so it's possible to easily add roles and features at a later time. (To see what roles and features are available for Server Core, see Table 7.1 earlier in this chapter.) Type **start /w ocsetup <feature-name>** to install a feature. Remember that the role and features names are case-sensitive. The following examples show the installation commands for all the features that can be installed on Server Core

- BitLocker drive encryption, *start /w ocsetup* BitLocker.
- BitLocker remote administration tool, *start /w ocsetup BitLocker-Remote AdminTool.*

- Cluster service, *start /w ocsetup FailoverCluster-Core.*

- Removable Storage Management, *start /w ocsetup Microsoft-Windows-RemovableStorageManagementCore*

- MultipathIo, *start /w ocsetup MultipathIo.*

- Network Load Balancing (NLB), *start /w ocsetup NetworkLoadBalancing HeadlessServer.*

- Quality Windows Audio/Video Experience, *start /w ocsetup QWAVE.*

- SNMP, *start /w ocsetup SNMP-SC.*

- Subsystem for Unix-based applications, *start /w ocsetup :SUACore.*

- Telnet client, *start /w ocsetup TelnetClient.*

- Windows Activation Service, *start /w ocsetup WAS-Windows ActivationService.*

- Windows Backup, *start /w ocsetup WindowsServerBackup.*

- Wins, *start /w ocsetup WINS-SC.*

Administrating Server Core

After installing and configuring the Server Core machine, it's time to administer it. This can be done remotely with WINRM/WINRS or you can use the MMCs that become available after you install the Remote Server Administration Tools or RSAT. It's up to the administrator which tools he or she prefers. To be honest, if I have to choose between the command *dnscmd.exe* or the DNS MMC snap-in, I prefer the snap-in. It's quicker and there's less room for error. The following sections detail the administration tools available for Server Core.

Remote Server Administration Tools (RSAT)

Server Manager is the single all-in-one tool that you generally use to administer a Server 2008 machine. You can only open the tool if you connect via RDP or sit behind the console. Server Manager is not available on a Server Core installation because it needs .NET Framework 2.0 and MMC 3.0, and these two components are not installed on Server Core. Because the option *connect to a different computer* is not available within Server Manager, it isn't possible to connect with this tool to a Server Core machine or even a regular Server 2008 installation.

One of the options available to you to administer Server Core is to use Remote Server Administration Tools (RSAT). You can compare RSAT with the legacy "Adminpack.msi," which was used to administer Windows Server 2003. The RSAT tools are actually a collection of MMC tools. RSAT is a feature component within Windows Server 2008. If you install a role or feature in the GUI-version of Server 2008, the corresponding "RSAT tool" or MMC snap-in is automatically installed. To install all management tools for the Roles available in Server 2008, use the command *ServerManagerCmd.exe -install RSAT-Role-Tools.* To install all feature management tools, use the command *ServerManagerCmd.exe -install RSAT-Feature-Tools.* So, even if a role or feature is not installed on a server, it's possible to install management tools to connect to other servers—for example, Server Core.

> **NOTE**
>
> RSAT is in public beta testing at the moment of writing and can only be installed on Windows Vista SP1. With RSAT tools installed, you'll be able to manage Windows Server 2008 servers, including Server Core. With many RSAT tools, it's also possible to manage servers running Windows Server 2003. RSAT will be released as an Out of Band component shortly after Vista SP1 is released.

WINRM/WINRS

WINRM/WINRS has many similarities with psexec. To explain what WINRM/WINRS is, we must first take a look at what psexec actually does. Many of you are familiar with the Sysinternals command-line tools, better know as pstools (from Mark Russinovich). For the download location, click the following link: http://technet. microsoft.com/en-us/sysinternals/bb896649.aspx. One utility of the pstools suite is psexec, which is easy to use. The command *psexec \\192.168.1.230 cmd.exe* starts a remote command session to a server with IP address 192.168.1.230. The big advantage is that you don't have to install any client software. The disadvantage is that psexec doesn't traverse well through firewalls. Here's where WINRM/WINRS comes in. WINRM/WINRS has capabilities similar to those of psexec. WINRM stands for Windows Remote Management, while WINRS stands for Windows Remote Shell. We first need to create a listener with the command *winrm quickconfig.* After executing this command, a listener is created on port 80. With the following command, we can connect from a remote host to this listener: *winrs –r:<servername> <command>*. In Figure 7.14, you can see we are trying to connect to the server with IP address 192.168.1.230, this time using Winrs. If you get the same error, you're probably working in a workgroup and the default Kerberos authentication mechanism won't work.

Figure 7.14 A WINRM Error

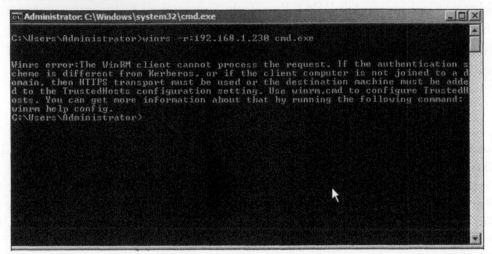

To loosen the security, run the following commands:
Run on the server and client side:

- winrm set winrm/config/service/auth @{Basic="true"}
- winrm set winrm/config/client @{TrustedHosts="<local>"}.

Run on the client side:

- winrm set winrm/config/client @{TrustedHosts="RemoteHost"} and winrm set winrm/config/client @{TrustedHosts="Servername"}.

Be careful, the syntax is case-sensitive. For more configuration details, see the command *winrm help config*.

Managing Server Core with Group Policy

If you have a large amount of Server Core machines, the absolute easiest way to administer Server Core is by using group policy. Just put all the Server Core machines in the right OU and you're done. This will likely prove to be a little more convenient than having to edit the settings on each system individually.

The number of policy settings that can be done has increased from approximately 1,700 in Windows 2003 to around 2,400 in Windows 2008. If you want to do some troubleshooting or other group policy–related tasks, the tools *gpupdate, gpresult*, and *secedit* are still available.

PowerShell

As said before, PowerShell running on Server Core isn't supported. PowerShell requires the .NET Framework, and because the framework has a lot of GUI dependencies, it can't be installed on Server Core. But that doesn't mean you can't use PowerShell from your management workstation to administer a Server Core machine. You are allowed to use the Windows Management Instrumentation (WMI) or Active Directory Services Interface (ADSI) within PowerShell to administer the Server Core box. At the time of this writing, Microsoft was developing a light version of .NET Framework. The expectation is that PowerShell will probably be part of Server Core in a future release.

Installing Active Directory Domain Services on Server Core

So, here is where things get a little tricky. When installing the Directory Services role on a full server installation, we simply open up a **Run** window and type in **Dcpromo**. Then, we follow the prompts for configuration (domain name, file location, level of forest/domain security), and finally restart the system. Installing the role in Server Core isn't that simple, but on the other hand, it's not exactly rocket science either. In order to make this installation happen, we need to configure an *unattended installation file*. An unattended installation file (see Figure 7.15) is nothing more than a text file that answers the questions that would have been answered during the Dcpromo installation. So, let's assume you've created the unattended file and placed it on a floppy disk, CD, or other medium, and then inserted it into the Server Core server. Let's go ahead and install Directory Services:

1. Sign in to the server.

2. In the console, change drives to the removable media. In our example, this is drive E.

3. Once you have changed drives, type **dcpromo.exe /answer:e:\unattended.txt**. Unattended.txt is the name of our unattended file (see Figure 7.15).

Figure 7.15 A Simple Unattended File

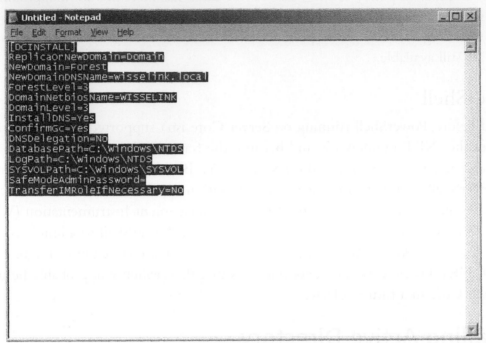

This is the only way to install Active Directory Domain Services on Server Core. If you don't know how to configure the settings in an unattended file in order to install a domain controller, you can still create an unattended file after typing Dcpromo.exe on a normal Windows 2008 machine. Walk through the screens until you see the one displayed in Figure 7.16. Click the **Export Settings** button and save the file to a suitable location. Afterward, cancel the Dcpromo setup.

Figure 7.16 The Active Directory Domain Services Installation Wizard

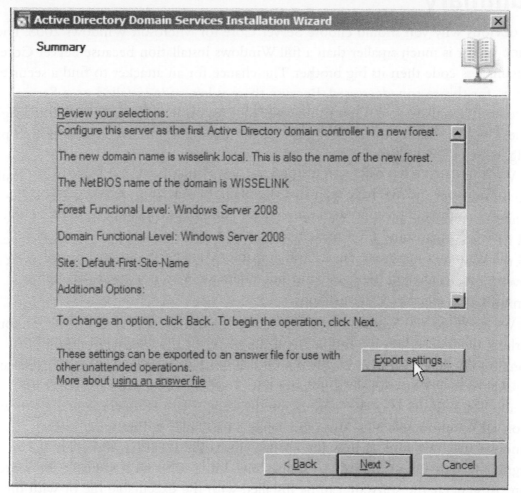

Summary

It's obvious why you should choose Server Core for Microsoft Windows 2008. The attack vector is much smaller than a full Windows installation because Server Core contains less code then its big brother. The chance for an attacker to find a security hole is, for this reason, decreased. Because there is less code installed on a Server Core machine, there is also less to manage. This results in a decreased patch managing cycle. The low disk footprint can help you free up some time when you have to plan a big Server Core rollout.

We've learned what roles and features are and which roles and features are available for Server Core. We have seen that the main console from Server Core is the Windows command prompt. We know which components belong to Server Core and have seen that some GUI tools, like Notepad, two Control Panel applets, regedit, and the Windows logon screen, are still available. Most DOS commands still work on Server Core, so reading the command-line reference A–Z is a good start before administrating a Server Core machine.

We provided you with some tips to help you easily recognize which server you're working on, like adding the hostname of the server to the command prompt or changing the background color for the most important servers. If no commands are available to help you with the configuration of Server Core, you can always use regedit. Many of the Registry settings are the same if you compare Server Core with a normal Windows machine. You can change a particular setting on a normal Windows machine, look at how the change affects the Registry, and apply the Registry change on a Windows Core machine. Little software is available for Server Core. In general, the software can be installed with the executable file or with the command msiexec /i productname.msi. Before installing software on a Server Core machine, it's best to first check the official installation instructions. Instead of typing long commands, use the resource kit tool choice.exe to create menu-send batch files. For those administrators out there with less scripting knowledge, it's now easier to administer Server Core because you don't have to remember all those long or difficult commands. You only have to press a number that corresponds to the command.

In the chapter's final section, we learned how to administer Server Core. The section was divided into three separate parts: installing, configuring, and administrating Server Core. After reading the first paragraph, you should have quickly concluded that installing Server Core is rather easy. You can install it manually or unattended. Command-line freaks should have had a lot of fun with the section on configuring

Server Core since all the command-line options are covered there. After the initial configuration is done, you saw that administrators can manage their Server Core machines with the normal MMC tools (or Remote Server Administration Tools RSAT), WS-management, or with group policies.

Solutions Fast Track

Server Core Features

- ☑ Server Core is a stripped-down version of Windows Server 2008. Most of the installing, configuring, and maintenance must be done using the command line.

- ☑ Server Core has fewer services installed and is, for this reason, less vulnerable to exploits and outside attacks.

- ☑ It's expected that the total number of patches will be reduced by 60 percent because the components that require the greater burden of servicing are removed.

- ☑ Server Core uses only 2GB of disk space for operations, and because of this it's a good candidate for large datacenters.

Server Core Components

- ☑ You can divide Server Core into *hardware support components* (disk, net card), a *Coresubsystem* (RPC, Winlogon File Systems, TCP/IP), *infrastructure features* (command shell, performance counters, WINRM/WINRS), and some thin *management tools* to configure IP addresses, join a domain, create users, and so on.

- ☑ With the command *oclist.exe*, you can see what roles and features are installed on the Server Core machine.

- ☑ The following roles are available for Server Core: Active Directory Domain Services (AD DS), Active Directory Lightweight Directory Services (AD LDS), DHCP Server, DNS Server, File Services, Streaming Media Services, Print Server, Web Server (IIS), and Hyper-V.

- ☑ Server Core doesn't support managed code like .NET Framework. For this reason, PowerShell isn't supported on Server Core like the command *servermanagercmd.exe*. *servermanagercmd.exe* is replaced by *ocsetup.exe*. This command lets you install and uninstall roles and features on Server Core.

Server Core Best Practices

☑ With a Registry change, you can adjust the default layout from the command prompt. This helps you distinguish the command prompts when you have several remote command boxes open.

☑ You can connect to a Server Core machine with Remote Desktop. It's also possible to create an RDP file, which starts (after double-clicking it) a remote command shell session to a Server Core machine.

☑ Creating menu-send DOS menus can help you more easily administrate Server Core.

Server Core Administration

☑ You can install Server Core unattended or by booting the Windows Server 2008 DVD and selecting Server Core as an installation option.

☑ You can remotely manage Server Core machines with the Remote Server Administration Tools (RSAT) installed on Windows Vista with Service Pack 1. RSAT is also a built-in feature component of the full installation version of Windows Server 2008. If you install a role or feature, the corresponding RSAT tool or MMC will be installed on the full version of Windows Server 2008. If you use WINRM/WINRS, you are able to remotely administer Server Core command lines. Just like the previous versions of Windows, it's possible to administer Server Core with group policies.

Frequently Asked Questions

Q: Why should I install Server Core?

A: Because it's more secure due to fewer installed DLLs and services, making it less vulnerable to attacks. Server Core requires less software maintenance than a regular Windows machine and requires only 2GB of disk space.

Q: Which roles are available for Server Core?

A: Active Directory Domain Services, Active Directory Lightweight Directory Services (AD LDS), DHCP Server, DNS Server, File Services, Streaming Media Services, Print Server, Web Server (IIS), and Hyper-V.

Q: How can I see which roles are installed or uninstalled?

A: Execute the command *oclist* at the command prompt.

Q: How do I install a role or feature?

A: Use the command *start /w ocsetup <server role name/feature name>*.

Q: How do I install Active Directory on Server Core if there is no RUN in the Start menu where we can type DCPROMO?

A: First of all, the name Active Directory has been changed to Active Directory Domain Services (AD DS), and you can only install Active Directory Domain Services unattended.

Q: How do I install software on Server Core?

A: If the application has an executable, you can run that. If it is an MSI file, you can use *Msiexec.exe /i <msipackage>*. It's a best practice to install applications in silent mode.

Q: How do you uninstall software on Server Core if there is no Add/Remove Programs?

A: Use *Msiexec.exe /x <msipackage>*. If the application isn't an MSI file but an executable, look for the product documentation. Or type *application.exe /?* for the de-installation options.

Q: Do I have to learn a new scripting language because all the administering and configuring must be done at the command prompt?

A: No. Many commands that were also available in previous versions of Windows can be used on Server Core. A good start is the command-line reference A–Z, which can be found at http://technet2.microsoft.com/windowsserver/en/library/552ed70a-208d-48c4-8da8-2e27b530eac71033.mspx?mfr=true.

Q: Do I have to activate Windows Server Core?

A: Yes, you must activate Windows Server Core within 60 days of installation.

Chapter 8

Configuring Windows Server Hyper-V and Virtual Machines

Solutions in this chapter:

- Configuring Virtual Machines
- Migrating from Physical to Virtual Machines
- Backing Up Virtual Machines
- Virtual Server Optimization

- ☑ Summary
- ☑ Solutions Fast Track
- ☑ Frequently Asked Questions

Introduction

In previous versions of Windows Server, Virtual PC and Virtual Server were utilized to run multiple operating systems on the same computer. Windows Server 2008 provides you with very useful and powerful methods of running multiple virtualized operating systems that you must be familiar with. One of these new features is a next-generation hypervisor-based virtualization platform called Hyper-V for Windows Server 2008. *Hyper-V* is a powerful new role that we will explain further in this chapter.

In this chapter, we will discuss Hyper-V as well as how to configure and back up virtual machines using the new methods available with Windows Server 2008. We will also go over how to migrate from physical to virtual machines using the Hyper-V role for virtualization. In addition we will explore all the new virtualization options available with Windows Server 2008 and how they compare to older virtualization suites. To begin with, we will discuss some of the concepts of virtualization available to previous Windows Server builds and the new features offered by Windows Server 2008.

Advancing Microsoft's Strategy for Virtualization

Microsoft is leading the effort to improve system functionality, making it more self-managing and dynamic. Microsoft's main goal with virtualization is to provide administrators more control of their IT systems with the release of Windows Server 2008 and Hyper-V.

This includes a faster response time to restore that is head and shoulders above Microsoft's competition. Windows Server 2008 provides a total package of complimentary virtualization products that range in functionality from desktop usage to datacenter hubs. One of their major goals is to provide the ability to manage all IT assets, both physical and virtual, from a single remote machine. Microsoft is also forwarding an effort to cut IT costs with its virtualization programs to better help customers take advantage of the interoperability features its products have to offer as well as data center consolidation. This also includes energy efficiency due to the use of less physical machines. This fact alone reduces the consumption of energy in the data center and helps to save money long term. By contributing to and investing in the areas of management, applications, and licensing, Microsoft hopes to succeed in this effort.

Windows Server 2008 has many of these goals in mind, providing a number of important assets to administrators. The implementation of Hyper-V for virtualization allows for quick migration and high availability. This provides solutions for scheduled and unscheduled downtime, and the possibility of improved restore times. Virtual storage is supported for up to four virtual SCSI controllers per virtual machine, allowing for ample storage capacity. Hyper-V allows for the import and export of virtual machines and is integrated with Windows Server Manager for greater usability options.

In the past compatibility was always an issue of concern. Now the emulated video card has been updated to a more universal VESA compatible card. This will improve video issues, resulting in noncompatibility with operating systems like Linux. In addition Windows Server 2008 also includes integration components (ICs) for virtual machines. When you install Windows Server 2008 as a guest system in a Hyper-V virtual machine, Windows will install the ICs automatically. There is also support for Hyper-V with the Server Core in the parent partition allowing for easier configuration. This as well as numerous fixes for performance, scalability, and compatibility make the end goal for Hyper-V a transparent end user experience.

Notes from the Underground…

Windows Hypervisor

With Windows Server 2008 Microsoft introduced a next-generation hypervisor virtualization platform. Hyper-V, formerly codenamed Viridian, is one of the noteworthy new features of Windows Server 2008. It offers a scalable and highly available virtualization platform that is efficient and reliable. It has an inherently secure architecture. This combined with a minimal attack surface (especially when using Server Core) and the fact that it does not contain any third-party device drivers makes it extremely secure. It is expected to be the best operating system platform for virtualization released to date.

Compared to its predecessors, Hyper-V provides more options for specific needs because it utilizes more powerful 64-bit hardware and 64-bit operating systems. Additional processing power and a large addressable memory space is gained by the utilization of a 64-bit environment. It also requires no need for outside applications, which increase overall compatibility across the board.

Hyper-V has three main components: the *hypervisor*, the *virtualization stack*, and the new *virtualized I/O model*. The hypervisor (also known as the *virtual machine monitor* or *VMM*) is a very small layer of software that interacts directly with the processor, which creates the different "partitions" that

Continued

each virtualized instance of the operating system will run within. The virtualization stack and the I/O components act to provide a go-between with Windows and with all the partitions that you create. Hyper-V's virtualization advancements will only help to further assist administrators in quicker easier responses to emergency deployment needs.

Hyper-V is a new feature for Microsoft in Windows Server 2008. It is a role that Microsoft is pushing very hard, and it is a feature that has many uses in day-to-day operations. Although you may be familiar with past methods of virtualization such as Virtual PC and Virtual Server, these virtualization suites operate very differently from Hyper-V. Many of the terms and user features may appear similar to past versions but have been changed, updated, or completely overhauled. Be sure to familiarize yourself with these updated features and terms, especially how virtualization works in regards to Hyper-V.

Understanding Virtualization

At times, you will need a method to hide the physical characteristics of the host system from the way in which other systems and applications interact with it. This includes the way end users will interact with those resources as well. For example a single server, operating system, application, or storage device may need to appear to function as multiple logical resources. You may also want to make multiple physical resources (such as storage devices or servers) appear as a single logical resource as well. This method is known as *virtualization* and is achieved in Windows Server 2008 by the installation of Hyper-V and the creation of virtual machines.

Virtualization is a broad term that deals with many aspects of its use. The trouble is being able to understand different types of virtualization. This includes what these types offer for you and how they can help accomplish your individual goals. There are currently three major types of virtualization that are available for use with Windows Server 2008 with Hyper-V role installed. Here is a simple explanation of each:

- **Server Virtualization** is the when the physical server hardware is separated from Guest operating systems (servers).

- **Network Virtualization** involves creating the illusion that all resources on the network are part of the user's desktop computer by moving network applications, localizing them in a seamless fashion through virtualization.

- **Storage Virtualization** involves hiding disk storage complexities by creating a Storage Area Network, which is responsible for redirecting storage requests from end users through virtualization.

Hyper-V allows virtual machine technology to be applied to both server and client hardware. It enables multiple operating systems to run concurrently on a single machine. Hyper-V specifically, is a key feature of Windows Server 2008. Until the release of Windows Server 2008, many x86-based operating systems seeking to use a Microsoft solution achieved virtualization via Virtual PC 2007 and Virtual Server 2005.

Tools & Traps...

Understanding Virtual PC and Server

Before Windows Server 2008 there were other options for virtualization and emulation. Two of the most common that you should be aware of are Virtual PC and Virtual Server 2005. Both are virtualization suites for the PC and emulations suites for use in Mac OS X. They allow the cross-platform use of a variety of PC applications and operating systems. Virtual Server 2005 and Virtual PC 2007 mimic standard Intel Pentium 4 processors with an Intel 440BX chipset. Thus, they can be used to emulate certain applications for the PC on a Mac PowerPC. Virtual PC 2007 is a recent release that allows the emulation and virtualization of Microsoft Vista. However, issues can arise when trying to install uncommon operating systems that have not been specifically targeted in the development of Virtual PC or Virtual Server.

Virtual PC for the Mac uses dynamic recompilation in order to translate the x86 code used by a standard PC. It translates this code into the equivalent PowerPC code used by a Mac. Virtual PC for Windows also uses the same type of dynamic recompilation. Instead it takes kernel mode and real mode x86 code and translates it into x86 user mode code. The original user mode and virtual 8086 mode code runs natively, allowing fluidity.

Both Virtual PC and Virtual Server were useful in the development of the virtualization trend but received some complaints. Both seemed to fall short in specific areas of compatibility, especially in regards to Linux and uncommon application usage. Another drawback is that Virtual Server 2005 and Virtual PC 2007 are compatible for hosts with x64 processors but cannot run guests that require x64 processors running a 64 bit OS. Both of these products are commonly utilized but have been slowly declining in popularity due to free virtualization software such as VMware and Xen. Windows Server 2008 is Microsoft's solution to this issue by offering more options than its free competitors via the new features available through Hyper-V.

Virtualization creates virtual machines, each of which is capable of running a different operating system on a single physical machine while the virtual machines run without interference behind partitions. This can be used to simulate multiple native environments and most of the benefits that would normally require multiple machines and deployments. Virtualization is a growing trend that can greatly reduce deployment costs. It allows a single machine to run multiple operating systems simultaneously while allowing you to dynamically add physical and virtual resources to those machines as needed. For example, you can install multiple virtualized operating systems on the host computer and each virtualized operating system will run in isolation from the other operating systems installed.

Notes from the Underground...

Expanding the Limits of Hyper-V Virtualization

Hyper-V has many features that surpass previous virtualization software packages as a stand alone virtualization suite installed on Windows Server 2008. Hyper-V allows for greater application compatibility than previous software of its kind. Because of this, Hyper-V can utilize and take advantage of other tools and applications to create an even more versatile and dynamic experience. This greatly increases the options for administrators to customize their virtual network to their own specific needs for their company.

There are many scenarios that can test the limits of Hyper-V that Microsoft is only beginning to speculate on. As an example of the options available with Hyper-V, consider this scenario. Many of you may be familiar with Virtual PC 2007 and use it as a solution for running a virtualized Windows 98 operating system. You may find it interesting to know that although this scenario is not supported by Microsoft using Hyper-V, it is possible to run a Windows Server 2008 with Hyper-V with Windows 2003 installed on a virtual machine. By then installing Virtual PC 2007 onto that virtual machine you can in turn use Virtual PC 2007 to run Windows 98. Both Virtual PC and Virtual Server work in this scenario and have better than expected performance. Microsoft plans on expanding their support of Hyper-V to eventually cover more of these unique scenarios.

Although virtualization has existed in many incarnations it is not a catch-all fix for all networking needs. There are still many precautions that are required when working with Hyper-V or any virtualization suite. For example, if the machine acting as a host for your virtual network is not part of some failover group or you do not have a method of back up such as a hot spare, you could find yourself with a total network outage if that computer fails. There will always be a need for redundancy of some kind for no other reason than to be thorough and prove due diligence. Also note that the Hyper-V requires heavier system requirements such as enterprise class hardware and training that must also be factored into your company's cost considerations.

The potential of virtual machine technology is only beginning to be harnessed and can be used for a wide range of purposes. It enables hardware consolidation, because multiple operating systems can run on one computer. Key applications for virtual machine technology include cross-platform integration as well as the following:

- **Server consolidation** Consolidating many physical servers into fewer servers, by using host virtual machines. Virtual machine technology can be used to run a single server with multiple operating systems on it side by side. This replaces the need for multiple servers that were once required to run the same applications because they required different operating systems to perform their tasks. The physical servers are transformed into virtual machine "guests" who occupy a virtual machine host system. This can be also called Physical-to-Virtual or P2V transformation.

- **Disaster recovery** Physical production servers can use virtual machines as "hot standby" environments. Virtual machines can provide backup images that can boot into live virtual machines. This allows for application portability and flexibility across hardware platforms. It changes the traditional "backup and restore" mentality. These VMs are then capable of taking over the workload of a production server experiencing an outage.

- **Consolidation for testing and development environments** Virtual machines can be used for testing of early developmental versions of applications without fear of destabilizing the system for other users. Because each virtual machine is its own isolated testing environment it reduces risks incurred by developers. Virtual machines can be used to compare different versions of applications for different operating systems and to test those applications in a variety of different configurations. Kernel development and operating system test course can greatly benefit from hardware virtualization, which can give root access to a virtual machine and its guest operating system.

■ **Upgrading to a dynamic datacenter** Dynamic IT environments are now achievable via the use of virtualization. Hyper-V, along with systems management solutions enables you to troubleshoot problems more effectively. This also creates IT management solution that is efficient and self-managing.

In past Windows versions there were specific limitations on these virtual machines created. In Windows Server 2008 with Hyper-V installed each virtual operating system is a full operating system with access to applications. You can also run non-Microsoft operating systems in the virtualized environment of Windows Server 2008.

Understanding the Components of Hyper-V

Hyper-V has greater deployment capabilities to past versions and provides more options for your specific needs because it utilizes specific 64-bit hardware and a 64-bit operating system. Additional processing power and a larger addressable memory space is gained by the utilization of a 64-bit environment. Hyper-V has three main components: the *hypervisor*, the *virtualization stack*, and the new *virtualized I/O model*. The hypervisor also known as the *virtual machine monitor*, is a very small layer of software that is present directly on the processor, which creates the different "partitions" that each virtualized instance of the operating system will run within. The virtualization stack and the I/O components act to provide a go-between with Windows and with all the partitions that you create. All three of these components of Hyper-V work together as a team to allow virtualization to occur. Hyper-V hooks into threads on the host processor, which the host operating system can then use to efficiently communicate with multiple virtual machines. Because of this, these virtual machines and multiple virtual operating systems can all be running on a single physical processor. You can see this model in Figure 8.1.

Figure 8.1 Viewing the Components of Hyper-V

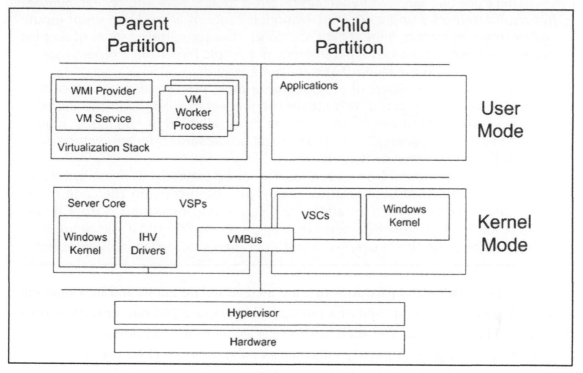

Tools & Traps…

Understanding Hypercalls in Hyper-V

In order to better understand and distinguish the basis for Hyper-V virtualization, let's try to get a better idea of how hypercalls work. The hypervisor uses a calling system for a guest that is specific to Hyper-V. These calls are called *hypercalls*. A hypercall defines each set of input or output parameters between the host and guest. These parameters are referred to in terms of a memory-based data structure. All aspects of input and output data structures are cushioned to natural boundaries up to 8 bytes. Input and output data structures are placed in memory on an 8-byte boundary. These are then padded to a multiple of 8 bytes in size. The values inside the padding areas are overlooked by the hypervisor.

Continued

There are two kinds of hypercalls referred to as *simple* and *repeat*. *Simple hypercall* attempts a single act or operation. It contains a fixed-size set of input and output parameters. *Repeat hypercall* conducts a complicated series of simple hypercalls. Besides having the parameters of a simple hypercall, a repeat hypercall uses a list of fixed-size input and output elements.

You can issue a hypercall only from the most privileged guest processor mode. For x64 environment, this means the protected mode with the Current Privilege Level (CPL) of zero. Hypercalls are never allowed in real mode. If you attempt to issue a hypercall within an illegal processor mode, you will receive an undefined operation exception.

All hypercalls should be issued via the architecturally defined hypercall interface. Hypercalls issued by other means including copying the code from the hypercall code page to an alternate location and executing it from there could result in an undefined operation exception. You should avoid doing this altogether because the hypervisor is not guaranteed to deliver this exception.

The hypervisor creates partitions that are used to isolate guests and host operating systems. A partition is comprised of a physical address space and one or more virtual processors. Hardware resources such as CPU cycles, memory, and devices can be assigned to the partition. A *parent partition* creates and manages child partitions. It contains a *virtualization stack*, which controls these child partitions. The parent partition is in most occasions also the root partition. It is the first partition that is created and owns all resources not owned by the hypervisor. As the root partition it will handle the loading of and the booting of the hypervisor. It is also required to deal with power management, plug-and-play, and hardware failure events.

Partitions are named with a partition ID. This 64-bit number is delegated by the hypervisor. These ID numbers are guaranteed by the hypervisor to be unique IDs. These are not unique in respect to power cycles however. The same ID may be generated across a power cycle or a reboot of the hypervisor. The hypervisor does guarantee that all IDs within a single power cycle will be unique.

The hypervisor also is designed to provide availability guarantees to guests. A group of servers that have been consolidated onto a solitary physical machine should not hinder each other from making progress, for example. A partition should be able to be run that provides telephony support such that this partition continues to perform all of its duties regardless of the potentially contrary actions of other partitions. The hypervisor takes many precautions to assure this occurs flawlessly.

For each partition, the hypervisor maintains a *memory pool* of RAM SPA pages. This pool acts just like a checking account. The amount of pages in the pool is called the *balance*. Pages are *deposited* or *withdrawn* from the memory pool. When a hypercall that requires memory is made by a partition, the hypervisor withdraws the required memory from the total pool balance. If the balance is insufficient, the call fails. If such a withdrawal is made by a guest for another guest in another partition, the hypervisor attempts to draw the requested amount of memory from the pool of the latter partition.

Pages within a partition's memory pool are managed by the hypervisor. These pages cannot be accessed through any partition's Global Presence Architecture (GPA) space. That is, in all partitions' GPA spaces, they must be inaccessible (mapped such that no read, write or execute access is allowed). In general, the only partition that can deposit into or withdraw from a partition is that partition's parent.

WARNING

Remember not to confuse partitions with virtual machines. You should think of a virtual machine as comprising a partition together within its state. Many times partitioning can be mistaken for the act of virtualization when dealing with Hyper-V.

We should note that Microsoft will continue to support Linux operating systems with the production release of Hyper-V. Integration components and technical support will be provided for customers running certain Linux distributions as guest operating systems within Hyper-V. Integration components for Beta Linux are now available for Novell SUSE Linux Enterprise Server (SLES) 10 SP1 x86 and x64 Editions. These components enable Xen-enabled Linux to take advantage of the VSP/VSC architecture. This will help to provide improved performance overall. Beta Linux Integration components are available for immediate download through http://connect.microsoft.com. Another additionally noteworthy feature is, as of this writing, Red Hat Fedora 8 Linux and the alpha version of Fedora 9 Linux, which are both compatible and supported by Hyper-V. The full list of supported operating systems will be announced prior to RTM.

Configuring Virtual Machines

We have discussed the many benefits and concept of virtualization and touched on how it can benefit you in terms of server consolidation, energy efficiency, and simpler management and deployment.

All these aspects of efficiency make virtualization an important tool. The root of virtualization is its use of *virtual machines.* Virtual machines are by definition software emulations within a computer that executes programs and applications like a real machine. Windows Server 2008 with Hyper-V allows the creation of multiple virtual machines, each running multiple operating systems also called *guest operating systems,* from a single physical machine.

The two main advantages of a Virtual Machine (VM) are:

- Multiple OS environments can share the same computer while still being strongly isolated from each other and the virtual machine

- They can provide an *instruction set architecture* (ISA) that is fairly contrary to that of the actual machine.

One of the main and most popular uses for VMs is to isolate multiple operating systems from a single machine, which consolidates servers and reduces interference between conflicting operating systems. This is referred to as Quality-of-Service (QoS) isolation.

Hyper-V supports isolation in terms of a partition that is a logical unit of isolation. This is supported by the hypervisor, in which operating systems execute. A hypervisor instance has to have at least one root partition, running Windows Server 2008. Hardware devices are accessed directly by the virtualization stack in the root partition. Guest operating systems are hosted on child partitions that are created by the root partition. A child partition can also create additional child partitions. A host or parent partition creates child partitions using the hypercall, *application programming interface (API).*

Windows Server 2008 includes a new tool to manage your virtual machines called the Hyper-V Manager.

Installing Hyper-V

As you have seen so far in this chapter, Hyper-V is a versatile new feature for Windows Server 2008. Before explaining how to create, configure, and delegate hard drive space to virtual machines you must first be able to install the Hyper-V feature to your machine. Hyper-V has many prerequisites that must be met before installation can occur. We will now discuss the proper method for installing the virtualization features of Hyper-V.

NOTE

Hyper-Vs require 64-bit hardware and a 64-bit version of the Windows Server 2008 operating system to implement.

In order to utilize virtualization you must have a clean install of Windows Server 2008 Enterprise with Hyper-V installed onto the host machine. Remember that Hyper-V requires 64-bit hardware and a 64-bit version of the operating system. You must also ensure that you have hardware-assisted virtualization enabled prior to installation. If BIOS configuration changes were made to the machine to enable these features, a full cycle power down must be completed to proceed. Once we are sure all these prerequisites are met, we can go over the steps required to install Hyper-V.

Configuring & Implementing...

Avoiding Common Bios Problems with Hyper-V

Hyper-V requires hardware-assisted virtualization. If you have an x64 Intel processor that supports hardware virtualization you should have no BIOS configuration issues. These processors come preconfigured for hardware virtualization. Hardware-assisted virtualization may need to be enabled on some processors. This may require altering the BIOS configuration of the host computer.

Intel Virtualization Technology and AMD Pacifica are both compatible with Hyper-V usage out of the box. However if you are using an x64 AMD processor there are known configuration issues that have yet to be addressed. If you are using this type of processor you should consult the online documentation located at http://techreport.com/discussions.x/13721 for your specific processor.

A BIOS update will more than likely be necessary. There is a fairly simple way of determining if you will need to update your BIOS in this case. You should check the "stepping" value for your processor using a CPU validation tool such as CPUID, which is available at http://www.cpuid.com. After running the tool consult the stepping value of your CPU. If the stepping value is 2 you will require a BIOS update. If the stepping value is 3 or higher you should have no need to update the BIOS to install Hyper-V to your machine.

www.syngress.com

This is the procedure for installing the Hyper-V role on Windows Server 2008:

1. Click **Start** and click to open Server Manager.

2. Locate the Roles node of the main Server Manager window.

3. Click **Add Roles**.

4. On the Specific Server Roles page click **Add Hyper-V** (as shown in Figure 8.2). Follow the prompts to finish installing the Role and click **OK** when finished.

Figure 8.2 Adding Hyper-V on the Specific Server Roles Page

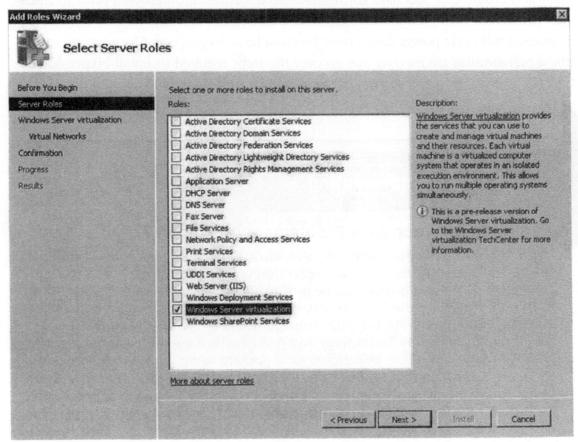

5. Once installed, you will need to access the Virtualization Management Console to configure virtual machines. You can find the VMM within the Administrative Tools menu in the Start menu. Once opened, you can use the Create Virtual Networks page to select the network

adapters that you wish to make connections available to virtual machines. Also note that you should leave one network adapter free for remote access. Only Ethernet (802.3) network adapters are supported.

6. Click **Install** on the Confirm Installation Selections page.

7. Upon completion, click **Close** to end the installation.

8. Click **Yes** to restart the system.

Also note that when you open Hyper-V Manager for the first time, you must accept the end-user license agreement (EULA) using an account that is a member of the local Administrators group. If you fail to do so you will not be able to use the snap-in to perform any tasks. Be sure to log on to the computer using an appropriate account before you open the snap-in for the first time. If this problem occurs simply close Hyper-V Manager and log on to the computer using an appropriate account. Once you have done this you may open Hyper-V Manager without incident.

Installing and Managing Hyper-V on Windows Server Core Installations

The Windows server core installation option of Windows Server 2008 and Windows Server virtualization are two new features of Windows Server 2008 that work together to a mutually beneficial end. Windows server core installation option is a new shell-less and GUI-free installation option for Window Server 2008 Standard, Enterprise, and Datacenter Editions. It will lower the level of management and maintenance required by an administrator. The Windows server core installation option provides several advantages over a full installation of Windows Server 2008. It is intended to act as a complement to Windows Server virtualization. Hyper-V is compatible with Server Core installations but requires certain preparation to install. In order to take advantage of this installation process you must be aware of certain procedures before installing. If you wish to install Hyper-V on to a Server Core, run the following command: **Start /w ocsetup Microsoft-Hyper-V**. Once installed you can manage Hyper-V on a Server Core installation, by doing the following:

1. Use Hyper-V Manager to connect to the Server Core installation remotely from a full installation of Windows Server 2008 on which the Hyper-V role is installed.

2. Use the Windows Management Instrumentation (WMI) interface to manage the installation process.

> **NOTE**
>
> WMI is used to define a nonproprietary set of environment-independent specifications. By doing this it allows management information to be shared between management applications that run in both similar and dissimilar operating system environments.

We should now be familiar with the installation process of Hyper-V. Let us now get a better grasp of the bigger picture behind virtual machines. We can start with what a virtual network is and how it is set up using Windows Server 2008 with Hyper-V enabled.

Virtual Networking

A *virtual network* is the organization of a group of networks in such a way that it appears to the end user to be a singular larger network. It ideally contains a consistent user interface, which allows for the user to communicate both remotely and locally across similar and dissimilar networks. This concept can also be applied to the way the network is administrated and managed as well. This is often referred to as *network virtualization*. Deployed correctly, an administrator could manage and monitor all the resources of a virtualized network from a single network administrator's console. In an ideal configuration, all the servers and services in the network would act as a single pool of resources that the administrator could rearrange and redeploy in real time as required by his changing needs. Today's enterprises are comprised of diverse groups of users, each with specific needs. The different business needs of these groups make way for an array of network requirements. These requirements can be so far reaching it requires different groups to be treated as completely separate customers by IT departments.

Many business drivers that encourage the virtualization of networks, including the following:

- Gains in productivity that are derived from providing visitors with access to the Internet so that they can connect to their own private networks.

- The need to quarantine hosts that are infected or not compliant with the security policies to increase availability.

- Providing personnel connectivity to the Internet and select internal resources to in-house consultants, partners, or even contractors of a business.

- The necessity for secure network areas that are partially or totally isolated.

- Consolidation of multiple networks onto a single infrastructure.

- A simple, logical collocation of competing customers on a shared infrastructure.

- Integration of subsidiaries and acquisitions.

- Meeting the requirements of next-generation business models that are aimed at improving efficiencies, reducing costs, and generating new streams of revenue. In such a situation the IT department could become a revenue-generating service provider.

NOTE

Be sure to familiarize yourself with the benefits of network virtualization in different business environments. The end goal of network virtualization is to have a transparent, always accessible, dedicated network with resources and security policies that are not codependent. Bear this definition in mind when looking at how a business can benefit from virtualization.

Network virtualization is an innovative approach to providing an isolated networking environment for each group within the enterprise. Each of these logical environments will be maintained across a single shared network infrastructure. Each network allows for the corresponding group of users to have full network access similar to those provided by a traditional network. The overall goal from an end-user perspective is having access to an always accessible transparent dedicated network with individual resources and independent security policies. So in short, network virtualization requires the logical division of all network devices and network services.

Let's take an overview of what key elements comprise a virtual network:

- Network hardware, such as switches and Network adapters, also known as network interface cards (NICs)

- Networks, such as virtual LANs (VLANs)

- Containers such as virtual machines

- Network storage devices.

- Network transmission media, such as coaxial cable

Windows Server 2008 Hyper-V is the hypervisor-based virtualization feature included as a role of Windows Server 2008. It contains everything needed to create a virtual network. These virtual networks enable IT organizations to reduce costs, to improve server utilization and to create a more dynamic IT infrastructure. This enables you to create a nimble and multifunctional datacenter and progress toward achieving self-managing dynamic systems.

Windows Server 2008 comes equipped with integrated virtual switches to help you accomplish these goals. These switches play different roles than their past incarnation in Virtual Server and those of traditional hardware switches. Integrated Virtual Switches are new to Windows Server 2008 and were not included in previous Windows Servers. This also means that networking is quite different than it previously was in past Windows Servers. All the integrated switches come with Virtual Local Area Network (VLAN) support. There are three integrated virtual switches in Windows Server 2008. Here is a brief definition of the switches uses:

- The first virtual switch is bound to the physical adapter, which means any virtual machines connected to this virtual switch can access the physical network.

- The second virtual switch is connected to the host or parent partition, which allows virtual machines to communicate with each as well as the host partition.

- The third virtual switch is purely virtual or unbound and allows only the virtual machines connected to this switch to communicate without packets hitting the wire.

Virtualization Hardware Requirements

Windows Server 2008 has a variety of necessary requirements that you will need to be aware of when troubleshooting, installing, or configuring the functionality of virtual machines and Hyper-V. Hyper-V is available with Windows Server 2008 Enterprise x64. Unlike previous virtualization software Hyper-V is a hypervisor virtualization platform that requires hardware-supported virtualization, specific hardware requirements, and BIOS configuration updates for certain processors.

The hypervisor itself has several hardware tests that it performs prior to runtime. The hypervisor obtains information about the underlying physical hardware from three sources:

- **Boot-time input parameters** When the hypervisor is booted, parameters are provided about some aspects of the physical hardware. The hardware aspects that are described to the hypervisor at boot time include the number of potential logical processors, the status of hyperthreading capabilities in the BIOS, and the present RAM SPA ranges. RAM SPA is the systems physical address range that is populated with RAM when the hypervisor is booted.

- **Dynamic discovery** The hypervisor can discover information concerning the physical hardware at runtime. This is done by using architecturally defined mechanisms, for example CPUID instruction on x64 processors.

- **Root partition input** The hypervisor is required to be told about hardware changes by code running within the root partition. This includes hardware changes such as power management and hot add/removal.

There are two key hardware requirements for installation of Hyper-V platform. One is the need to ensure that the server is a 64-bit environment. The second is that the server supports hardware-assisted virtualization technology. More specifically, a 64-bit system with hardware-assisted virtualization enabled and data execution prevention (DEP) is required.

Hyper-V runs on a 64-bit (x64) server platform and requires support of either AMD64 or Intel IA-32e/EM64T (x64) processors with hardware-assisted virtualization support. It is important to note that Hyper-V does not support Itanium (IA-64) processors. Hyper-V can support both single processor and multiprocessor configurations in the virtual machine environment. For an updated list of Microsoft compatibility tested hardware see the information listed in http://download.microsoft.com/download/e/4/8/e48d5cff-53d2-4eed-85bf-4af50e25b78c/relnotes.htm.

Virtual Hard Disks

When dealing with virtual machines, virtual storage plays a large role in reaping the benefits of virtualization. A virtual machine relies on virtual hard disks much in the same way a physical machine would rely on a physical hard disk. Because of this it is critical to understand and master the creation and configuration of virtual hard disks.

Hyper-V allows you to designate and connect *Virtual Hard Disks* (VHD) to the virtual machines that you create. The virtual hard disk (VHD) format is a block-based format that stores the contents of a virtual machine. VHDs use the *.vhd file that simulates the properties of a physical hard drive. Virtual hard disks can be created during the VM creation using Hyper-V Manager. VHDs can also be customized and created prior to the creation of the virtual machine. To do this Hyper-V offers the *New Virtual Hard Disk wizard* as shown in Figure 8.3. This is a wizard that allows you a great deal of configuration options to create the ideal virtual hard disk for your requirements.

Figure 8.3 New Virtual Hard Disk Wizard

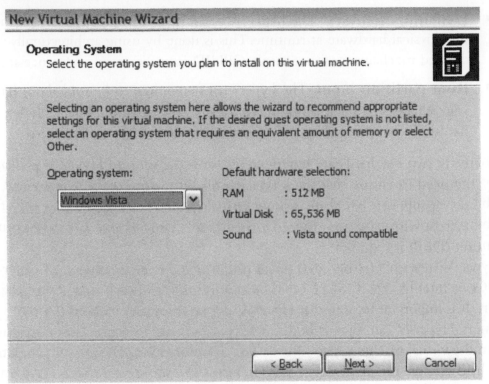

Here is an overview of the functions available to you with the New Virtual Hard Disk Wizard:

- **Before You Begin** This page of the wizard explains the purpose of the wizard. From this pane you can create a default virtual hard disk without working through the rest of the wizard. By clicking **Finish** on this page, the wizard will create a dynamically expanding virtual hard disk with a storage capacity of 127 gigabytes by default.

- **Choose Disk Type** From this page you can choose one of the three types of virtual hard disk that you would like to create based on the functionality you require.

- *Dynamically expanding virtual hard disks* provide storage capacity as needed to store data. The size of the *.vhd file is small when initially created and expands as data is added. The size does not shrink automatically, however, when data is deleted. In order to decrease the *.vhd file size you must compact the disk after data is deleted by using the *Edit Virtual Hard Disk Wizard*.

- *Fixed virtual hard disks* provide storage via a size-specified *.vhd file when the disk is created initially. The size of the *.vhd file remains fixed regardless of the amount of data stored. In order to change the size of this type of disc you must use the Edit Virtual Hard Disk Wizard to increase the size of the virtual hard disc.

- *Differencing virtual hard disks* provide storage to enable you to make changes to a parent virtual hard disk without altering that disk. The size of the *.vhd file for a differencing disk grows as changes are stored to the disk.

- **Specify Name and Location** This page is used to provide a name and location for your new virtual hard disk. You can also specify a shared location if you plan to cluster the virtual hard disk to a virtual machine.

- **Configure Disk** This page allows you to adjust the configuration of the VHD based on the type of disk you selected in the Choose Disk Type window.

  - For fixed and dynamically expanding virtual hard disks, you have the option to copy the contents of an available physical disk.

  - For a differencing disk, you can specify the location of the disk you want to use as the parent virtual hard disk.

- **Completing the New Virtual Hard Disk Wizard** This page gives you the all the configuration details that you selected from all the previous pages. The new virtual hard disk is created when you click **Finish.** This process can take a considerable amount of time depending on the configuration options you choose for your virtual hard disk.

The New Virtual Hard Disk Wizard can be an invaluable resource creating as well as backing up virtual machines. Once a virtual machine is created by the New Virtual Hard Disk Wizard you can use the Edit Virtual Hard Disk wizard to make adjustments to it. This wizard has a number of options including Compact, Convert, Expand, Merge, and Reconnect, based on the type of VHD you have created.

Here is a summation of each of these functions:

- **Compact** This function applies only to dynamically expanding virtual hard disks and differencing virtual hard disks. It reduces the size of the *.vhd file by removing blank space left from where data was deleted.

- **Convert** This function converts a dynamically expanding virtual hard disk to a fixed virtual hard disk or vice versa.

- **Expand** This function increases the total storage capacity of a dynamically expanding virtual hard disk or a fixed virtual hard disk.

- **Merge** This feature applies only to differencing disks and merges the parent partition with the differencing disk for back up purposes.

- **Reconnect** This function applies to differencing disks only. It allows you to choose a differencing disk to reconnect to. This page will appear automatically when the parent virtual hard disk cannot be located.

Now that we have a better understanding of how to create and configure virtual hard disks we are ready to move on to the creation of virtual machines with the Hyper-V role.

Adding Virtual Machines

When attempting to add virtual machines on a Windows Server 2008 you must first be sure that the Hyper-V is installed and correctly set up on the machine. Remember that Hyper-V requires 64-bit hardware and a 64-bit version of the operating system with hardware assisted virtualization enabled to implement virtualization. Be sure that the hardware options of the machine match this criteria and that you are running Windows Server 2008 x64 before attempting to use virtualization options. Also before installing a virtual machine you should go over this quick checklist before moving forward.

- Do you have the proper operating system media available for the virtual machine you are installing?

- By what media type (.ISO, physical media, or remote server image) is the operating system being installed? The virtual machine will be configured according to this information.

- How much memory do you plan on allotting to the virtual machine?

- What do you plan on naming the virtual machine and where it will you store it?

Organization is always critical to success and these will be questions that will be asked of you during the installation process. After the Hyper-V role is enabled, Hyper-V Manager will become available as a part of Administrative Tools. From the Hyper-V Manager users can easily create and configure virtual machines.

To begin creating virtual machine:

1. Click **Start** and proceed to Administrative Tools. Click on **Hyper-V Manager** as shown in Figure 8.4.

Figure 8.4 Hyper-V Manager

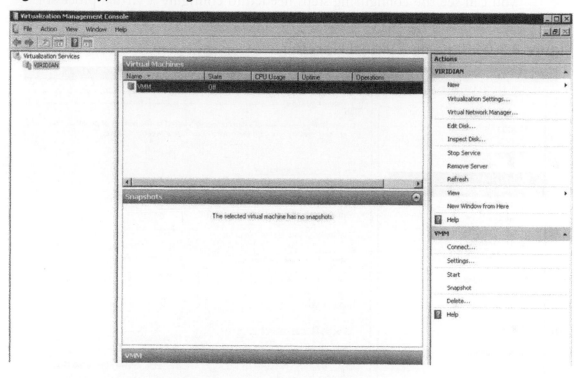

2. Click **New** from the Action Pane and proceed by clicking **Virtual Machines**. Doing this will open the New Virtual Machine wizard.

3. Use the information from your checklist to create a name and storage location for the virtual machine on the Specify Name and Location page.

4. Consult the checklist again for the amount of memory you wish use for the virtual machine. This should be based on the operating system requirements that the virtual machine will be running. After double-checking this information, enter it on the Memory page.

5. To establish connectivity at this point go to the Network page and connect the network adapter to an existing virtual network. If you wish to install your operating system on your virtual machine remotely, select **External Network**.

6. Create a Virtual Hard disc by specifying a name, size, and location on the Connect Virtual Hard Disc. Be sure to account for enough free space to install the operating system on your virtual machine.

7. You can also configure Virtual Processors in the VMM as well. In Figure 8.5, you can see the configuring steps needed to configure a virtual processor.

Figure 8.5 Configuring a Virtual Processor

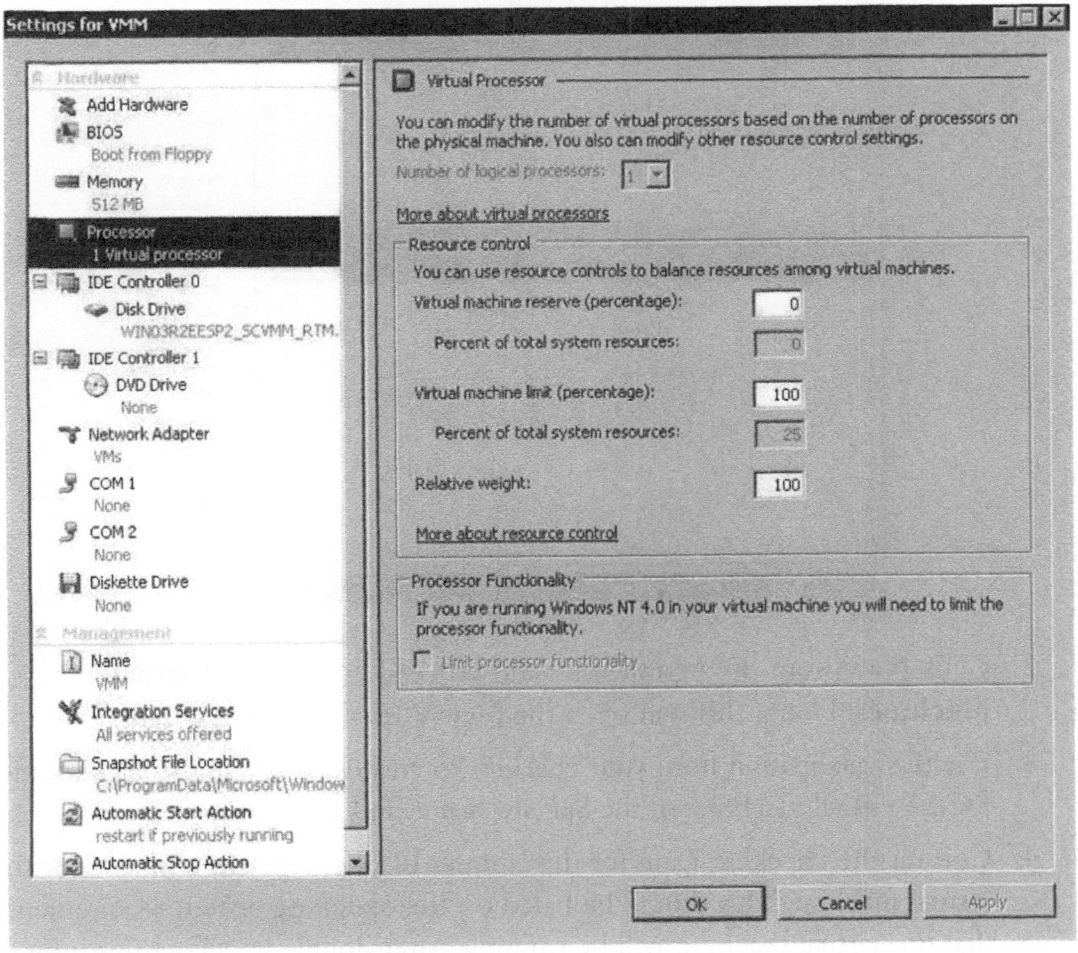

Windows Hyper-V allows you to attach virtual hard discs to each of the virtual machines you create. This allows you to customize and control the storage resources for each VM you create. By default each virtual machine is created with a single virtual hard disk with a maximum of 256 virtual hard disks per Virtual SCSI controller. This feature allows you to add multiple SCSI controllers per virtual machine that you create. With the current limitations on Hyper-V you can add up to a petabyte of storage per virtual machine. Administrators need to configure VHD files on the host system. Tasks such as inspecting virtual hard drive files, compacting virtual hard drive files, or moving storage locations can be accomplished this way. Administrators can mount a virtual hard drive and change a file in the virtual hard drive without starting the associated virtual machine. This ability is invaluable for conducting changes to deactivated images, which would normally require reactivation.

To add hard drive space to your virtual machine:

1. Click **Add Hardware**.
2. Click **Add a virtual SCSI controller**.
3. Then find the Tab labeled **Add Virtual Disc Drive**.
4. Select the amount of storage you wish to add from the list.

TIP

Consult the checklist you made during this section for the amount of memory you wish to allot to a virtual machine. This should be based on the operating system requirements that the virtual machine will be running. Remember that Hyper-V allows for 256 virtual hard disks per Virtual SCSI controller. This means that you can add up to a Petabyte of storage per virtual machine created.

Setting the number of virtual processors that a guest partition uses, adding virtual hard disks or network cards, or adjusting the memory allocation for a virtual machine can be done through the individual virtual machine manager. Administrators can change these settings by using the virtual machine manager or by editing the .VMC files directly. Bear in mind that some of these changes are dynamic, such as adding virtual processors or network adapters. Other changes made such as memory allocation, will require a restart of the virtual computer to take effect.

Installation of Hyper-V and of virtual machines is conducted through the Hyper-V Manager window. Hyper-V utilizes a new method as the main interaction point for dealing with virtual machines. It is called the *Virtual Machine Connection* menu. Using this interface we can create a backup snapshot, edit and alter VMs, and execute a number of configuration changes to virtual machines we have created. This is the primary user interface that you will use when interacting with a virtual machine in Hyper-V role (unlike Virtual Server, which used Virtual Machine Remote Control Client). The Virtual Machine Connection window wraps the standard Remote Desktop Client (RDC).

You may use this interface to connect to a virtual machine, update VM details, and configurations concerning it. As we have discussed previously in this section Hyper-V installation and configuration has been streamlined and made very simple for the administrator to take advantage of it. The Virtual Machine Connection can be toggled between full and normal screen modes for ease of use and accessibility. It can also use key combination to accomplish frequent tasks.

Virtual Machine Connection has its own set of native key combinations for easier usage. These can prove invaluable when configuring multiple virtual machines from a remote host, while also swapping between multiple applications or for nothing other than simplistic ease of use. When first familiarizing yourself with Virtual Machine Connection and its key combinations, be sure to toggle the Virtual Machine Connection to full screen mode when using the standard Windows key combinations. They key combinations will not get sent to the virtual machine, unless you are in the full screen mode. This is the default setting for Hyper-V, which you can change so that key combinations are always sent to the virtual machine as long as the Virtual Machine Connection has focus. This can be accomplished as follows:

1. Open the Hyper-V Manager.
2. Click **Hyper-V Server Settings**.
3. Click **Keyboard**.
4. Click the **Use on the Virtual Machine** option.

If you choose to do so you can change the Focus Release key from it normal setting to a custom configuration as follows:

1. Open Hyper-V Manager.
2. Click Hyper-V Settings.
3. Click Release and choose from the drop-down menu options.

Table 8.1 includes a brief summary of the key combinations that can be used with the Virtual Machine Connection and their standard Windows key combinations.

Table 8.1 Key Combinations

Standard Windows Key Combination	Virtual Machine Connection Key Combination	Explanation
CTRL + ALT + DEL	CTRL + ALT + END	This displays the Task Manager or Windows Security dialog box on Windows. This will also prompt to the log in screen if available.
ALT + TAB	ALT + PAGE UP	This switches between programs in order from left to right.
ALT + SHIFT + TAB	ALT + PAGE DOWN	This switches between programs in order from right to left.
ALT + ESC	ALT + INSERT	This will cycle through programs in the chronological order in which they were started.
CTRL + ESC	ALT + HOME	This displays the Windows Start menu.
N/A	CTRL + ALT + PAUSE	This swaps the Virtual Machine Connection window back and forth between full screen mode and normal.
N/A	CTRL + ALT + LEFT ARROW	This releases the mouse and keyboard focus from the Virtual Machine Connection window for other tasks.

Installing Hyper-V and Creating Virtual Machines

In this chapter you learned how virtualization works, how to install the Hyper-V role for Windows Server 2008, and how to create and configure virtual machines. In this section you will familiarize yourself with the process of installing Hyper-V to Windows Server 2008 and creating a new virtual machine.

1. Begin by reviewing the hardware requirements, BIOS compatibility, and other system requirements described in this section for the install process for the Hyper-V role.

2. When ready, begin installing the Hyper-V role to your system. Remember to start with a clean install of Windows Server 2008 and follow the steps described in this section.

3. Attempt an installation of Hyper-V on a Server Core install of Windows Server 2008 by following the procedures listed in this section.

4. Once Hyper-V is installed, create a checklist like the one described in this section. Factor in the memory and virtual hard drive requirements to create three virtual machines. Assume each VM will be running a different operating system and have a different installation plan.

5. Using your checklist and the information learned in this section, create and name three virtual machines. Attach the virtual hard drives to the machines and install their operating systems. Use an .ISO file, a physical media, and remote server image, respectively, for installation of the operating systems.

6. Navigate through the configuration process using Virtual Machines Connection (VMC) tool, and use key combinations to interface with the VMs.

Migrating from Physical to Virtual Machines

Before discussing the methodology behind migration it is important to understand when it is most effective to migrate to virtual machines. Research indicates that each layer of virtualization technology has merits when applied properly with the right end goal in mind. Virtualization technology is not a quick fix for everything that is required in all situations. Every case has its own individual needs and requirements based on their particular needs. Many organizations choose to go to the time and trouble to adopt some form of virtualization technology with the wrong objectives in mind.

One end solution that virtualization can help is availability or reliability. Virtualization technology often is deployed in an attempt to make outages, planned or unplanned, invisible to users. Hyper-V can help in the areas of access virtualization, application virtualization, processing virtualization, network virtualization, storage virtualization, and tools to manage its virtualized environment. Past virtual machine software could not achieve this goal without numerous issues.

As we mentioned, consolidation is a huge goal when deploying virtual machines and operating system virtualization technology. Both help organizations increase the amount of usage from physical resources by consolidating applications onto a much smaller number of systems. However virtual machines alone will not completely resolve a solution. You will need to have access to more virtualization technology to really gain all of the benefits mentioned. Hyper-V helps in this with a large number of tools and compatibility with other virtual machine technology and tool sets. Without all these other tools, you would soon find that they had a patchwork network system that was difficult manage and maintain.

Another virtualization goal is performance. Hyper-V is focused on allowing multiple functions to share the same physical resources. Always consider the type of performance goal you wish to increase. Hyper-V is one of the most apt choices if the goal is higher levels of application performance.

Obtaining the maximum in scalability is a task for which virtualization often is utilized. This is normally obtained by spreading a single workload over many physical machines. Hyper-V's application virtualization combined with workload management software would achieve the best results in this scenario.

Organizations will often rush to agree that the deployment of virtual machines is the correct choice for them. This often occurs without much planning or research. Your goal is to learn when to take advantage of virtualization offered by the Hyper-V role in Windows Server 2008. Many organizations ultimately face significant challenges because they are not prepared to use the virtualization software they are deploying to the best means for their situation. Before migration occurs ensure that you have a successful deployment of the technology. This can be accomplished by the following methods of organization:

- Organize your management team and try to assess the total needs for your deployment. Account for both unified and diverse management teams. Some organizations contain separate groups that manage application development, system infrastructure, network infrastructure, and web infrastructure. A fragmented management team always makes implementation of virtualization technology more difficult.

- Organize your development team so that you can assess the total needs of your deployment. Account for separate groups that develop mainframe applications, midrange applications, Windows applications, Linux applications, Web-based applications, and so on. A fragmented development makes the task of deploying virtualization technology much more difficult.

- Do not accept virtualization as the end-all solution. As you know, the most common IT environments with be hybrids of physical and virtual resources. Your organization will need tools to discover and manage all its diverse IT assets. Through organization and determining who is responsible for operations and administration of each of these resources, you can ensure a much more successful deployment.

With all this considered we can now move on to talking about the most effective methods of migration from physical to virtual machines using Hyper-V.

Configuring & Implementing...

Determining When Virtualization Is the Right Solution

As we mentioned, virtualization is not a catch-all technology. It has very beneficial and wide reaching uses but is not always the ideal choice of deployment. Distributed services may not be suitable for virtualization unless the host computers are also distributed. In a virtualization scenario that places all DNS servers in a single central IT environment that serves multiple sites, an increase in network traffic and reduced service reliability may occur.

Continued

On the other hand, if these sites all consist of multiple servers that offer file and print, database, DNS, and Active Directory services, then virtualization of these servers would be of great benefit. By consolidating all the virtual computers onto one physical host you can then be assured of a more efficient performance.

Always rely on pilot virtualizations where possible, to assess and verify real resource usage figures and gains in efficiency. Comparing these figures against the predictions you made will help give you a better idea of what sort of benefit virtualization will yield. As with most processes, predictions cannot be entirely accurate because the simulated clients may not match the workload that the physical server experiences in daily usage. Always attempt to factor these statistics in your deployment plan. Remember it may not be possible to simulate some client workloads.

We have discussed that one of the main goals in virtualization is consolidation. *Server consolidation* is the process of migrating network services and applications from multiple computers to a singular computer. This consolidation can include multiple physical computers to multiple virtual computers on one host computer. You can consolidate computers for several reasons, such as minimizing power consumption, simplifying administration duties, or reducing overall cost. Consolidation can also increase hardware resource utilization. This will increase the return on investments for the IT department of an organization. Service consolidation involves moving multiple network services onto a single computer. This is most efficiently done by means of a virtual network. However, distributed services, such as DNS and Active Directory, have additional issues, such as availability, security, and network topology. For this reason virtualization is safer for organizations that may not want to concentrate these network services onto a single physical computer.

TIP

Although you may not immediately think of this, consolidation is one way of increasing security. It works by reducing the opportunities for possible attackers to gain physical access to servers. Consolidation of servers typically involves centralization. Centralization allows organizations to justify the cost of investing in higher levels of security protection. These security measures can include stronger physical security or two-factor authentication systems.

Application consolidation works by moving several business applications onto a single physical computer. If you have invested in high-availability hardware to run your company's single line of business applications, then it is logical to use that hardware to run multiple applications. However, problems can occur if the application requirements conflict. This method is completely impossible if the applications run on different operating systems altogether. Virtualization provides a method to consolidate applications onto a single physical computer. This avoids operating system and other resource conflicts. By migrating from physical to virtual machines using a virtualization model, administrators can create a virtual network that maps to the original physical computers. The host computer can easily run these virtual computers as if they were autonomous physical computers. This way the application environments remain completely unaltered.

Hyper-V allows migration from one physical host system to a virtual machine with minimal downtime, leveraging familiar high-availability capabilities of Windows Server and System Center management tools. In order to prepare to do this, let's go over the hardware requirements for migration with Hyper-V.

The planned guest partition (virtual machine) must be able to function with the standardized hardware that Hyper-V provides. This hardware should include an advanced system with a uniprocessor or multiprocessor configuration, a virtualized network card, and a virtualized hard disk. Hardware that is not supported includes parallel port dongles, almost all universal serial bus devices, and hardware-based authentication. The physical computer you are using for the migration must also contain more than 96 MB RAM. It should also run the NTFS file system.

The host machine for migration should also meet or exceed the following specifications:

- At least one virtual processor core for every child partition
- One dedicated core for the parent partition
- 8 GB of RAM or more
- An iSCSI attachment to network-based storage devices, for example a Storage Area Network (SAN)
- Multiple gigabit network cards (NICs)
- A clean install of Windows Server 2008v Server 64-bit edition
- Redundant and uninterruptible power supplies
- A fast dedicated attachment to backup system

Planning a P2V Migration

This section details the planning of a physical-to-virtual (P2V) migration and the possible advantages and disadvantages of virtualization. In this section you will plan out a fictional migration of a group of physical machines to virtualized machines for server consolidation purposes.

Plan out a strategy using the earlier guidelines for the migration using the following tactics:

1. Assess the total needs for your deployment. Account for both unified and diverse management teams. Some organizations contain separate groups that manage application development, system infrastructure, network infrastructure, and web infrastructure. A fragmented management team always makes implementation of virtualization technology more complicated.

2. Assess the training requirements needed to undergo the migration both for staff and end user education.

3. Identify any applications that may require special needs for deployment or that require specific resources from your virtual network

4. Confirm that all hardware and software is compliant to the requirements of Windows Server 2008 and Hyper-V. Remember to check both the host and guest clients.

5. Estimate the total downtime required to complete the migration and the services that will be affected by its deployment.

6. Decide which method of backup you plan to use to ensure availability resources for the network.

7. Attempt a small-scale test of the deployment using a test lab to ensure your familiarity with all the requirements and configuration methods that we have discussed.

8. Create a checklist based on your research and information gathering that can be used during the real migration. It should detail the number of VMs required, the OS that each will be using, and the amount of storage each VM will require based on applications that are being run.

Backing Up Virtual Machines

Deploying virtualization technology requires diligence and research on the part of the administrator. One of the main objectives is to create a more efficient and cost-effective environment. To do so, changes and updates must constantly occur to optimize the settings and need prior to deployment. This is similar the methodology used for physical computers. Backup for virtual computers is as important as with physical computers.

The Windows 2008 Volume Shadow Copy Service (VSS) is a feature available for NTFS volumes. VSS is used to perform a point-in-time backup of an entire volume to the local disk. This backup can be used to quickly restore data that was deleted from the volume locally or through a network-mapped drive or network file share. VSS also is used by Windows Server Backup and by compatible third-party backup applications to back up local and shared NTFS volumes.

VSS can make a point-in-time backup of a volume, including backing up open files. This entire process is completed in a very short period of time but is powerful enough to be used to restore an entire volume, if necessary. VSS can be scheduled to back up a volume automatically once, twice, or several times a day. This service can be enabled on a volume that contains Distributed File System (DFS) targets and standard Windows 2008 file shares.

The following approaches can be applied to backing up virtual computers with the Hyper-V role installed:

- Install the Windows Server Backup role in Windows Server 2008. Using the Windows Server Backup role you can take full and incremental backups of the disks that contain the virtual hard disks. This is the recommended method for utilizing this feature.

- The Volume Shadow Copy Service (VSS) as seen in Figure 8.6 on Windows Server 2008 can be used to take shadow copies of running virtual computers. Use incremental backups, to minimize the size of these backup files and not affect the operations of the virtual machine. This can be done by configuring the VSS as seen in Figure 8.7. Also VSS on Windows Server 2008 will avoid the inconsistency issues that might occur with VSS backing up virtual computers on Windows Server 2003 and Virtual Server 2005.

Figure 8.6 Volume Shadow Copy Service (VSS) Utility for Windows Server 2008

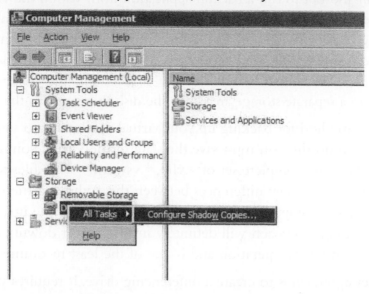

Figure 8.7 Configuring the VSS

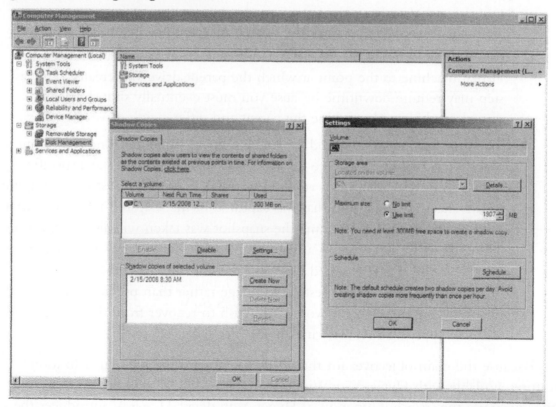

- You can also opt to run a backup application from within the virtual machine you are attempting to back up. This will provide you consistency with the existing backup strategy of an organization. The main problem with this method is that it does not provide you with a snapshot of the data at a particular instance. You should be sure that the virtual computer creates the backup image on a separate storage area from the disk that contains the *.vhd file.

- Another method for backing up your virtual machine is to suspend and copy the VM. To do this you must save the state of the virtual computer. Then you would copy the complete set of *.vhd, *.vsv, and *.vmc files to another location. To avoid any differences between the *.vhd and the *.hsv files, copy all the virtual computer files on a single pass and stop the image from restarting. This approach will definitely involve server downtime during the save state and copy operation and is one of the least recommend.

- Another approach is to create a differencing drive. It requires you to shut down the virtual computer and creates a new differencing drive for the virtual hard disk or disks. This can be accomplished via the New Virtual Hard Disk wizard. You then restart the virtual machine immediately. All changes are made to the differencing drive, which makes it possible to back up to the parent drive by using the XCOPY command. Next you would restore the virtual machine to the point at which the parent drive was created. The last step may require downtime because you must eventually shut down the virtual machine and combine the parent and differencing drives together.

- The final and newest method for backing up a virtual machine is creating a snapshot. A snapshot can save the state of a virtual computer at a specific instant in time whether it is running or not. You can then restore a computer to the exact configuration that was captured in the snapshot taken. The data settings that existed at the time the snapshot was taken will also be restored. The only main downside to a snapshot is that it requires the existence of a suitable *.vhd file. This *.vhd file will act as a parent file for the snapshot. Snapshots are best used to restore an image rather than provide data integrity. Snapshots are invaluable to you if you wish to recover from the unexpected effect of applying a security update process or service pack.

Because the main objectives for this chapter deal with the new virtualization features available with Hyper-V in Windows Server 2008, we will discuss how to effectively use the snapshot function of Hyper-V in detail. Hyper-V introduces the concept of virtual machine snapshots. This is best defined as a point in time image of a VM that you can resume to at any stage. Snapshots are implemented in the virtualization layer. Any guest operating system can take a snapshot at anytime including during installation. Snapshots can be taken whether the virtual machine is running or stopped. If a virtual machine is running when the snapshot is taken no downtime will occur while creating the snapshot.

To create a snapshot, you will need to use the Hyper-V Manager. This is accomplished in the following way:

1. Open the Hyper-V Manger and select a **virtual machine**.

2. Click the **Snapshot** button in the toolbar of the Virtual Machine Connection window or open the Action menu in Hyper-V manager and select **Snapshot**.

Creating a snapshot from the Virtual Machine Connection window will open a dialog that allows you to enter a custom label for the snapshot. Be sure to name the snapshot appropriately to the purpose you will be using it for. If you plan on testing new configurations be sure to logically notate what the purpose for the snapshot is. Virtual Machine Connection will also allow you to skip this dialog and opt to have the snapshot use an auto-generated name. Auto-generated naming conventions consist of the name of the virtual machine followed by the date and time when the snapshot was taken. All snapshots created from the Hyper-V Manager will be created with an auto-generated name. Always be aware of the naming convention you decide to use so that you can effectively return to this back up.

Created snapshots can be viewed in the Snapshot pane of the Hyper-V Manager. This is accomplished by selecting the virtual machine that the snapshot is associated with. The display method for Snapshots in the Snapshot pane is hierarchal and describe the order in which the snapshots where taken. The last snapshot to be taken will have a green arrow head on top of it. This will be last one to be taken or applied to the virtual machine.

Once you have a snapshot selected there will be two main options available to you in the Action panel:

- **Settings**: This will open the Virtual Machine Settings dialog, which will contain all the settings that the virtual machine had at the time the snapshot was taken. Essentially this snapshot is read only, so all settings will be disabled at this time. From here you can change the snapshot name and the notes associated with the snapshot.

- **Apply**: This option allows you to copy the complete virtual machine state from the snapshot to an active virtual machine. If you select this process any unsaved data in the currently active virtual machine will be lost. However, you will be asked before applying if you want to create a snapshot of your current active virtual machine. If you do so this will occur before the selected snapshot is applied.

Appling the virtual machine snapshot to an active virtual machine will result in the active virtual machine being either in a saved state or stopped state. This will depend on whether the snapshot was taken of a running or stopped virtual machine. If wish to change settings before starting the updated virtual machine you can make them now. Follow this procedure to make changes to your newly updated virtual machine before starting it:

1. Select the updated **virtual machine**.

2. Open the **Virtual Machine Settings**.

3. Select **Rename** to rename a snapshot without having to open the Virtual Machine Settings.

4. Select **Delete Snapshot** if you no longer wish to restore the virtual machine to that point in time.

Tip

It is very important for you to understand that deleting a snapshot will never affect any other snapshots. It will also not affect the current state of the virtual machine. The only thing that will be erased by deleting the snapshot is the selected snapshot itself. This will have no effect on any VM actively running that snapshot.

A snapshot associated with a virtual machine now allows you access to the Revert option. The Revert option will roll back a virtual machine to the last snapshot that was taken or applied to it. Revert will also delete any changes that have been made since that snapshot was taken.

Backing Up a Virtual Hard Drive

This section shows you a variety of methods on how to back up a virtual hard drive, including the new method of snapshots introduced by Hyper-V for Windows Server 2008. For this exercise let's attempt to use what we have learned to create different virtual machine backups using the different methods available with Windows Server 2008 and the Hyper-V role.

Attempt to use the following methods to create backups of your virtual machines:

1. Use Window Server Backup Role.
2. Use Volume Shadow Copy Service.
3. Run a back up application from the virtual machine you are copying.
4. Create a differencing drive.
5. Suspend and Copy the VM.
6. Create a Snapshot using the Hyper-V Manager.

For each of these back up methods identify what strengths and weaknesses each has, and in which situations each would work best.

Virtual Server Optimization

Windows Server 2008 presents many options to you as an administrator for virtualization of your network. As with all networks, your virtualized network will only be as functional as the diligence invested into the optimization of its functions. Even though optimization is a current trend, it is something that has existed in theory for a good deal of time. Due to compatibility and processor requirements, virtualization in the past has been impractical to deploy in many situations. Before deciding to utilize the virtualization features that Hyper-V has to offer, be sure that it is the proper option for your IT department. As we mentioned previously, steps should be taken to determine if your business is a match for this particular method of deployment.

The simplest way to optimize an existing network is through logical organization of its resources and needs. Optimizing any network involves organization and a logical deployment procedure that accounts for all the security, resource, and access requirements of the project. The same holds true of virtual networks as well. As administrator it is up to you to be diligent in your research and testing of the server.

In this section we will discuss some steps and stages of optimization for virtual machine based servers.

The first stage of optimization is to collect a record of previous performance information for your virtual machine workload. This will help to better quantify your servers needs. Optimize virtual machine placement by collecting a record of previous performance information concerning the preexisting physical or virtual computers in the network. Also tools such as System Center Operations Manager (SCOM) 2007 as seen in Figure 8.8 can be used to record and analyze performance information. This includes both physical and virtual computers, which will help you in both consolidation and virtualization.

Figure 8.8 System Center Operations Manager (SCOM) 2007

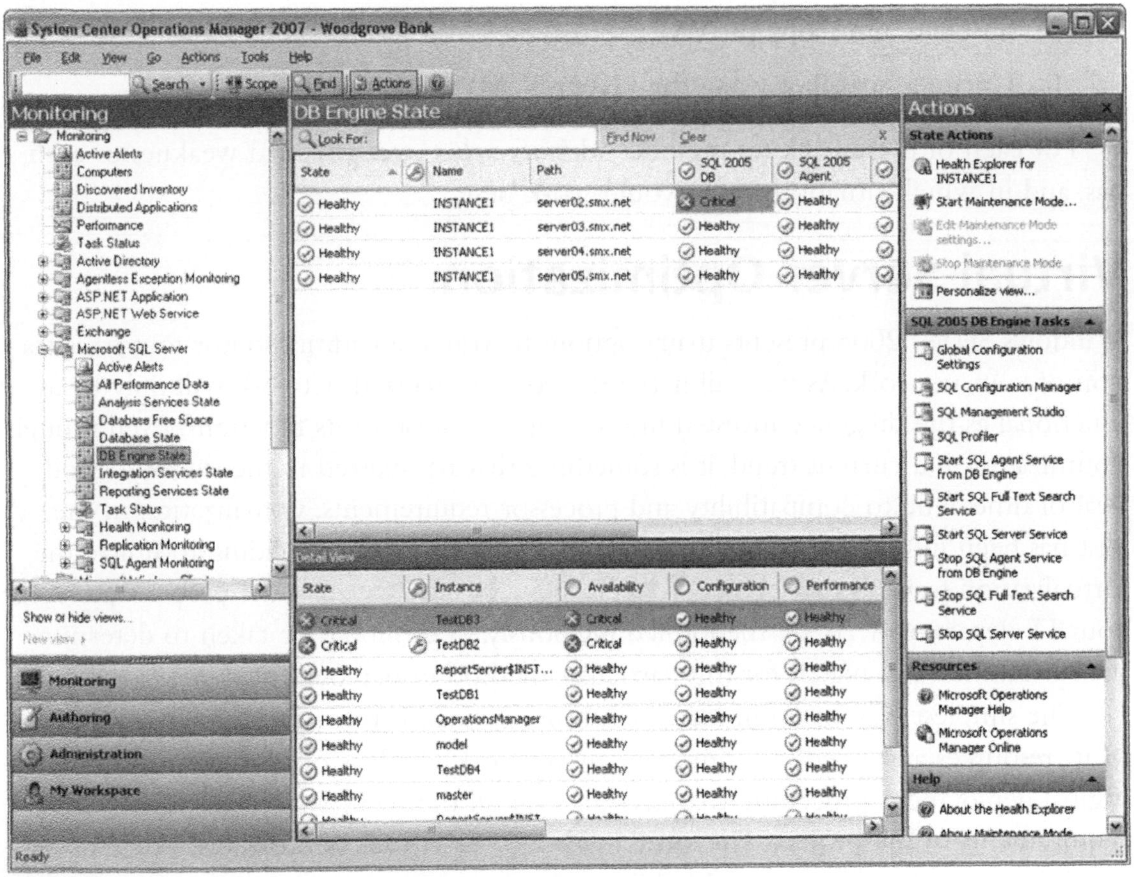

The second stage of optimizing server performance is to verify the minimum required resources for configuration of the virtual machines in your network and adjusting configurations accordingly. For each virtual machine, check the minimum requirements for processors, memory, hard disk space, and network bandwidth. You can calculate the host memory usage by adding an additional 32 MB of memory for each virtual computer. This is considered memory overhead.

The third stage requires you to calculate the total amount of virtual machines the host computer can support running simultaneously. Remember to account for factors such as total memory. Always allow 512 MB for the parent partition alone. Also account for the number of virtual processors you plan to use and how you plan to assign them. Do you plan to assign a processor core to an individual virtual machine in dual-core or quad-core computers? Another factor in this stage is to account for virtual hard disk storage and expected file growth. Be sure to plan ahead for the future needs of the network as well. Also make sure to localize network connectivity by placing computers with large mutual data transfer requirements on the same host computer.

In the fourth stage you will begin resource maximization or load balancing. This will optimize your server for resource maximization requirements. By placing virtual machines on a host computer until the resources of the host computer are fully assigned you can more easily balance workloads.

TIP

Bear in mind that queuing theory will prevent you from maximizing certain specific areas of resource usage. This will include processor activity. Optimize for load balancing and assign virtual computers to two or more host computers so that each host will split the resource usage evenly. This will help compensate for things that you can't account for in your optimization stages.

In the fifth stage you will monitor resource usage and compare the measured figures to the research and predictions you have made in previous stages. Take note of each virtual machine as it starts and as you make changes to the configurations. Monitor static resource usages such as memory. When switching clients over to the virtual images, monitor active resource usage. Take note of things such as processor and network loading. From this point, continue to monitor and adjust virtual machine placements if necessary.

Entering the sixth stage you can begin to accumulate data concerning the server by using SCOM to measure performance data. Ensure this research accounts for high loading times and frequent periods of usage. Certain applications may have specific usage times once a week or only one day out of the month. Familiarize yourself with the high load times of applications of your server. Databases and e-mail servers may have even less frequent maintenance operations that increase resource usage only once in a while.

Lastly in the seventh stage, fine tune your resource consumption using SCOM. Monitor the virtualized computers and the host computers more intricately. Use this information to identify excessive resource consumption and eliminate these sources of consumption where possible.

Summary

In this chapter, we discussed Hyper-V, a new virtualization role exclusive to Windows Server 2008. You should now be familiar with all the aspects and features that Hyper-V can offer you when using Windows Server 2008. We have talked about how Hyper-V and its parts produce transparent virtualization by creating virtual machines that can run multiple operating systems on a single physical host. We discussed how this is accomplished using Hyper-V's three parts: the hypervisor, the virtualization stack, and they virtual I/O model. In addition we explored all the new virtualization options available with Windows Server 2008 and how they compare to older virtualization suites such as Virtual Server and Virtual PC. We discussed all the major benefits and drawbacks of virtualization, including hardware and software requirements specific to Hyper-V. We have also learned how to install and manage Hyper-V in a Windows Server 2008 environment.

As with any large deployment of new technology, we have learned that there are many steps needed to plan a P2V migration. This includes the need to weigh the gains and drawbacks of virtualization. We stressed the value of organization and knowing exactly the needs of your particular network. We talked about how to estimate costs and what overall benefits can be expected from such a migration. We also discussed how this migration may affect your end users and the way your current network may operate. We also talked about a list of scenarios that were best suited for virtualization.

In addition to the installation and planning for the implementation of Hyper-V, we learned how to configure and back up virtual machines using the new methods available with Windows Server 2008 and the Hyper-V role. You should now be aware of the various steps needed to configure a virtual processor and how to allot virtual storage to any VM that you create using the Hyper-V Manager. You should also have knowledge about virtual snapshots and Volume Shadow Copy Services (VSS) and how each could be used to back up virtual machines you have created in case of emergency or outages.

Last but not least we talked in detail about the various steps and stages required to optimize your virtual network. As we have learned, research and data collection are of utmost importance to the successful administration of a virtual network. We discussed ideal goals to strive for when deploying virtualization in your network and how to maintain the highest levels of efficiency for these types of deployments. We talked about how tools such as SCOM 2007 can help gather data that will be invaluable to your assessment and optimization of your virtual network.

After reading this chapter you should have a sound knowledge of all the features, methods, and requirements necessary to implement a virtual network using Windows Server 2008 and the Hyper-V role.

Solutions Fast Track

Configuring Virtual Machines

☑ Hyper-V is a key feature of Windows Server 2008. It offers a scalable and highly available virtualization platform that is efficient and reliable. It has an inherently secure architecture with a minimal attack surface and does not contain any third-party device drivers.

☑ Hyper-V has three main components: the *hypervisor*, the *virtualization stack*, and the new *virtualized I/O model*. The hypervisor, also know as the *virtual machine monitor*, is a very small layer of software that is present directly on the processor, which creates the different "partitions" within which each virtualized instance of the operating system will run.

☑ The Hyper-V role requires a clean install of Windows Server 2008 Enterprise on the host machine. Hyper-V requires 64-bit hardware and a 64-bit version of the operating system. You must also ensure that you have hardware-assisted virtualization enabled prior to installation.

☑ Virtual machines are created in the Hyper-V role of Windows Server 2008 via the Hyper-V manager. They can be configured for via the Virtual Machine Connection or through the Hyper-V manager.

☑ Virtual hard disks can be created and managed via the Hyper-V manager or via the New Virtual Hard Disk Wizard. VHDs can be edited using the Edit Virtual Hard Disk wizard. Hyper-V allows for 256 virtual hard discs per Virtual SCSI controller. This means that you can add up to a Petabyte of storage per virtual machine created.

Migrating from Physical to Virtual Machines

☑ Server consolidation is the process of migrating network services and applications from multiple computers to a singular computer. This consolidation can include multiple physical computers to multiple virtual computers on one host computer. You can consolidate computers for several reasons, such as minimizing power consumption, simplifying administration duties, or reducing overall cost. Consolidation can also increase hardware resource utilization.

☑ The planned guest partition (virtual machine) used for migration should include an advanced system with a uniprocessor or multiprocessor configuration, a virtualized network card, and a virtualized hard disk. Hardware that is not supported includes parallel port dongles, almost all universal serial bus devices, and hardware-based authentication. The physical computer you are using for the migration must also contain more than 96 MB RAM. It should also run the NTFS file system.

☑ Virtualization technology often is deployed in an attempt to make outages, planned or unplanned, invisible to users. Hyper-V can help in the areas of access virtualization, application virtualization, processing virtualization, network virtualization, storage virtualization, and tools to manage its virtualized environment.

Backing Up Virtual Machines

☑ The Windows 2008 Volume Shadow Copy Service (VSS) is a feature available for NTFS volumes. VSS is used to perform a point-in-time backup of an entire volume to the local disk.

☑ VSS is also used by Windows Server Backup and by compatible third-party backup applications to back up local and shared NTFS volumes.

☑ A differencing drive may be created and used as a back up using the New Virtual Hard Disk wizard, which makes it possible to back up to the parent drive by using the XCOPY command.

☑ Snapshots are implemented in the virtualization layer. Any guest operating system can take a snapshot at anytime including during installation. Snapshots can be taken whether the virtual machine is running or stopped. If a virtual machine is running when the snapshot is taken no downtime will occur while creating the snapshot.

☑ Virtual Machine Connection can be used to organize and edit snapshots taken.

Virtual Server Optimization

☑ The simplest way to optimize an existing network is through logical organization of its resources and needs. Optimizing any network involves organization and a logical deployment procedure that accounts for all the security, resource, and access requirements of the project. The same holds true of virtual networks as well.

☑ The first stage of optimization is to collect a record of previous performance information for your virtual machine workload. This will help to better quantify your servers needs.

☑ The second stage of optimizing server performance is to verify the minimum required resources for configuration of the virtual machines in your network and adjusting configurations accordingly. For each virtual machine, check the minimum requirements for processors, memory, hard disk space, and network bandwidth. You can calculate the host memory usage by adding an additional 32 MB of memory for each virtual computer. This is considered memory overhead.

☑ The third stage of optimization requires you to calculate the total amount of virtual machines the host computer can support running simultaneously. Remember to account for factors such as total memory.

☑ The fourth stage of optimization requires you to begin resource maximization or load balancing. This will optimize your server for resource maximization requirements.

☑ In the fifth stage of optimization you monitor resource usage and compare the measured figures to the research and predictions you have made. Take note of each virtual machine as it starts and as you make changes to the configurations.

Frequently Asked Questions

Q: How does virtualization with Hyper-V differ from other virtualization software available?

A: Hyper-V has greater deployment capabilities to other software and provides more options for your specific needs. It utilizes a hypervisor-based virtualization with 64-bit hardware assistance and 64-bit operating systems. Hyper-V has three main components: the *hypervisor*, the *virtualization stack*, and the new *virtualized I/O model*. The hypervisor, also known as the *virtual machine monitor*, is a very small layer of software that is present directly on the processor, which creates the different "partitions" within which each virtualized instance of the operating system will run. The virtualization stack and the I/O components act to provide a go-between with Windows and with all the partitions that you create. All three of these components of Hyper-V work together as a team to allow virtualization to occur. Hyper-V hooks into threads on the host processor, which the host operating system can then use to efficiently communicate with multiple virtual machines. Because of this these virtual machines and multiple virtual operating systems can all be running on a single physical processor with complete isolation and limited compatibility issues.

Q: What are the greatest benefits of virtualization?

A: The main benefits of virtualization include:

- Server consolidation: Consolidating many physical servers into fewer servers, by using host virtual machines.

- Disaster recovery: Physical production servers can use virtual machines as "hot standby" environments. Virtual machines can provide backup images that can boot into live virtual machines.

- Consolidation for testing and development environments: Virtual machines can be used for testing of early developmental versions of applications without fear of destabilizing the system for other users.

- Upgrading to a dynamic datacenter: Dynamic IT environments are now achievable via the use of virtualization. Hyper-V, along with systems management solutions, enables you to troubleshoot problems more effectively.

Q: What are the two main benefits of the Hyper-V role for Windows Server 2008?

A: The two main benefits of Hyper-V include:

- Multiple OS environments can share the same computer while still being strongly isolated from each other and the virtual machine.

- An *Instruction Set Architecture* (ISA) that is fairly contrary to that of the actual machine.

Q: What new backup methods are offered by Hyper-V for Windows Server 2008 and how do they work?

A: In addition to the Windows Server Backup role in windows Server 2008, Hyper-V offers the new feature of snapshots. A snapshot saves the state of a virtual computer at a specific instance in time whether it is running or not. You can then restore a computer to the exact configuration that was captured in the snapshot taken.

Q: What are the main components of a virtual network?

A: The key elements that constitute a virtual network are:

- Network hardware, such as switches and Network adapters, also known as network interface cards (NICs)

- Networks, such as virtual LANs (VLANs)

- Containers such as virtual machines

- Network storage devices

- Network media, such as Ethernet

Q: What is the best method for optimizing a virtual server?

A: The best way to optimize an existing network is through logical organization of its resources and needs. Optimizing a virtual network or server involves organization and a logical deployment procedure that accounts for all the security, resource, and access requirements of the project. Be diligent in your research and testing of the server.

Chapter 9

Microsoft Windows Server 2008: Terminal Services Changes

Solutions in this chapter:

- Terminal Services RemoteApp
- Terminal Services Gateway
- Terminal Services Web Access

☑ Summary

☑ Solutions Fast Track

☑ Frequently Asked Questions

Introduction

Many organizations choose to run applications on terminal servers rather than installing them locally on each workstation. The advantage to doing so is that the application runs on the server, and only video images are sent to the workstations. This makes it much easier for an administrator to maintain the applications. The terminal services are good for security as well, because applications are much more resistant to user tampering since they do not actually reside on the user's workstations.

In this chapter, you will learn how to configure and monitor the Terminal Services Resources. You'll also learn about Terminal Services Gateway, which allows remote users to connect to internal resources securely. You'll then learn about configuring TS RemoteApp, which publishes the applications that can be accessed remotely.

Terminal Services RemoteApp

Terminal Services (TS) **RemoteApp Manager** is a tool that enables you to provide access to Windows-based programs and applications for remote users. Remote users need only an Internet connection. Modern hand-held devices powered with the Windows Mobile operating system supports Remote Desktop Connection (RDC) client. Access to applications hosted centrally in the corporate networks is made available to these hand-held devices without consuming much of the network bandwidth. Only keyboard depressions, mouse clicks, and screen changes travel across the network. You can publish applications and manage it centrally in a scenario where branch offices may not have IT staff to install and configure applications.

TS RemoteApp can be considered a synonym to terminal service. TS RemoteApp publishes the network applications that can be remotely accessed through clients running RDC clients or through the Web. Only keyboard clicks, mouse movements, and display information is transmitted over the network. Users can see only their sessions. Remote applications can be executed along with local applications. Users get seamless access to the remote applications instead of accessing a remote desktop to open applications. Multiple remote applications can be run in a single terminal service session utilizing resources efficiently. While accessing remote applications through TS Web Access, remote applications appear as Web links. Remote Desktop Protocol (.rdp) files can be created by administrators and distributed over the network for remote users to install and access applications.

Benefits of TS RemoteApp include:

- Provide applications from a central location to remote offices

- Support branch offices with inadequate IT staff to offer system administration

- Install applications centrally and access from anywhere

- Manage frequently updated, difficult to manage, or infrequently used applications efficiently

- Improve performance even under limited network-bandwidth scenarios

- Offer applications through hand-held devices (such as Windows mobile powered phones/PDAs) with RDC Client

- Allow multiple versions of same applications to exist (in some scenarios that demand such co-existence)

Configuring TS RemoteApp

Configuring TS RemoteApp includes installing applications in a terminal-server aware mode (on the Terminal Server), enabling remote control configuration, configuring application parameters, adding users, and publishing it on TS Web for Web access.

To install an application in the Terminal Server mode:

1. Click **Start | Control Panel** and double-click on **Install Application on Terminal Server** (see Figure 9.1). It is recommended to install any new applications only after installing terminal services on the server. Microsoft applications *(.msi packages)* are terminal services aware and can be installed directly without going through the Install Application on Terminal Server option.

Figure 9.1 Windows 2008 Control Panel Option to Install Applications on Terminal Server

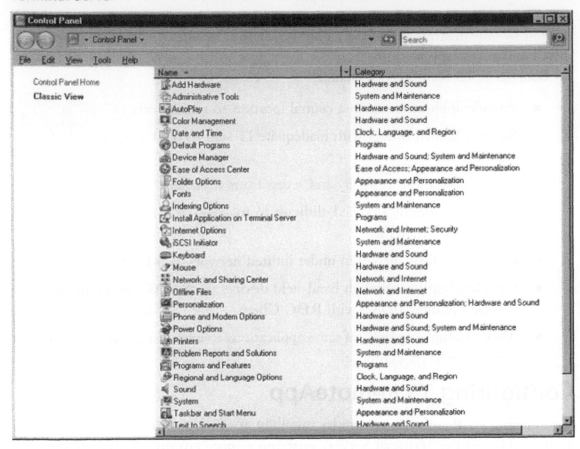

2. Click **Next** on the **Install program From Floppy Disk or CD-ROM** screen of the wizard (see Figure 9.2).

Figure 9.2 Installing Applications on Terminal Server

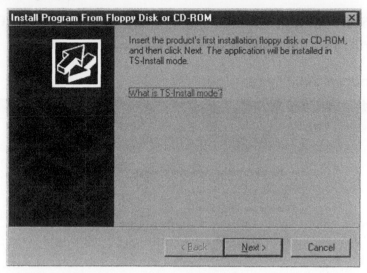

3. Type the location of the set-up file of the application (for example, *d:\setup.exe*) or click on **Browse** to locate the set-up file.

4. Wait until the installation of the software completes. The Finish button will turn gray until the application completes the installation. Do not close this screen until the Finish button becomes active (see Figure 9.3). Click **Finish** to complete the installation. Now you can use TS Remote App manager to publish the application you have installed.

Figure 9.3 Terminal Server Application Wizard Transferring Control to Application

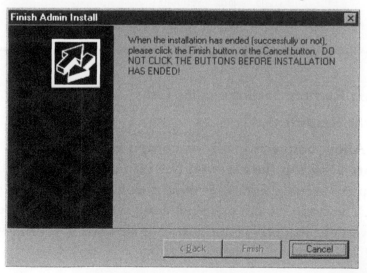

To verify the remote connection settings:

1. Click **Start | Run**, and then type **control system** into the **Open** box. This will open the **System** tool (see Figure 9.4).

Figure 9.4 Windows 2008 System Tool

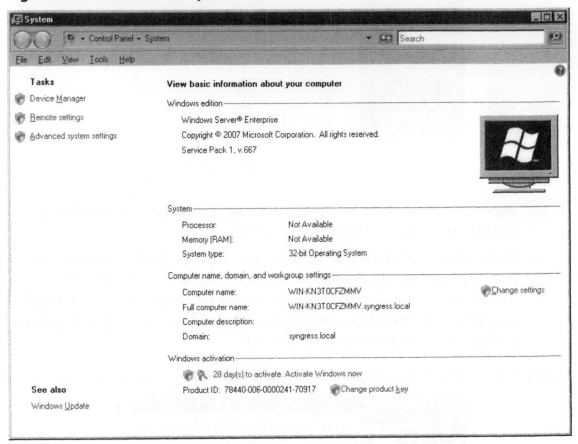

2. Click on **Remote Settings** under **Tasks**.

3. Click the **Remote** tab.

4. Select **Allow connections from computers running any version of Remote Desktop (less secure)** (see Figure 9.5). This will allow remote desktop connections from your present setup consisting of Windows XP clients. This option is also preferred when you are not sure about the RDP client versions that may connect to your network. If your network consists

of Windows Vista and Windows 2008 or Windows XP with the latest RDP client, you can choose the more secure option, **Allow connections only from computers running Remote Desktop with Network Level Authentication (more secure)**.

Figure 9.5 Remote Desktop Configuration

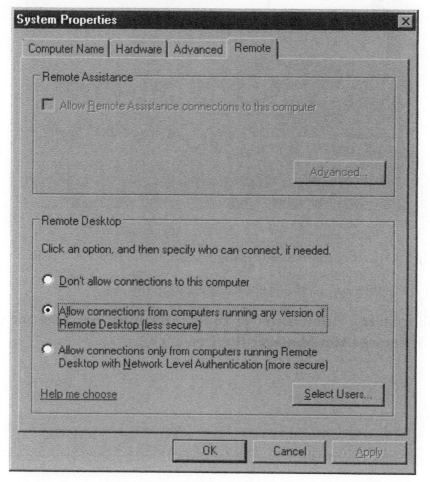

5. Click on **Select Users** and then click **Add**. Locate the Users or User groups (see Figure 9.6) and double-click to add.

Figure 9.6 RDP Users Configuration

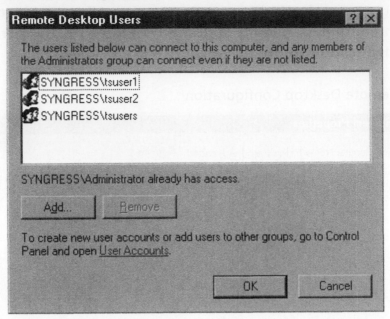

6. Click **OK** to complete the configuration.

To add an application to the RemoteApp Programs:

1. Click **Start** | **Administrative Tools** | **Terminal Services**, and then select **TS RemoteApp Manager** (see Figure 9.7).

Figure 9.7 TS RemoteApp Manager

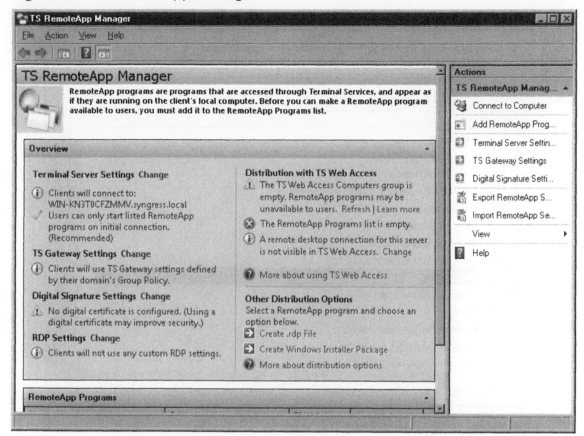

2. Click on **Add RemoteApp Programs** from the **Actions** pane (right). This will start the **RemoteApp wizard**.

3. Click **Next**.

4. Click on the check boxes on the left of the applications you want to publish for remote access. For this example we've installed Microsoft Word 2007 (see Figure 9.8).

Figure 9.8 Choosing Applications for Remote Access

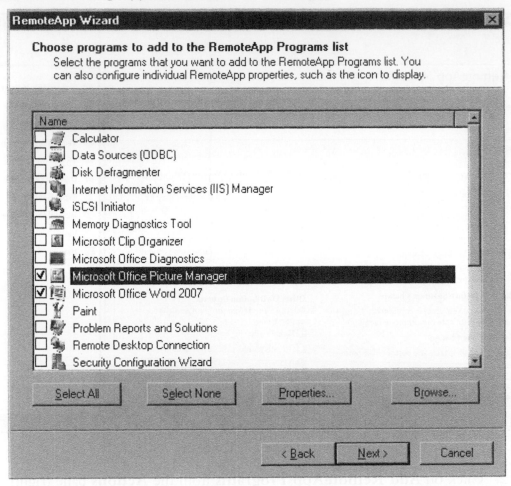

5. Click on **Properties** (see Figure 9.9).

Figure 9.9 Configuration Applications for Remote Access

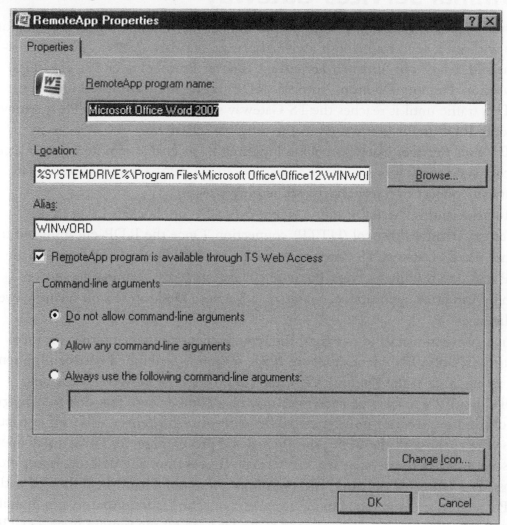

6. Select the **RemoteApp program is available through TS Web Access** check box. This will enable the application to be accessed by the users through Terminal Service Web Access (discussed later in this chapter).

7. You also have the option to **Change Icon** (if required).

8. Click **Finish** after you review the settings on the Review Settings screen. On the main screen of RemoteApp Manager now you can see Microsoft Office Word 2007 added to the RemoteApp Programs list. Repeat these steps to publish all the applications that require remote access.

Terminal Services Gateway

Terminal Services Gateway enables you to offer secure connection to your remote users without a need to establish a virtual private network (VPN). Any Internet-connected device can initiate a Hypertext Transfer Protocol over SSL (HTTPS) connection. Remote Desktop Protocol (RDP) traffic is encapsulated into the HTTPS traffic until it reaches the TS Gateway server and then HTTPS is removed and only RDP traffic gets passed to the terminal servers.

Terminal Services Gateway helps administrators to enable remote users to access the corporate applications without a need to setup a VPN. Users with the RDC client can connect to internal network resources securely.

To achieve this, the RDP traffic is sent over a Secure Sockets Layer (SSL) Hypertext Transfer Protocol (HTTP) connection. Once the RDP-encapsulated traffic reaches the TS Gateway, TS Gateway strips the HTTPS headers and forwards the RDP traffic to terminal servers. Remote clients can access terminal servers or RemoteApp listed applications, or initiate a Remote Desktop session securely over the Internet.

In a conventional VPN network, the remote client runs an Internet Protocol Security (IPSec) VPN client. A secure IPSec session is established between the remote user terminating at the Firewall/VPN appliance or server. However, managing mobile user VPN for a large enterprise may be a cumbersome task due to managing and distributing security policies across the enterprise. Moreover, users are restricted to use the client with the VPN pre-installed and pre-configured. TS Gateway liberates users from device restrictions and can virtually access from any desktop, laptop from a trusted or untrusted network, and even from the mobile hand-held devices with RDP client. Apart from establishing a secure connection, administrators can granularly control which network resources need to be accessed by the remote users. HTTP and HTTPS are allowed by most corporate firewalls, therefore there is no need to open the RDP 3389 port on the firewall.

In addition to this, TS Gateway provides resource authorization policies for remote user terminal connections.

Figure 9.10 shows the scenario where different types of users establish a secure connection over HTTPS carrying RDP traffic.

Figure 9.10 TS Gateway Server Deployment Scenario

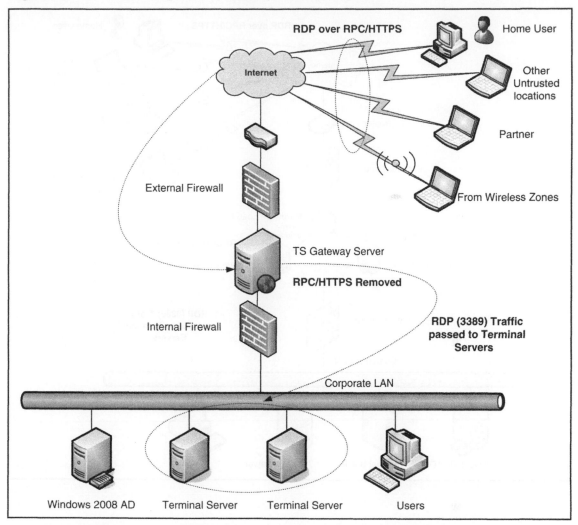

For large enterprises with a huge number of remote user sessions, TS Gateway can be deployed in a high-available load-balancing environment. Dedicated load-balances such as F5 FirePass controllers may be deployed with multiple TS Gateway servers to ensure continuous availability of remote user sessions. Figure 9.11 is an illustration of an environment with a dedicated hardware load balancer with two TS Gateway servers. HTTPS connections are load balanced between both of the TS Gateway servers. After HTTPS encapsulation is removed RDP traffic is passed to the terminal servers.

Figure 9.11 TS Gateway Server Deployment Scenario

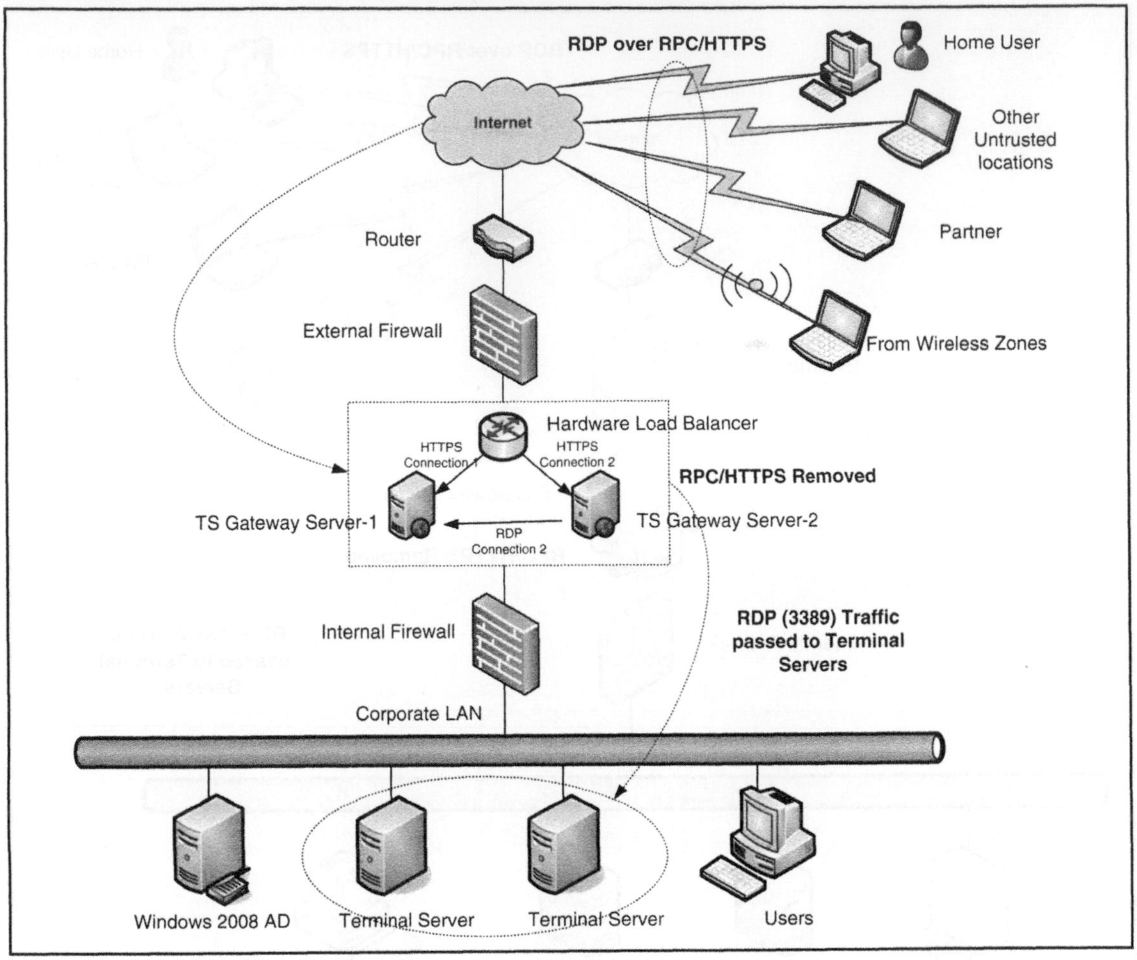

TS Gateway configuration involves the following procedure:

1. Install a SSL certificate (obtained through a trusted third party such as Verisign or create a self-signed certificate for the organization).

2. Map the SSL certificate to the TS Gateway Server.

3. Join the TS Gateway Server to an AD domain.

4. Create a Connection Authorization Policy (CAP)

5. Create a RAP.

Terminal Services Web Access

Terminal Services Web Access provides a Web platform to access remote applications through a Web site. Remote applications appear as a Web link on the corporate Web site. When users click on the link the remote application opens up.

TS Web Access enables you to make RemoteApp programs appear as a link on the Web site and make them available to remote users. TS Web Access also provides direct access to remote access through the Web browsers.

Install the TS Web Access server role if you have not already done so. You can add the TS Web Access Web page as a Web Part to your corporate Web site. IIS is required by TS Web Access. All applications that need to be available through RemoteApp have to be installed only after installing Terminal Service.

If you have not installed TS Web Access role service, install it through Server Manager.

Notes from the Underground…

Remote Desktop Connection (RDC) Client 6.1

Client computers running RDC client 6.1 can access TS Web Access. RDC client 6.1 is included in Windows Server 2008, Windows Vista with SP1, and Windows XP with SP3 Beta or Windows XP with SP3 operating systems.

To configure TS Web Access:

1. Open the Internet Explorer browser.
2. Type **http://server_name/ts** (**In this example, win-kn3t0cfzmmv. syngress.local/ts**) (see Figure 9.12).
3. Click on the **Configuration** link.
4. Provide the name of the Terminal Server in the **Terminal server name** text box under **Editor Zone** and then click **Apply**.

Figure 9.12 TS Web Access Configuration

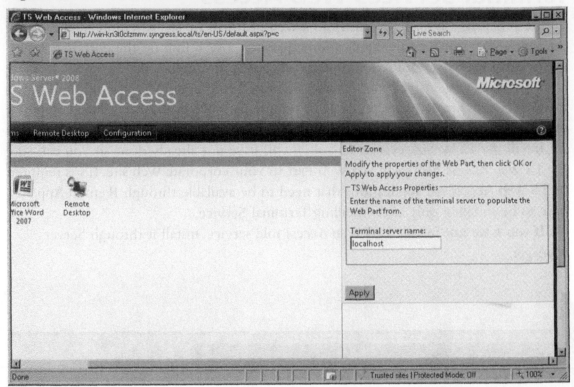

5. You will find the list of published applications in the **RemoteApp Programs** (see Figure 9.13) link.

Figure 9.13 Applications Through TS Web Access

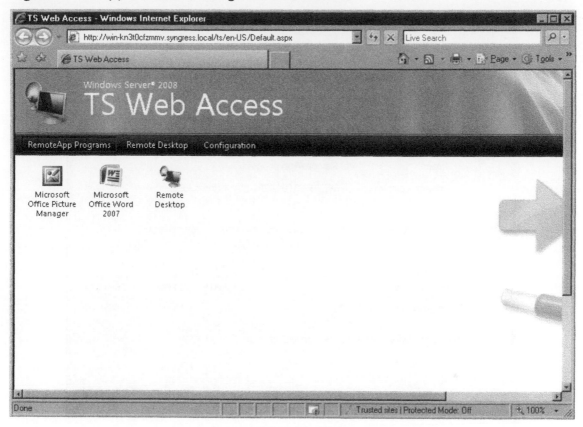

6. Click on the **Microsoft Office Word 2007** icon to start the remote application.

7. Provide the terminal server user name and password (*tsuser1*).

8. You may see a warning window (see Figure 9.14). Click on **Connect**.

Figure 9.14 RemoteApp Warning Message

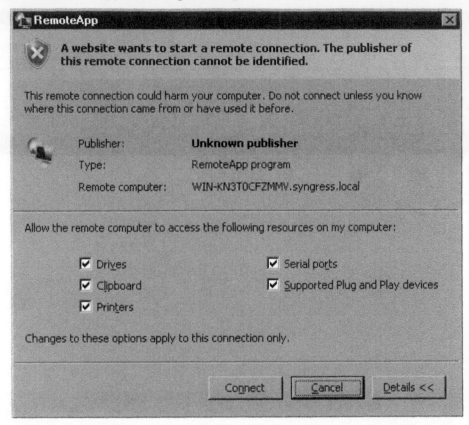

9. Microsoft Office Word 2007 should open with the look and feel of accessing a local application.

10. If you encounter an error message (**ActiveX control not installed or not enabled**) (see Figure 9.15), it's possibly due to the RDP client version running on your system. RDP client version 6.1 is required to access TS Web service. Presently in the Windows 2008 RC1 version clicking on the visit Web site link takes you to a blog suggesting some solution. You may click on Install ActiveX control without much success. Hopefully this will be resolved in the final release. To install the latest RDP client software, visit this link: http://support.microsoft.com/default.aspx/kb/925876.

Figure 9.15 ActiveX Error Message

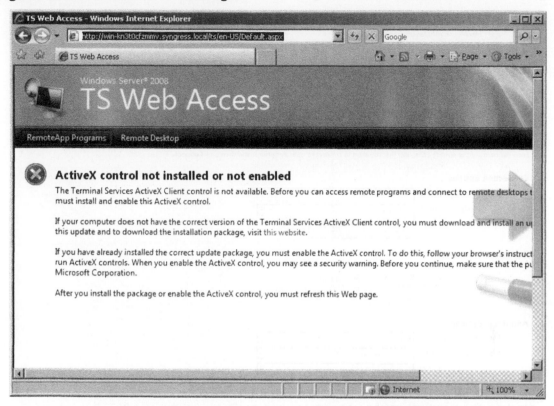

11. The RDP client (Terminal Services Client 6.0) is available for Windows Server 2003, Windows Server 2003, x64, Windows XP, and Windows XP, x64.

Configuring TS Remote Desktop Web Connection

TS Remote Desktop Web connection is a feature of TS Web Access that allows remote users to connect to a remote desktop, taking full control of the remote system instead of just accessing the remote applications (see Figure 9.16).

To configure TS Remote Desktop Web Access:

1. Open the Internet Explorer browser.

2. Type **http://server_name/ts** (in this **example, win-kn3t0cfzmmv.syngress. local/ts**).

3. Click on the **Remote Desktop** link.

4. Under the **Connection Options** provide the **Computer Name** or **IP address** of the Terminal Server.

Figure 9.16 Remote Desktop Configurations on TS Web Access

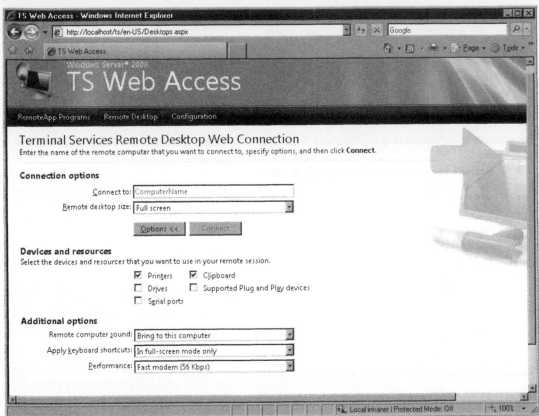

5. Choose from 800x600, 1024x768, 1280x1024, or 1600x1200 pixels for the **Remote desktop size**.

6. Click on **Options** to see other options available.

7. Choose the **Devices and resources** you want to use in the remote session (options are printers, clipboard, drives, supported plug-and-play devices and serial ports).

8. Choose **Additional Options** including **Remote Computer Sound** (Bring to this computer, Leave at remote computer, Do not play), **Apply keyboard shortcuts** (In full-screen mode only, On the local computer, On the remote computer), and **Performance** (Slow modem (28.8 Kbps), Fast modem (56 Kbps), Broadband (128 Kbps – 1.5 Mbps), and LAN (10 Mbps or higher).

9. Option for a legal disclaimer (**I am using a private computer that complies with my organization's security policy**) check box is available.

Summary

Monitoring any network service is an important task of an IT administrator. Fine-tuning and monitoring the Terminal Services ensures the network resources are utilized properly. In addition to that, users experience is enhanced while accessing remote applications. Installation of specific server roles, applications, enabling remote access, monitoring user sessions, and deploying load-balancing solutions are the Terminal Services administrator's tasks.

Solutions Fast Track

Terminal Services RemoteApp

- ☑ TS RemoteApp makes the network programs available over the LAN and Internet that can be remotely accessed through clients running RDC clients or through Web.

- ☑ TS RemoteApp is an easier way to deploy applications once and manage it across the enterprise. Remote offices with limited IT staff greatly benefit from this feature.

- ☑ TS RemoteApp helps organizations manage frequently updated, difficult to manage, or infrequently used applications efficiently.

Terminal Services Gateway

- ☑ Terminal Services Gateway helps administrators enable remote users to access the corporate applications without needing to set up a VPN.

- ☑ RDP traffic from the remote clients travel through a HTTPS encapsulation to reach TS Gateway, and later the HTTPS encapsulation is removed to pass only RDP traffic to the terminal servers.

- ☑ Configuration of TS Gateway servers includes installing SSL certificates and creating resource allocation policies CAP and RAP.

- ☑ Group Policy for Terminal Services defines finer security settings, connection and session limits, resource management, and licensing.

- ☑ RDC client parameters, connection, devices, and resource direction, licensing, printer redirection, user profiles, remote session environment, security, session time limits, temporary folders, and licensing are the options available for configuration.

☑ You need to group identical terminal servers into one GPO and place them under the OU to apply Group Policy settings.

Terminal Services Web Access

☑ Terminal Services Web Access provides a Web platform to access remote applications through a Web site. Remote applications appear as a Web link on the corporate Web site.

☑ TS Web Access enables you to make RemoteApp programs appear as a link on the Web site and make them available to remote users.

☑ TS Remote Desktop Web connection is a feature of TS Web Access that allows remote users to connect to a remote desktop, taking full control of the remote system instead of just accessing the remote applications.

Frequently Asked Questions

Q: What are the management tools available in Windows 2008 to manage Terminal Services environment?

A: Terminal Services Manager, TS RemoteApp Manager, TS Licensing Manager, TS Web Access Administration, and TS Gateway Manager. In addition to that, Windows System Resource Manager for managing system resources and NLB Manager for configuring load balancing are also available.

Q: What is the function of TS Gateway in the Terminal Services environment?

A: Terminal Services Gateway helps administrators to enable remote users to access the corporate applications without a need to setup a VPN. This is done through encapsulating RDP within HTTPS.

Q: What are the TS CAP and TS RAP?

A: A TS CAP allows you to specify who can connect to the TS Gateway Server, while TS RAP allows you to specify the resources users can connect through the TS Gateway Server.

Q: What are the two authentication modes supported by TS CAP?

A: Password and Smart Card are the two authentication modes supported by TS CAP.

Q: I am unable to see Group Policy Management in the Administrative Tools.

A: You can add the Group Policy Management feature through the Server Manager, Add Features option.

Q: I have installed Terminal Services role service on my Windows 2008. What should I do next to publish the applications?

A: Install the applications through **Control Panel | Install Application** on a Terminal Server. Publish it through TS RemoteApp Manager.

Q: What are the different RDP connection options available?

A: Don't allow connections to this computer, Allow connections from computers running any version of Remote Desktop (less secure), and Allow connections only from computers running Remote Desktop with Network Level Authentication (more secure) are the available options.

Q: What are the tasks involved in managing Terminal Services?

A: Configuring RDP permissions, session limits, connection limits, monitoring sessions and processes, log off, disconnect, or reset terminal service sessions are the management tasks.

Index

www.syngress.com

Syngress: *The Definition of a Serious Security Library*

Syn·gress (sin–gres): *noun, sing.* Freedom from risk or danger; safety. See *security*.

AVAILABLE NOW
order @

Syngress IT Security Project Management Handbook
Susan Snedaker

The definitive work for IT professionals responsible for the management of the design, configuration, deployment and maintenance of enterprise-wide security projects. Provides specialized coverage of key project areas including Penetration Testing, Intrusion Detection and Prevention Systems, and Access Control Systems.

ISBN: 1-59749-076-8
Price: $59.95 US $77.95 CAN

Combating Spyware in the Enterprise
Paul Piccard

AVAILABLE NOW
order @

Combating Spyware in the Enterprise is the first book published on defending enterprise networks from increasingly sophisticated and malicious spyware. System administrators and security professionals responsible for administering and securing networks ranging in size from SOHO networks up to the largest enterprise networks will learn to use a combination of free and commercial anti-spyware software, firewalls, intrusion detection systems, intrusion prevention systems, and host integrity monitoring applications to prevent the installation of spyware, and to limit the damage caused by spyware that does in fact infiltrate their networks.

ISBN: 1-59749-064-4
Price: $49.95 US $64.95 CAN

Practical VoIP Security
Thomas Porter

AVAILABLE NOW
order @

After struggling for years, you finally think you've got your network secured from malicious hackers and obnoxious spammers. Just when you think it's safe to go back into the water, VoIP finally catches on. Now your newly converged network is vulnerable to DoS attacks, hacked gateways leading to unauthorized free calls, call eavesdropping, malicious call redirection, and spam over Internet Telephony (SPIT). This book details both VoIP attacks and defense techniques and tools.

ISBN: 1-59749-060-1
Price: $49.95 U.S. $69.95 CAN

SYNGRESS®

Syngress: *The Definition of a Serious Security Library*

Syn·gress (sin‑gres): *noun, sing.* Freedom from risk or danger; safety. See *security*.

AVAILABLE NOW
order @

Cyber Spying: Tracking Your Family's (Sometimes) Secret Online Lives

Dr. Eric Cole, Michael Nordfelt, Sandra Ring, and Ted Fair

Have you ever wondered about that friend your spouse e‑mails, or who they spend hours chatting online with? Are you curious about what your children are doing online, whom they meet, and what they talk about? Do you worry about them finding drugs and other illegal items online, and wonder what they look at? This book shows you how to monitor and analyze your family's online behavior.

ISBN: 1‑93183‑641‑8

Price: $39.95 US $57.95 CAN

Stealing the Network: How to Own an Identity

Timothy Mullen, Ryan Russell, Riley (Caezar) Eller, Jeff Moss, Jay Beale, Johnny Long, Chris Hurley, Tom Parker, Brian Hatch

AVAILABLE NOW
order @

The first two books in this series "Stealing the Network: How to Own the Box" and "Stealing the Network: How to Own a Continent" have become classics in the Hacker and Infosec communities because of their chillingly realistic depictions of criminal hacking techniques. In this third installment, the all-star cast of authors tackle one of the fastest-growing crimes in the world: Identity Theft. Now, the criminal hackers readers have grown to both love and hate try to cover their tracks and vanish into thin air...

ISBN: 1‑59749‑006‑7

Price: $39.95 US $55.95 CAN

AVAILABLE NOW
order @

Software Piracy Exposed

Paul Craig, Ron Honick

For every $2 worth of software purchased legally, $1 worth of software is pirated illegally. For the first time ever, the dark underground of how software is stolen and traded over the Internet is revealed. The technical detail provided will open the eyes of software users and manufacturers worldwide! This book is a tell-it-like-it-is exposé of how tens of billions of dollars worth of software is stolen every year.

ISBN: 1‑93226‑698‑4

Price: $39.95 U.S. $55.95 CAN

SYNGRESS®

Syngress: *The Definition of a Serious Security Library*

Syn·gress (sin-gres): *noun, sing.* Freedom from risk or danger; safety. See *security.*

AVAILABLE NOW
order @

Phishing Exposed

Lance James, Secure Science Corporation,
Joe Stewart (Foreword)

If you have ever received a phish, become a victim of a phish, or manage the security of a major e-commerce or financial site, then you need to read this book. The author of this book delivers the unconcealed techniques of phishers including their evolving patterns, and how to gain the upper hand against the ever-accelerating attacks they deploy. Filled with elaborate and unprecedented forensics, Phishing Exposed details techniques that system administrators, law enforcement, and fraud investigators can exercise and learn more about their attacker and their specific attack methods, enabling risk mitigation in many cases before the attack occurs.

ISBN: 1-59749-030-X

Price: $49.95 US $69.95 CAN

Penetration Tester's Open Source Toolkit

Johnny Long, Chris Hurley, SensePost,
Mark Wolfgang, Mike Petruzzi

AVAILABLE NOW
order @

This is the first fully integrated Penetration Testing book and bootable Linux CD containing the "Auditor Security Collection," which includes over 300 of the most effective and commonly used open source attack and penetration testing tools. This powerful tool kit and authoritative reference is written by the security industry's foremost penetration testers including HD Moore, Jay Beale, and SensePost. This unique package provides you with a completely portable and bootable Linux attack distribution and authoritative reference to the toolset included and the required methodology.

ISBN: 1-59749-021-0

Price: $59.95 US $83.95 CAN

AVAILABLE NOW
order @

Google Hacking for Penetration Testers

Johnny Long, Foreword by Ed Skoudis

Google has been a strong force in Internet culture since its 1998 upstart. Since then, the engine has evolved from a simple search instrument to an innovative authority of information. As the sophistication of Google grows, so do the hacking hazards that the engine entertains. Approaches to hacking are forever changing, and this book covers the risks and precautions that administrators need to be aware of during this explosive phase of Google Hacking.

ISBN: 1-93183-636-1

Price: $44.95 U.S. $65.95 CAN

SYNGRESS®

Syngress: *The Definition of a Serious Security Library*

Syn·gress (sin-gres): *noun, sing.* Freedom from risk or danger; safety. See *security*.

AVAILABLE NOW
order @

Cisco PIX Firewalls:
Configure, Manage, & Troubleshoot

Charles Riley, Umer Khan, Michael Sweeney

Cisco PIX Firewall is the world's most used network firewall, protecting internal networks from unwanted intrusions and attacks. Virtual Private Networks (VPNs) are the means by which authorized users are allowed through PIX Firewalls. Network engineers and security specialists must constantly balance the need for air-tight security (Firewalls) with the need for on-demand access (VPNs). In this book, Umer Khan, author of the #1 best selling PIX Firewall book, provides a concise, to-the-point blueprint for fully integrating these two essential pieces of any enterprise network.

ISBN: 1-59749-004-0
Price: $49.95 US $69.95 CAN

Configuring Netscreen Firewalls

Rob Cameron

AVAILABLE NOW
order @

Configuring NetScreen Firewalls is the first book to deliver an in-depth look at the NetScreen firewall product line. It covers all of the aspects of the NetScreen product line from the SOHO devices to the Enterprise NetScreen firewalls. Advanced troubleshooting techniques and the NetScreen Security Manager are also covered..

ISBN: 1--93226-639-9
Price: $49.95 US $72.95 CAN

AVAILABLE NOW
order @

Configuring Check Point
NGX VPN-1/FireWall-1

Barry J. Stiefel, Simon Desmeules

Configuring Check Point NGX VPN-1/Firewall-1 is the perfect reference for anyone migrating from earlier versions of Check Point's flagship firewall/VPN product as well as those deploying VPN-1/Firewall-1 for the first time. NGX includes dramatic changes and new, enhanced features to secure the integrity of your network's data, communications, and applications from the plethora of blended threats that can breach your security through your network perimeter, Web access, and increasingly common internal threats.

ISBN: 1--59749-031-8
Price: $49.95 U.S. $69.95 CAN

SYNGRESS®

Syngress: *The Definition of a Serious Security Library*

Syn·gress (sin–gres): *noun, sing.* Freedom from risk or danger; safety. See *security.*

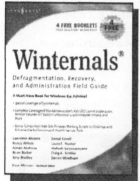

AVAILABLE NOW
order @

Winternals Defragmentation, Recovery, and Administration Field Guide

Dave Kleiman, Laura E. Hunter, Tony Bradley, Brian Barber, Nancy Altholz, Lawrence Abrams, Mahesh Satyanarayana, Darren Windham, Craig Schiller

As a system administrator for a Microsoft network, you know doubt spend too much of your life backing up data and restoring data, hunting down and removing malware and spyware, defragmenting disks, and improving the overall performance and reliability of your network. The Winternals® Defragmentation, Recovery, and Administration Field Guide and companion Web site provide you with all the information necessary to take full advantage of Winternals comprehensive and reliable tools suite for system administrators.

ISBN: 1-59749-079-2

Price: $49.95 US $64.95 CAN

AVAILABLE NOW
order @

Video Conferencing over IP: Configure, Secure, and Troubleshoot

Michael Gough

Until recently, the reality of videoconferencing didn't live up to the marketing hype. That's all changed. The network infrastructure and broadband capacity are now in place to deliver clear, real-time video and voice feeds between multiple points of contacts, with market leaders such as Cisco and Microsoft continuing to invest heavily in development. In addition, newcomers Skype and Google are poised to launch services and products targeting this market. *Video Conferencing over IP* is the perfect guide to getting up and running with video teleconferencing for small to medium-sized enterprises.

ISBN: 1-59749-063-6

Price: $49.95 U.S. $64.95 CAN

SYNGRESS®

Syngress: *The Definition of a Serious Security Library*

Syn·gress (sin–gres): *noun, sing.* Freedom from risk or danger; safety. See *security*.

AVAILABLE NOW
order @

How to Cheat at Designing Security for a Windows Server 2003 Network

Neil Ruston, Chris Peiris

While considering the security needs of your organiztion, you need to balance the human and the technical in order to create the best security design for your organization. Securing a Windows Server 2003 enterprise network is hardly a small undertaking, but it becomes quite manageable if you approach it in an organized and systematic way. This includes configuring software, services, and protocols to meet an organization's security needs.

ISBN: 1-59749-243-4

Price: $39.95 US $55.95 CAN

How to Cheat at Designing a Windows Server 2003 Active Directory Infrastructure

AVAILABLE NOW
order @

Melissa Craft, Michael Cross, Hal Kurz, Brian Barber

The book will start off by teaching readers to create the conceptual design of their Active Directory infrastructure by gathering and analyzing business and technical requirements. Next, readers will create the logical design for an Active Directory infrastructure. Here the book starts to drill deeper and focus on aspects such as group policy design. Finally, readers will learn to create the physical design for an active directory and network Infrastructure including DNS server placement; DC and GC placements and Flexible Single Master Operations (FSMO) role placement.

ISBN: 1-59749-058-X

Price: $39.95 US $55.95 CAN

AVAILABLE NOW
order @

How to Cheat at Configuring ISA Server 2004

Dr. Thomas W. Shinder, Debra Littlejohn Shinder

If deploying and managing ISA Server 2004 is just one of a hundred responsibilities you have as a System Administrator, "How to Cheat at Configuring ISA Server 2004" is the perfect book for you. Written by Microsoft MVP Dr. Tom Shinder, this is a concise, accurate, enterprise tested method for the successful deployment of ISA Server.

ISBN: 1-59749-057-1

Price: $34.95 U.S. $55.95 CAN

SYNGRESS®

Syngress: *The Definition of a Serious Security Library*

Syn·gress (sin–gres): *noun, sing.* Freedom from risk or danger; safety. See *security*.

AVAILABLE NOW
order @

Configuring SonicWALL Firewalls

Chris Lathem, Ben Fortenberry, Lars Hansen

Configuring SonicWALL Firewalls is the first book to deliver an in-depth look at the SonicWALL firewall product line. It covers all of the aspects of the SonicWALL product line from the SOHO devices to the Enterprise SonicWALL firewalls. Advanced troubleshooting techniques and the SonicWALL Security Manager are also covered.

ISBN: 1-59749-250-7

Price: $49.95 US $69.95 CAN

Perfect Passwords:
Selection, Protection, Authentication

Mark Burnett

AVAILABLE NOW
order @

User passwords are the keys to the network kingdom, yet most users choose overly simplistic passwords (like password) that anyone could guess, while system administrators demand impossible to remember passwords littered with obscure characters and random numerals. Author Mark Burnett has accumulated and analyzed over 1,000,000 user passwords, and this highly entertaining and informative book filled with dozens of illustrations reveals his findings and balances the rigid needs of security professionals against the ease of use desired by users.

ISBN: 1-59749-041-5

Price: $24.95 US $34.95 CAN

SYNGRESS®

Syngress: *The Definition of a Serious Security Library*

Syn·gress (sin-gres): *noun, sing.* Freedom from risk or danger; safety. See *security*.

AVAILABLE NOW
order @

Skype Me! From Single User to Small Enterprise and Beyond
Michael Gough

This first-ever book on Skype takes you from the basics of getting Skype up and running on all platforms, through advanced features included in SkypeIn, SkypeOut, and Skype for Business. The book teaches you everything from installing a headset to configuring a firewall to setting up Skype as telephone Base to developing your own customized applications using the Skype Application Programming Interface.

ISBN: 1-59749-032-6
Price: $34.95 US $48.95 CAN

Securing IM and P2P Applications for the Enterprise
Brian Baskin, Marcus H. Sachs, Paul Piccard

As an IT Professional, you know that the majority of the workstations on your network now contain IM and P2P applications that you did not select, test, install, or configure. As a result, malicious hackers, as well as virus and worm writers, are targeting these inadequately secured applications for attack. This book will teach you how to take back control of your workstations and reap the benefits provided by these applications while protecting your network from the inherent dangers.

ISBN: 1-59749-017-2
Price: $49.95 US $69.95 CAN

AVAILABLE NOW
order @

SYNGRESS®

Syngress: *The Definition of a Serious Security Library*

Syn·gress (sin-gres): *noun, sing.* Freedom from risk or danger; safety. See *security.*

How to Cheat at Managing Windows Server Update Services

Brian Barber

AVAILABLE NOW
order @

If you manage a Microsoft Windows network, you probably find yourself overwhelmed at times by the sheer volume of updates and patches released by Microsoft for its products. You know these updates are critical to keep your network running efficiently and securely, but staying current amidst all of your other responsibilities can be almost impossible. Microsoft's recently released Windows Server Update Services (WSUS) is designed to streamline this process. Learn how to take full advantage of WSUS using Syngress' proven "How to Cheat" methodology, which gives you everything you need and nothing you don't.

ISBN: 1-59749-027-X

Price: $39.95 US $55.95 CAN

AVAILABLE NOW
order @

How to Cheat at IT Project Management

Susan Snedaker

Most IT projects fail to deliver – on average, all IT projects run over schedule by 82%, run over cost by 43% and deliver only 52% of the desired functionality. Pretty dismal statistics. Using the proven methods in this book, you'll find that IT project you work on from here on out will have a much higher likelihood of being on time, on budget and higher quality. This book provides clear, concise, information and hands-on training to give you immediate results. And, the companion Web site provides dozens of templates for managing IT projects.

ISBN: 1-59749-037-7

Price: $44.95 U.S. $64.95 CAN

SYNGRESS®

SYNGRESS®

info security

Syngress is now part of Elsevier, publisher of *Infosecurity* magazine. *Infosecurity*'s UK-based editorial team provides information security professionals with strategy, insight and technique to help them do their jobs better.

Infosecurity's web-site runs online-only information security news and analysis, selected features from the magazine and free access to relevant articles from Elsevier's paid-for scientific journals.

And it now also offers exclusive columns from Syngress authors, along with extracts from their books.

For a deeper understanding of infosecurity, visit **www.infosecurity-magazine.com/syngress**

ELSEVI

Printed and bound by CPI Group (UK) Ltd, Croydon, CR0 4YY

03/10/2024

01040341-0012